LEGENDARY LOCALS

OF

YOSEMITE NATIONAL PARK AND MARIPOSA COUNTY

CALIFORNIA

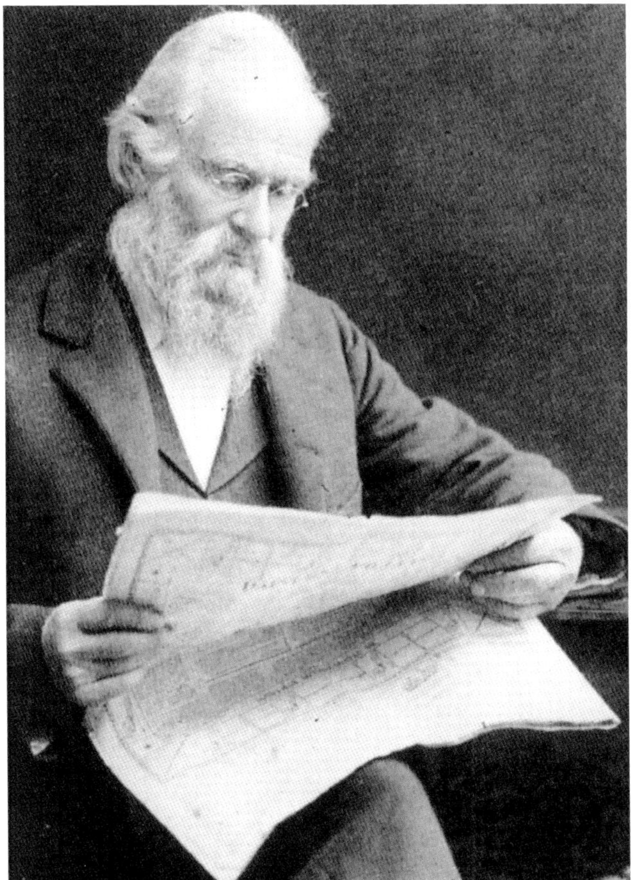

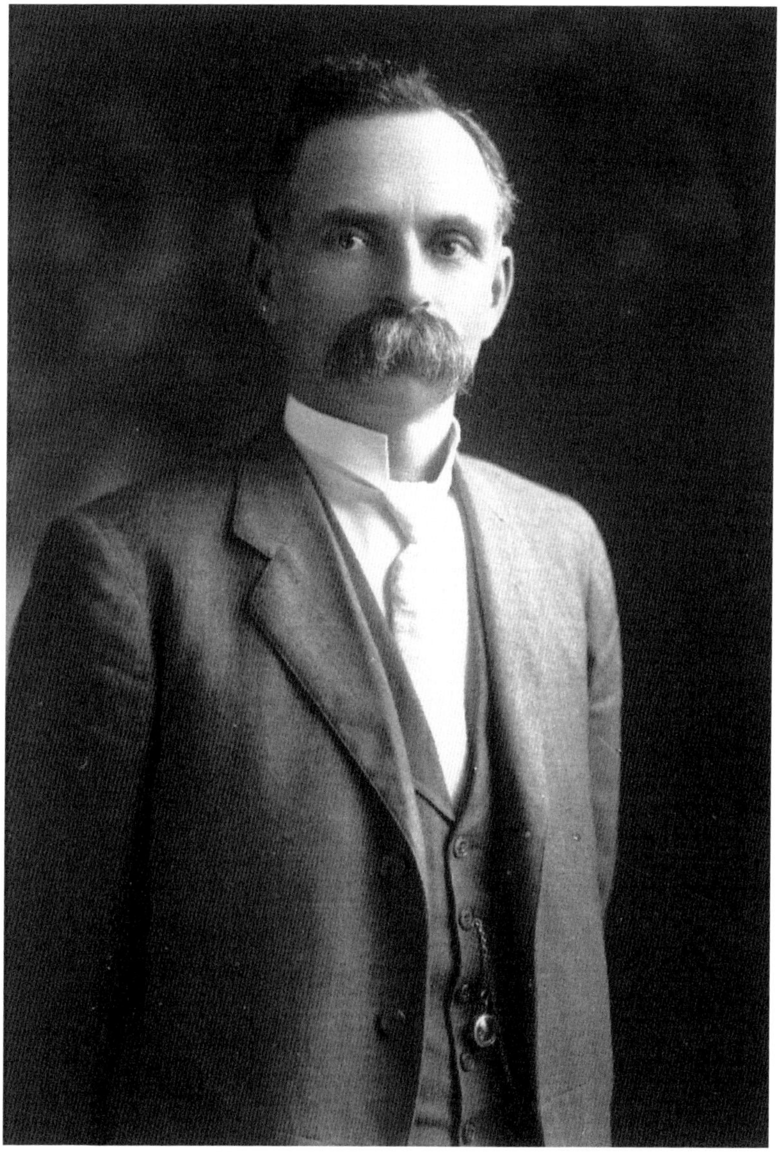

Superior Court Judge Joseph J. Trabucco

Joseph J. Trabucco was the son of immigrant merchants in Bear Valley. After law school, he became the superior court judge for Mariposa County for 35 years until his death in 1938. He was noted throughout California for his skill and wisdom as a jurist who served on a number of benches without ever having a decision overturned. He served Mariposa County from 1903 to 1938. (Author's collection.)

Page 1: Galen Clark, Guardian with Map

A physician diagnosed Galen Clark with consumption and informed him that he had little time to live. He chose to give up mining in the creeks of Mariposa and moved to the meadows of Pallahchun (Wawona) to live out his days. He went on to live many more years in the mountains; he loved discovering the Mariposa Grove of Big Trees and serving as guardian of the Yosemite Grant a number of times. (Author's collection.)

LEGENDARY LOCALS

OF

YOSEMITE NATIONAL PARK AND MARIPOSA COUNTY

CALIFORNIA

LEROY RADANOVICH

LEGENDARY LOCALS

ISBN 978-1-4671-0164-6

Legendary Locals is an imprint of Arcadia Publishing
Charleston, South Carolina

Printed in the United States of America

Library of Congress Control Number: 2014940867

For all general information, please contact Arcadia Publishing:
Telephone 843-853-2070
Fax 843-853-0044
E-mail sales@arcadiapublishing.com
For customer service and orders:
Toll-Free 1-888-313-2665

Visit us on the Internet at www.arcadiapublishing.com

Dedication
To the pioneers who crafted the legends of Mariposa County

On the Front Cover: Clockwise from top left:
Chief LeMee (Author's collection; see pages 114–116), Jessie Fremont (Author's collection; see page 12), Emile Trabucco (Photograph by author; see pages 59 and 60), George Monroe (Author's collection; see page 94), John Muir (Author's collection; see page 35), Jim Helm, Cowboy manager of livestock at Kenny Coffman Stables in Yosemite Valley about 1900 (Author's collection; see page 66), a Gordon family member, stage driver to the Mariposa Grove of Big Trees (Author's collection; see page 106), John C. Fremont (Author's collection; see page 12), Jim Tresidder, miner (Courtesy of June Meagher, see page 54).

On the Back Cover: From left to right:
John Dexter, editor of the *Mariposa Gazette* (Author's collection; see page 99), Judge J.J. Trabucco (Courtesy of Mariposa Museum and History Center, see page 111).

CONTENTS

Acknowledgments 6

Introduction 7

CHAPTER ONE A Gathering of Legends 9

CHAPTER TWO A Legendary Bandit and the Evolution of Mining 27

CHAPTER THREE Legends Following the Gold Rush 55

CHAPTER FOUR A Few Legends of Impact 69

CHAPTER FIVE The Legendary Educators 95

CHAPTER SIX Further Legends of Mariposa County 105

CHAPTER SEVEN Legends of Character in Mariposa County 113

Index 126

ACKNOWLEDGMENTS

The author wishes to acknowledge some of the people who have helped over the last 50 years to record the history of Mariposa County.

First, I am grateful for my late partner, Scott Pinkerton, who worked with me to begin translating our knowledge into a permanent available document. I also give thanks to Yosemite author Shirley Sargent, who served as a role model; Harold Rowney, photographer and friend, who taught me a great deal about photography; and Linda Milburn Parsons, who represents a family whose history is fundamental to the story of Mariposa County. Their direct connection to Las Mariposas, the Fremont Grant, through five generations of keeping track of the history and photographs of the mining activities helped form the county.

Then, there are countless photographers, historians, and ordinary people who preserved our history and were willing to see it preserved and passed on.

Thanks go to the Mariposa Museum and History Center, which has become the repository for our history, and to one special friend, Don Weston, who was instrumental in the establishment of the archival vault that will preserve what we accomplish forever.

To all, I say thank you.

INTRODUCTION

Yosemite National Park and Mariposa County are forever tied together.

Most of the developed parts of Yosemite are within the county, including well-known locations such as Yosemite Valley, Wawona, Mariposa Grove of Big Trees, Badger Pass Ski area, and Glacier Point. The northern half of the park is in Tuolumne County, which is largely undeveloped, and while still an important part of the natural area, it lends little to the human history of Yosemite—with the large exception of Joseph R. Walker and his troop, who crossed the Sierra just north of Yosemite Valley in 1833. It is thought that some of his men may have been the first white men to view the great valley. Perhaps it was the Merced River portion at Cascades or part of the valley west of El Capitan. Nonetheless, Walker and his men were part of the American experience in Yosemite.

Two notable events occurred in the world that changed man's ability to understand, interpret, and disseminate information about the natural world. Although the performance of lenses had been described prior to 1800, it was soon after the turn of that century that the discovery of the ability to transfer life images to materials such as leather and paper revealed itself. The sensitization of the receiving media using the salts of silver eventually resulted in the transference of the natural image. The permanence of such a product demanded years of experimentation but finally resulted in archival photographs.

The second unrelated event was the publishing a book by Charles Darwin called *On the Origin of Species*. Darwin introduced natural selection, diversity, and evolution to the world's understanding of its nature. No longer could the natural world be cataloged as a stable or fixed collection, but it had to be studied and understood as an ever-changing, evolving environment in which man lived and was a part of. Man developed a constant fascination with the need to utilize and change the natural world. Therefore, Yosemite Valley was not just a large rent in the earth, but a living laboratory of nature's diversity, which some thought needed to be protected from undue influence of man's need to impose his will. One solution to this was the establishment of natural reserves such as national parks. The intelligent management of these reserves then became the challenge.

Our collection of legendary locals includes the pioneer explorers, the Native Americans, the developers of Yosemite as a place of "rest and recreation" for the world, as well as those who seemed to understand the nature of this special place. Tying the discovery and development of Yosemite to the Gold Rush in Mariposa County gives the background for the development of the personalities who forever put their mark on our county and the Central Sierra.

Living more than 70 of my 80 years in Mariposa County, along with growing up in my father's drugstore in downtown Mariposa, introduced me to many of the pioneers and pioneer families of our county. I have known everyone from park rangers, gold miners, homesteaders, cattle ranchers, farmers, cowboys, packers, vintners, loggers, sawmill operators, road and trail builders, religious leaders, Native Americans, land developers and spoilers, pilots, airport builders, writers, historians, museum builders, politicians and government servants; newspaper editors, photographers, artists, firemen, sheriffs, law enforcement officers, hotel and motel keepers, cooks and bartenders, maids, and busboys. All passed my way. This is their story.

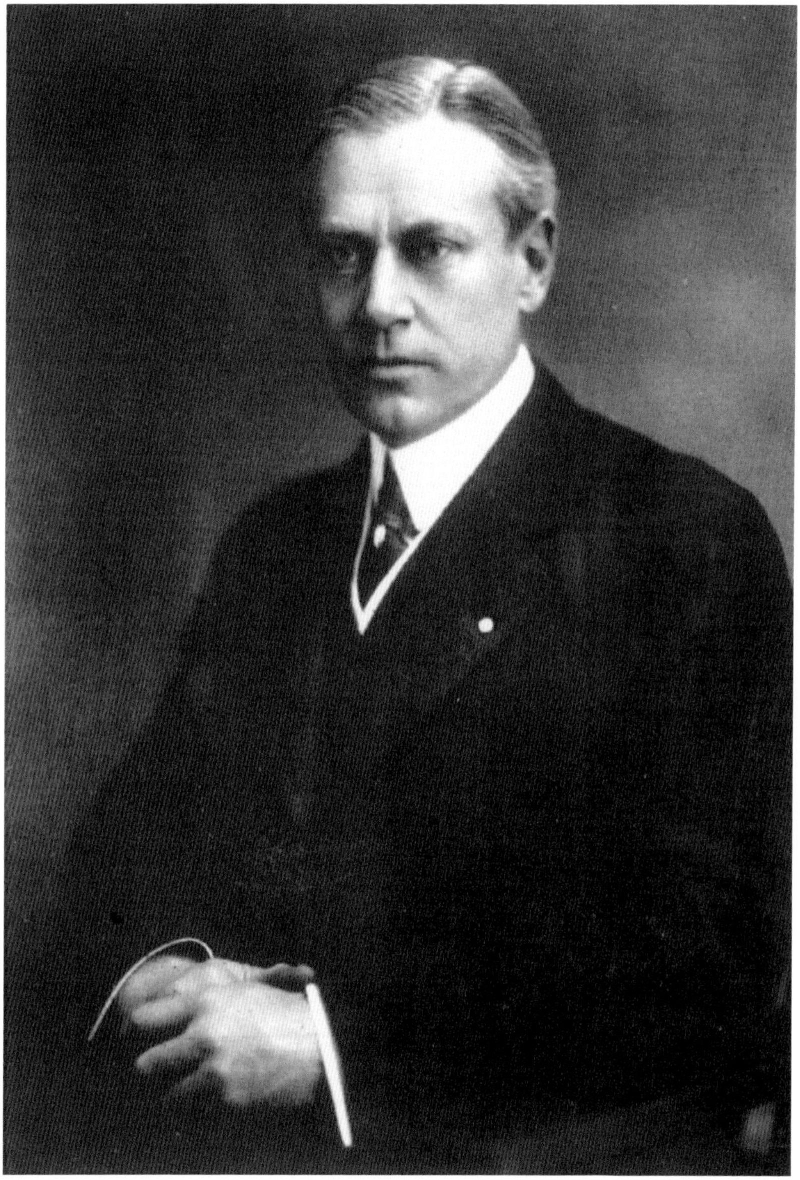

Stephen T. Mather

Though not a citizen of Mariposa County, his intense interest in Yosemite National Park, his personal wealth, and drive to preserve the public lands through use and involvement, Mather, as director of the National Park Service, must be recognized for his impact on the growth and development of the National Park System, including Yosemite National Park, and the future of Mariposa County. While he understood the preservation principles, he also recognized that the long-term viability of the National Park System depended heavily on public attention. He knew that it would take hotels, campgrounds, roads, trails, and services to satisfy public appreciation, which also translated into congressional commitment to the National Park System. He demonstrated this commitment by the investment of his personal wealth in such items as purchasing the Great Sierra Mine Road to become the Tioga Road and capital for building Yosemite's great hotel. (Courtesy of Yosemite Museum Library.)

CHAPTER ONE

A Gathering of Legends

No photographs exist of the significant early legends of Yosemite and Mariposa County. The technology had not reached California and the Sierra quite yet. The first photograph taken in Yosemite was by Charles Leander Weed in 1859.

Early in the 1800s, a young man was born, near Mono Lake in eastern California, to a Mono mother and a Miwok or Paiute father who lived in Yosemite Valley. He migrated with his mother to an area now called North Fork, south of Yosemite, where he grew up. As a young man, he traveled to Yosemite Valley, living with a group of varying origins who called themselves Awaneeches or Yosemites (the "grizzly bears"). They lived in the valley called Awahanee, a grassy place. As the young man aged, he became the chief of these people and was considered to be wise as well as crafty. Due to various depredations within the mining camps and at Col. James Savage's stores in early 1851, the colonel and members of the Mariposa Battalion set out to find those responsible—Chief Tenaya and his tribe.

Col. James Savage, Leader of Mariposa Battalion

The Mariposa Battalion was made up of three companies of young miners authorized by the State of California as a militia. They were led by Savage, a man who knew the native peoples about as well as anyone. By forming relationships, perhaps through marriage with their daughters, Savage became known as a friend as well as benefactor of the Native Americans. The fact that he had learned their language made him a valuable leader to the miners, but individual conflicts with Savage created a group of unhappy young Native Americans who destroyed his stores on the Fresno River and Mariposa Creek, just south of Mariposa, and killed his workers. Savage was prevailed upon to search for and gather these renegades and bring them to a gathering point on the Fresno River where they could be pacified and, in Savage's mind, protected.

From two of the three companies of the Mariposa Battalion, he selected a group of men to track down the old chief and gather his people. Chief Tenaya had spirited them away to Yosemite Valley and then came out of the valley by himself to try to divert Savage. Savage had Tenaya held while Savage and his men followed the old chief's tracks in the snow back to Yosemite Valley. Although the snow created great difficulties, the group of men reached the rim of the valley at approximately Inspiration Point and entered by way of a very dangerous and steep trail. (Author's collection.)

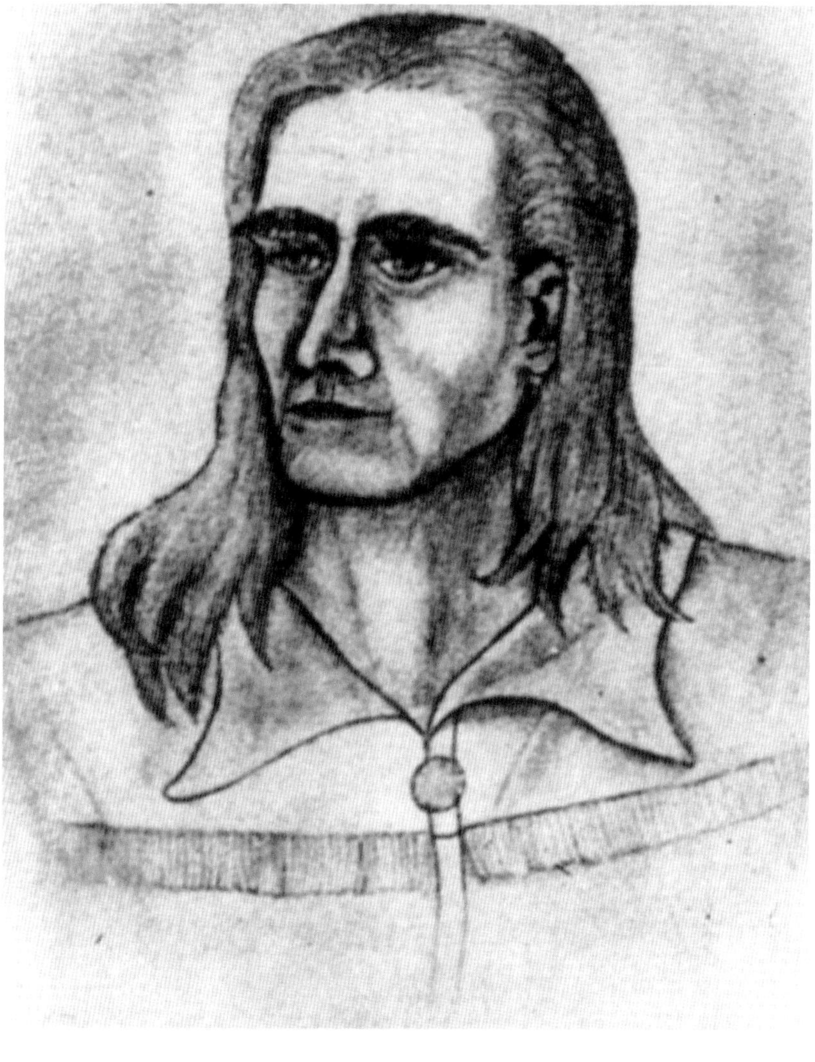

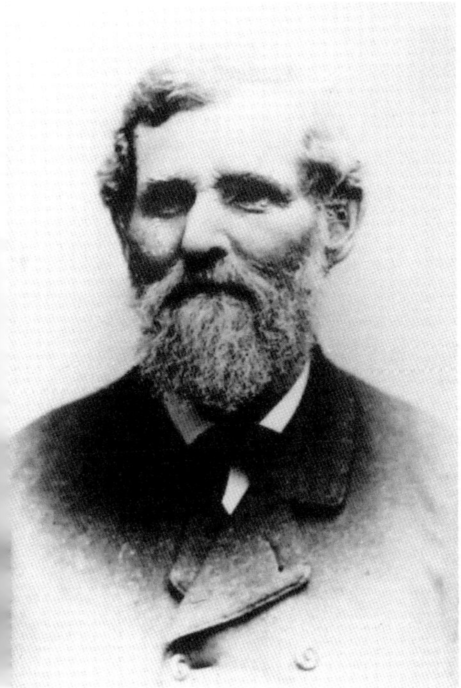

Lafayette H. Bunnell
Among the Mariposa Battalion was young gold miner Lafayette H. Bunnell, who had an interest in medicine. He served the medical needs of his fellow battalion members. Strangely, he seems to have been the only one to recognize the spectacular beauty of what was seen from the cliffs as they descended into the valley. Some 30 years later, he wrote his book, *Discovery of the Yosemite*, which has become the bedrock source on that early vision. He equated what he saw with the greatest scenes of nature. He mentioned that he had been able to see a bit of Half Dome from a trail down the Merced River, some miles away.

He did not stop there in his useful description of life in the West. In his book, he talks about mining and treatment of the Native Americans. He was well aware of the killing of James Savage by Judge Harvey of Tulare in a fight over the management of the Indian trust paid for by the federal government. Of these three men, only Bunnell lived long enough to have a picture taken. (Author's collection.)

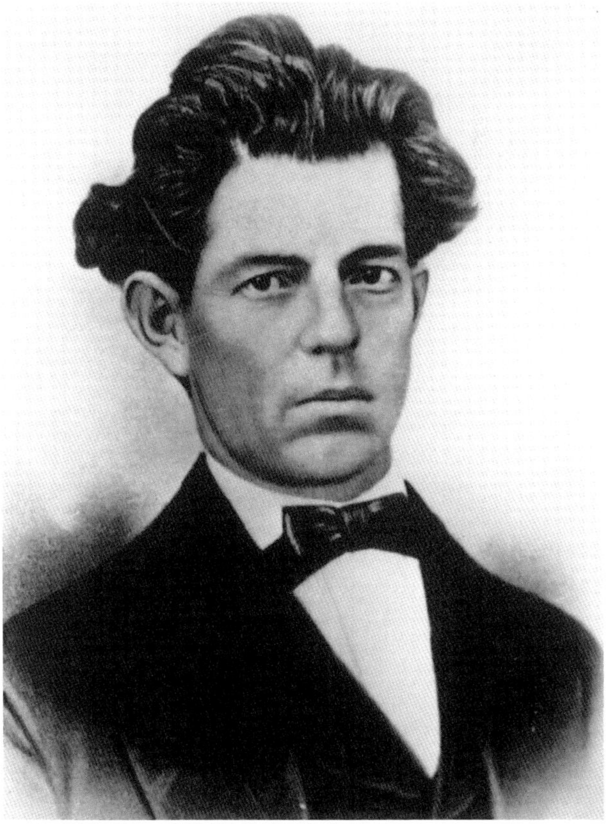

Capt. John Boling
While Savage and his troop neither found nor captured the Natives on their first trip to Yosemite Valley, a second trip, led by Capt. John Boling (later the sheriff of Mariposa County), resulted in the removal of the Indians. Thus, the American "Discovery of Yosemite" is complete. (Author's collection.)

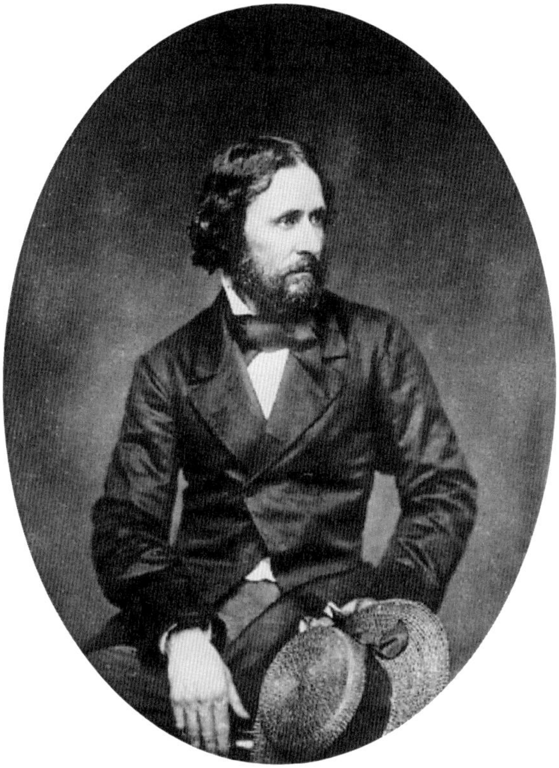

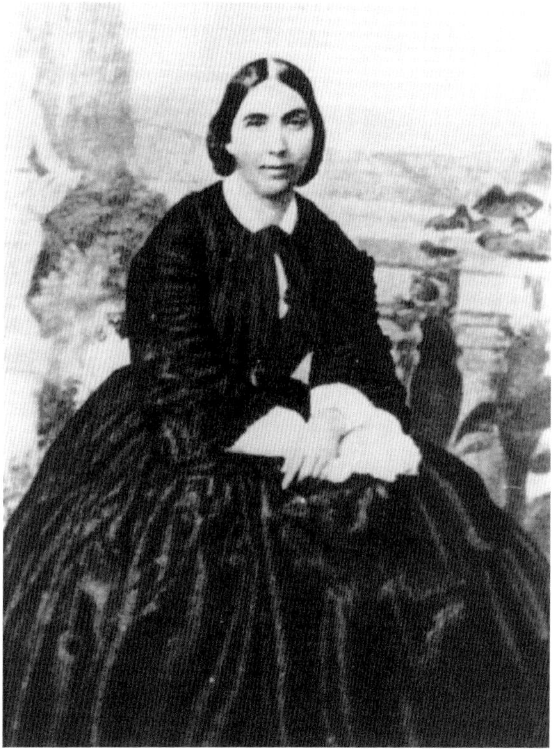

John C. Fremont and Jessie Fremont

In 1846, Col. John C. Fremont, "the Pathfinder" and Western explorer, and his wife, Jessie, provided Thomas Larkin, the American consul general in California, a sum of money for him to purchase farmland on their behalf. They preferred the purchase be near the San Francisco Bay area. For an unknown reason, Larkin purchased from the departing Mexican governor of California, Juan Bautista Alvarado, 10 square leagues of land that was a Mexican land grant that had not yet received a perfected title. Mexico, although still in possession of California at that time, was on the verge of losing control of this distant state. Within two years, California became a possession of the United States, the result of the treaty following the war with Mexico.

The grant that was purchased for Fremont had no fixed boundaries. It was only described as being located somewhere east of the San Joaquin River with the Merced River on the north; west of the Sierra and north of the Fresno River. The Mexican owner was in such a hurry to leave the state that he did not locate or perfect his grant. Therefore, Fremont acquired the land lacking the proper title even under Mexican law. He attempted to perfect the requirements by locating a farm along Mariposa Creek on the edge of the San Joaquin Valley. His agent encountered resistance from the Indians living in the area, and he withdrew. A second attempt was made, but it fared no better.

In the meantime, Mexico was losing control of California. By January, with the discovery of gold at Coloma, Fremont's focus was no longer on farming. His participation in California's Bear Flag Revolt gained him a court-martial as the result of his choosing the wrong leader to respond to. Gen. Stephen Watts Kearny charged Fremont with insubordination and escorted him to Washington, DC, where he was convicted and subsequently resigned his commission. He led an ill-fated trek, funded by his father-in-law, Thomas Hart Benton, senator from Missouri, into southern Colorado's San Juan Mountains searching for a railroad route West. Encountering difficulties and distress for his men, leading to a disastrous end, he left for Taos, New Mexico, and then California to meet wife, Jessie, who was waiting in San Francisco. In route to California, while crossing northern Mexico, Fremont encountered a group of Mexican miners from the state of Sonora who were headed to California to mine for gold. They knew of the discovery along the foothills of the Sierra near the grant land that he believed he owned. He engaged them to go to his property and begin the search. They arrived in the Mariposa area in the spring of 1849 and began placer mining. Fremont sent his trusted lieutenant Alexander Goday with the Mexicans. (Both, author's collection.)

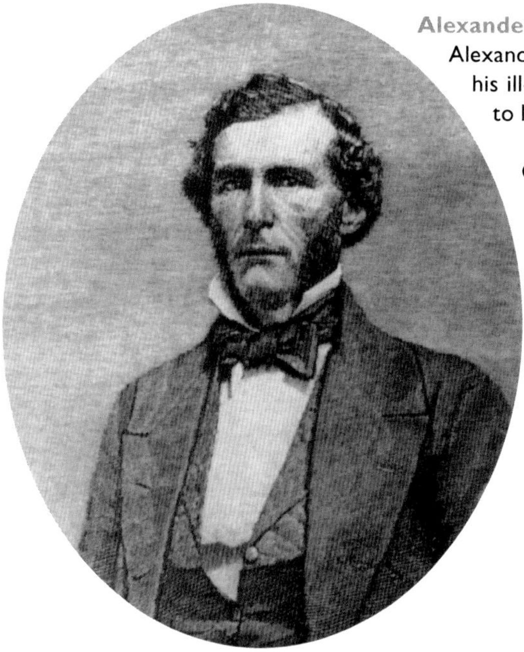

Alexander Goday

Alexander Goday was Fremont's second in command on his ill-fated Colorado expedition. Goday was trusted to lead Mexican miners to Mariposa.

They eventually enter the valley along Mariposa Creek, and there, they noticed the presence of gold containing quartz or "float." They crushed and processed the quartz gathering for themselves and Fremont many bags of gold. As of then, Fremont still had no title to the land that his charges were mining, and in fact, their discoveries determined the location of his title request. (Author's collection.)

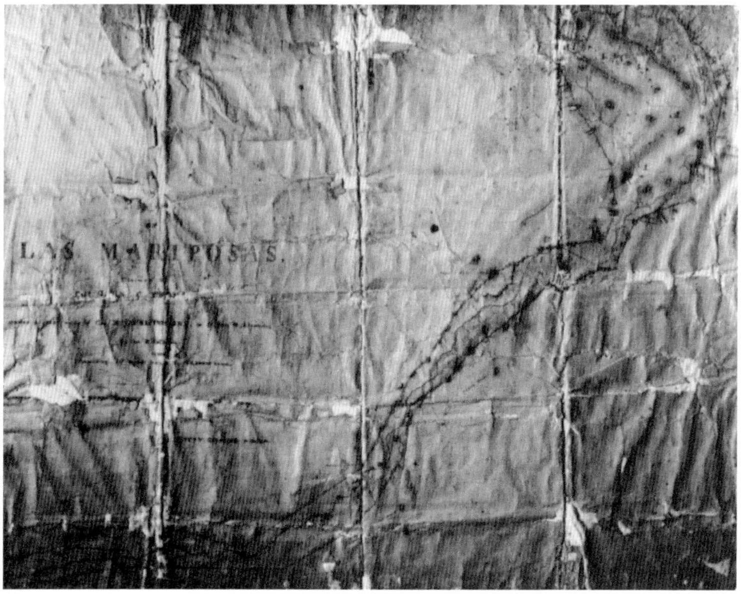

Fremont Grant Map

Here is Allexey von Schmidt's 1852 map of claim set out by Fremont at the direction of the California State Lands Commission.

Fremont met his wife, Jessie, in San Francisco, and then, in the spring of 1849, he traveled to Mariposa to establish his claim. By then, California, and thus Mariposa, was part of the United States, and Fremont had to gain an American title for the 44,386 acres. He set out the corners for establishing a fixed (instead of floating) grant. Instead of being in the San Joaquin Valley, he set the boundaries around the present town of Mariposa in what was Mariposa County and southern extent of the gold-rich Mother Lode. (Author's collection.)

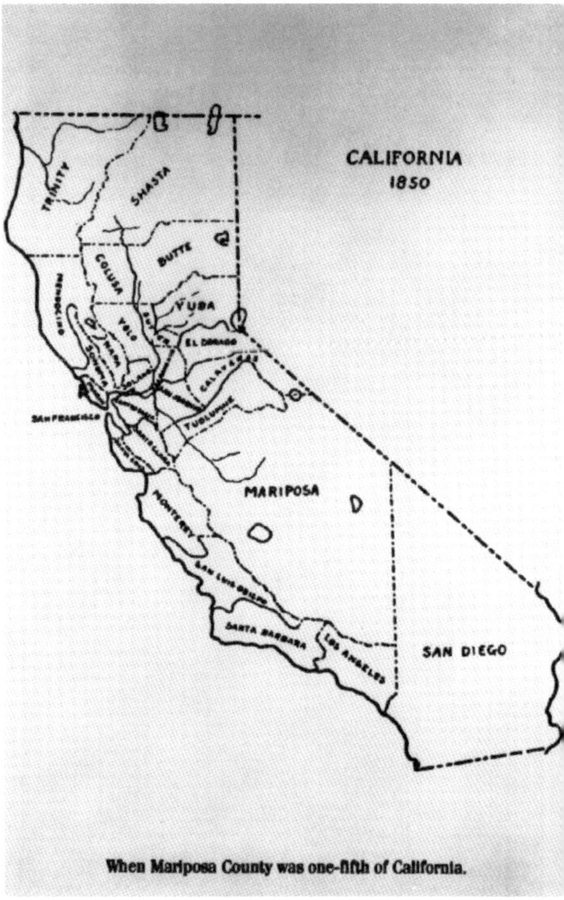

California, 1850

This map shows California when it entered the Union. Mariposa County occupied one-fifth of the state, and Fremont's grant was in north-central part. Mariposa County eventually divided into all or part of 11 counties.

By September 1850, statehood was granted to California, and Fremont now needed to apply for clear title for his Mexican claim under American law. His application to the newly formed California State Lands Commission required a survey. In 1852, state surveyor Allexey Von Schmidt created a map showing Fremont's claim extending around the new towns of Mariposa, Mount Bullion, and Bridgeport. Then, the claim followed Mariposa Creek into the San Joaquin Valley, incorporating the ranch and farmland that Fremont felt was needed to supply food and fodder to his projects. His claim was rejected; however, an appeal to the Supreme Court was accepted. The boundaries of the grant were modified before clear title was granted in 1855. Years of conflict, mismanagement, and legal costs created mounting debt that forced Fremont to sell the Las Mariposas Grant by 1861. (Author's collection.)

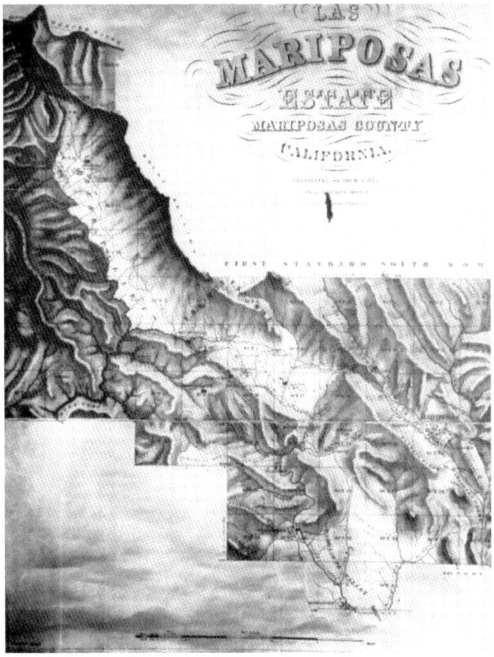

Final Fremont Grant Map

The Gold Rush and land activities of Fremont and others set the direction of activity in central Mariposa County for the next 100 years. (Author's collection.)

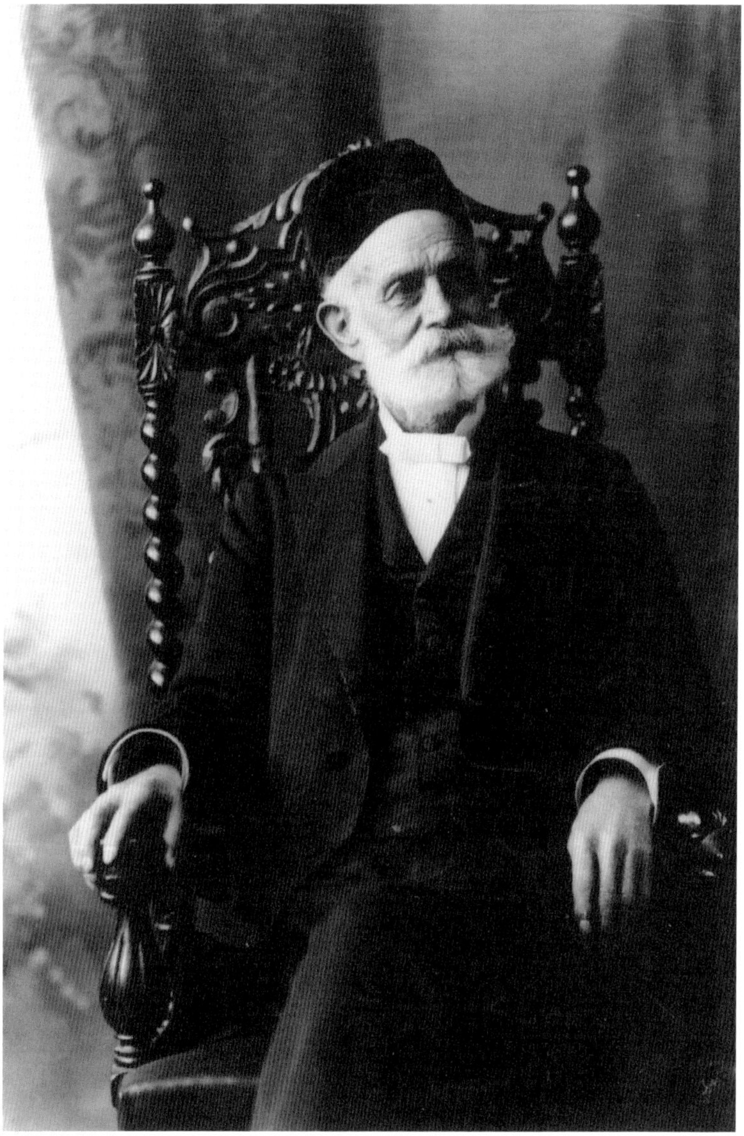

James Mason Hutchings

Accounts of the Mariposa Battalion trips to Yosemite were published in San Francisco newspapers and caught the eye of James Mason Hutchings. He understood the interest in the written word when he designed and sold a pamphlet offering a Miner's Ten Commandments. With capital from the sale of this card, he was able to begin publishing what became a popular tourist promotion periodical, *Hutchings California Magazine*.

Rumors of 1,000-foot waterfalls, soaring cliffs, and verdant meadows stimulated Hutchings to form a party to explore the mysterious valley. By 1855, Hutchings and his curious group of those first tourists visited Yosemite Valley using two Yosemite natives as guides. Starting in Mariposa, they proceeded over Indian trails to Wawona and Inspiration Point on the valley rim. Artist Thomas Ayers was brought along to sketch the features of Yosemite. Hutchings published the drawings in his new magazine, and the response was almost immediate. On subsequent trips, he brought Charles Leander Weed, who, in 1859, took the first photograph in Yosemite. (Author's collection.)

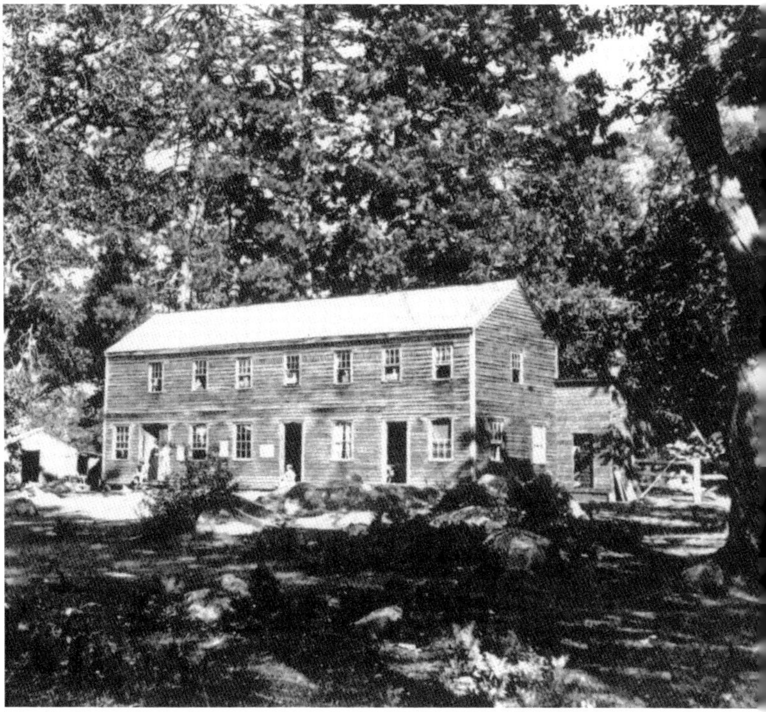

Upper House
Hutchings eventually owned Upper House, the first hotel in Yosemite Valley. This was one of two first photographs taken in Yosemite by Charles L. Weed.

In 1864, Hutchings purchased the first hotel, built in 1859, from Beardsley, and Gus Hite and began his years as a host in Yosemite. After Yosemite became a state park in 1864, Hutchings continued; however, he was unhappy with the state management. The governor formed a commission to manage the Yosemite Grant, and Hutchings served as a member for a time. He built a sawmill and hired John Muir to operate it. (Author's collection.)

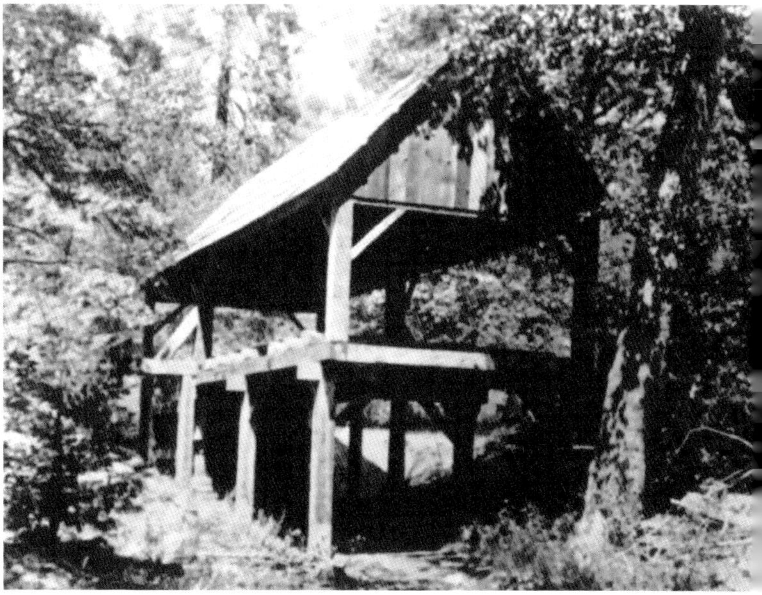

Hutchings Sawmill
In Hutchings Sawmill, logs were sawed into planks for building. John Muir worked this mill and built a loft at one end where he could live. This introduced Muir to Yosemite Valley full time. Following a band of sheep, Muir had come to Yosemite high country in 1869. (Courtesy of Yosemite Museum Library.)

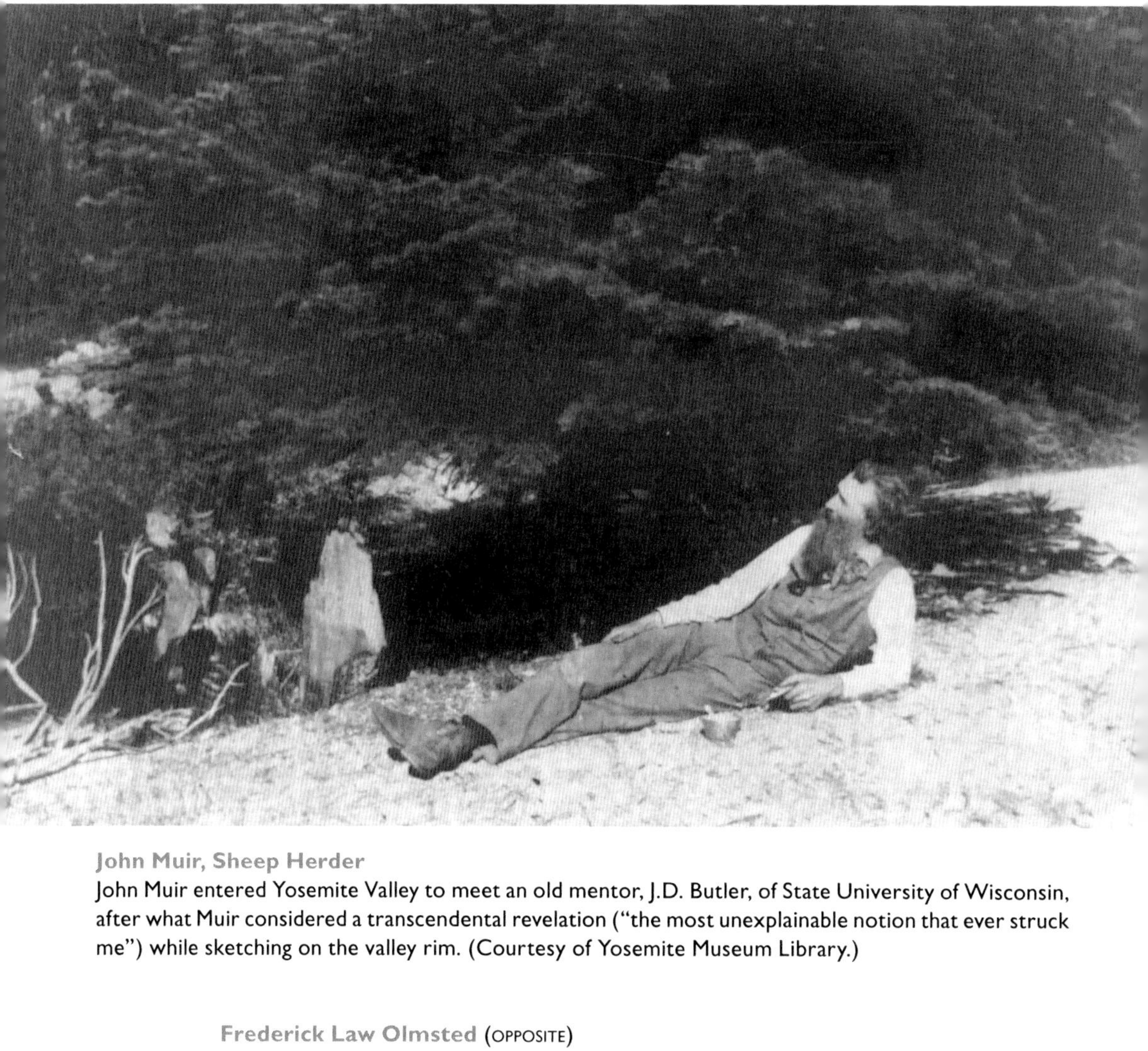

John Muir, Sheep Herder
John Muir entered Yosemite Valley to meet an old mentor, J.D. Butler, of State University of Wisconsin, after what Muir considered a transcendental revelation ("the most unexplainable notion that ever struck me") while sketching on the valley rim. (Courtesy of Yosemite Museum Library.)

Frederick Law Olmsted (OPPOSITE)
With the selling of the Las Mariposas Grant a new figure entered the Mariposa/Yosemite scene. Frederick Law Olmsted, landscape architect and developer of New York's Central Park, was sent by the new owners to manage the assets of the grant. On arrival, he found that Fremont had left behind many debts, and he was unable to purchase supplies both for the mines and the stores necessary to operate in a new country. Although lacking support from the new owners, Olmsted stayed in California for three years, attempting at first to resurrect the mining operations and then to collect his wage from the new owners.

While in California, Olmsted became chairman of the California commission for the management of the new Yosemite State Park Grant. Pres. Abraham Lincoln created this concession in 1864 at the behest of I.W. Raymond with such Californians as Galen Clark, Jessie Fremont, and Sen. John Conness applying support. Olmsted's task was the creation of a plan for the management of the new state park. He incorporated preservation concepts in the report that were not understood or popular in the manifest destiny environment. The report was largely ignored for many years but was rediscovered in the 1950s. Today, it forms the foundation for the management plans for the present and future of Yosemite National Park. (Author's collection.)

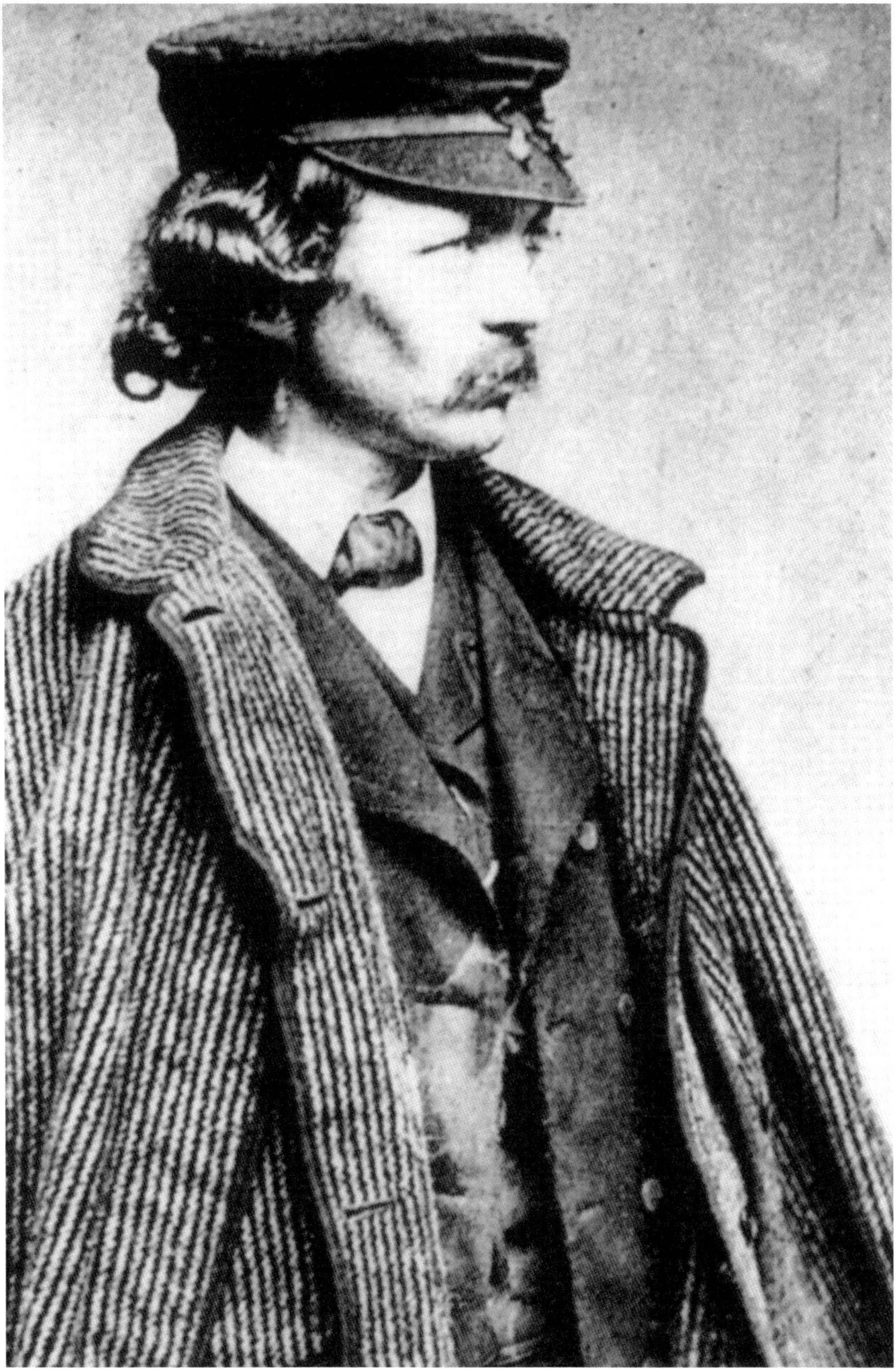

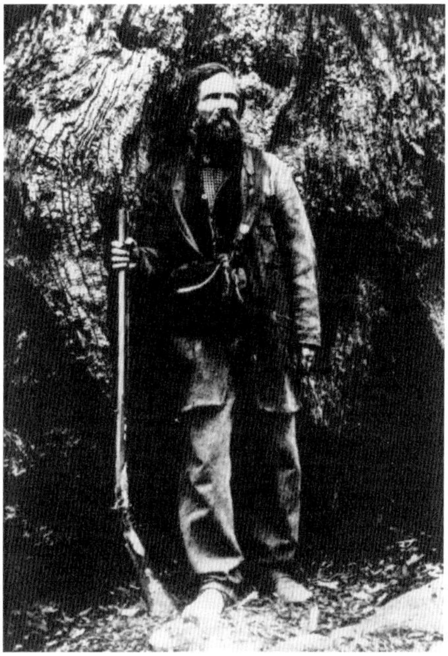

Galen Clark

Galen Clark had come to Mariposa County to mine for gold. But standing in cold running water and the physical stress of mining caused him to contract consumption. A doctor gave him only a few months to live, so he packed his belongings and moved over the mountains from Mariposa to Wawona (Pallahchun) on the South Fork of the Merced River. He was determined to finish out his final days in the beautiful calm of the meadows and mountains of Yosemite's south. But the clean air and adequate game for food revived his health, and he lived many more years. His only neighbors at first were the Indians. Then, travelers seeking Yosemite Valley would stop by looking for directions and, incidentally, something to eat. He realized the potential of catering to the people on the trail, so he established Clarks Ranch. Clark is pictured in Wawona at Mariposa Grove at the base of Grizzly Giant. (Photograph by Carleton E. Watkins, author's collection.)

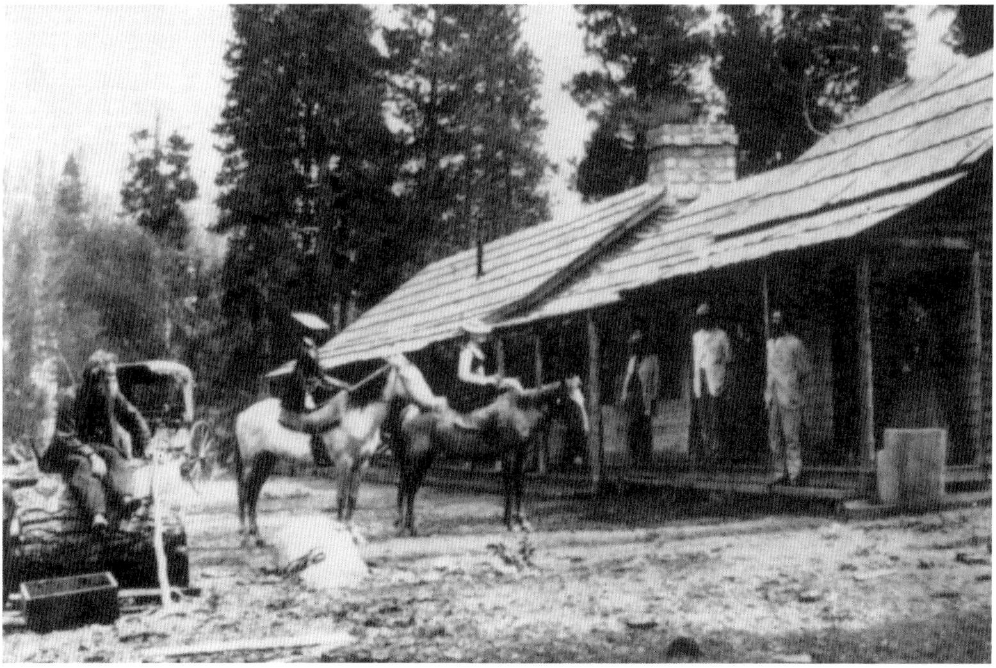

Clarks Ranch

Clark became acquainted with the Mann brothers, trail builders and stock providers in Mariposa. He agreed with them to build a trail to Wawona following many of the Indian routes. Soon, the demand grew to build a wagon road, which Clark provided. It then became natural to continue the trail building to Yosemite Valley, and the visitor business began. Clark and Milton Mann discovered the Mariposa Grove of Big Trees, filled with giant sequoias, and Clark built a cabin there. Clark is pictured here on the log with partners Edwin and Huldah Moore on the porch. (Courtesy of Yosemite Museum Library.)

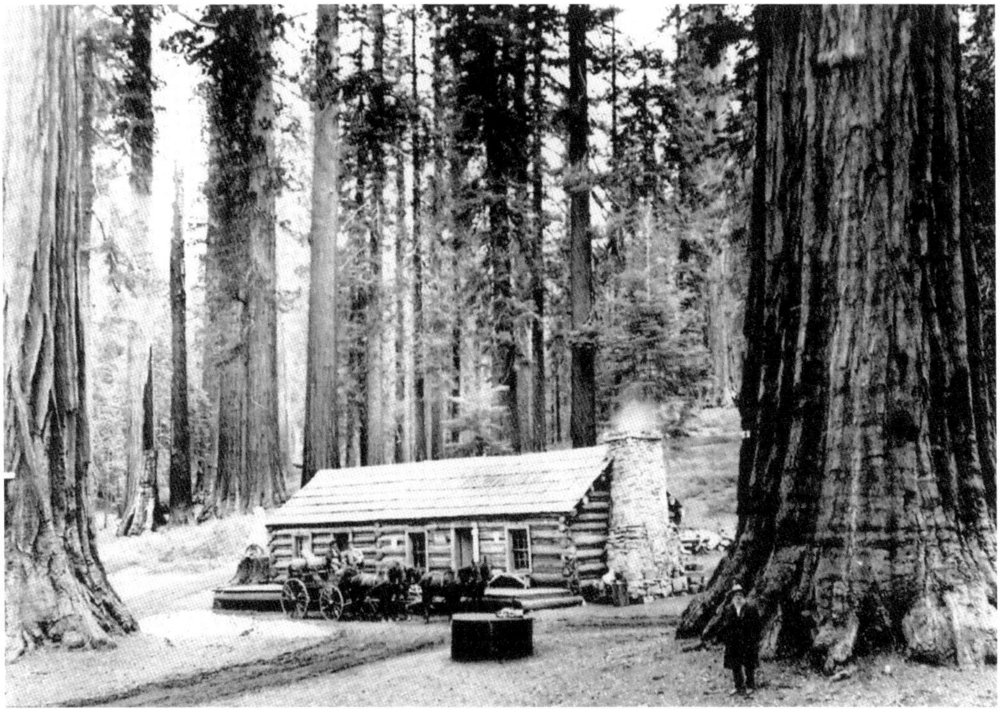

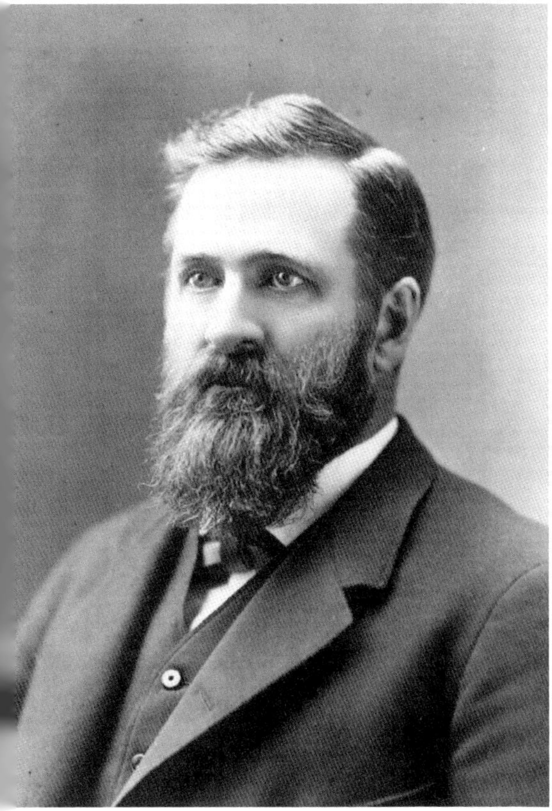

Clark in Mariposa Grove
Clark took partners in the form of Edwin and Huldah Moore for Clark's Ranch. But debt and management problems followed them, and he sold the Wawona properties to Alfred Henry Washburn, a Mariposa wagon provider who, in 1876, built the Wawona Hotel after fire destroyed Clark and Moore's ranch. In later life, Clark served as Yosemite guardian and is buried in the Pioneer Cemetery in Yosemite Valley surrounded by giant sequoias that he planted. Galen Clark is pictured in the upper grove near the site where his first cabin was erected. (Author's collection.)

Albert Henry Washburn
The 11th son of Seth Washburn of Vermont, Albert Henry traveled to Bridgeport, located below Mariposa, to join brother Seth Washburn Jr. in the mercantile and mining business. He soon became engaged in Mariposa in the livery business. (Author's collection.)

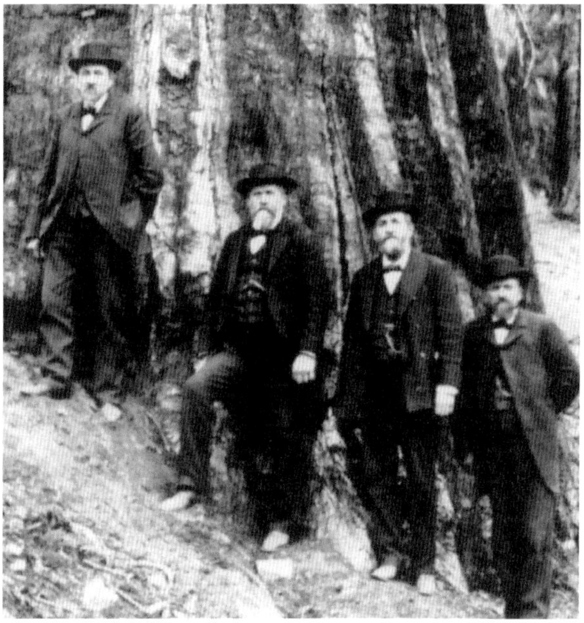

Seth, John, Edward, and Albert Henry Washburn at the Big Trees

Albert Henry married Jean Bruce, and with her came a skilled family who joined the Washburns in their projects. After acquiring Clark and Moore's ranch from Galen Clark, they began development of the property at Wawona. Fire destroyed Clark and Moore's buildings in 1878, and the Washburn and Bruce families rebuilt them, creating, in 1879, the main building of the Wawona Hotel, which is still in use. (Author's collection.)

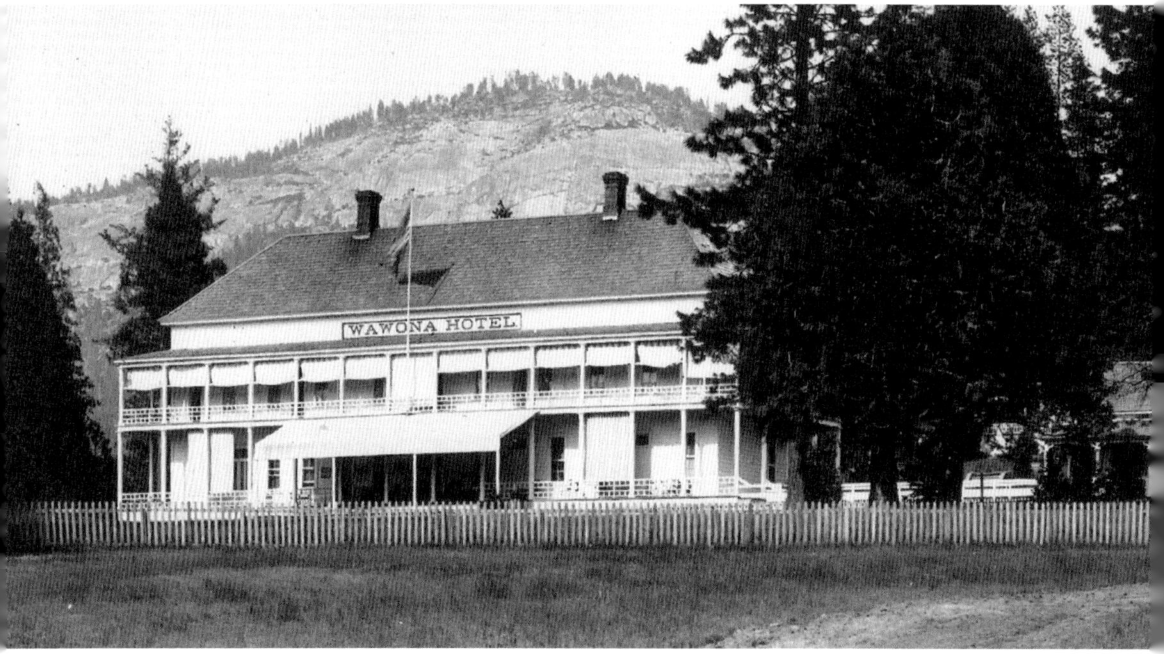

Wawona Hotel

Built in 1879, this hotel became the centerpiece of the Washburn family development.

The Washburn family continued ownership through three generations until 1932, expanding the hotel properties to include a farm, additional hotel units, a store, pavilion, tennis courts, golf course, swim tank, electrical system, and building the road from Wawona to Yosemite Valley, replacing the earlier horse trail. An art studio was created for Thomas Hill, outstanding Yosemite Artist. In 1932, the property was sold to the Department of Interior and added to Yosemite National Park. The golf course became the only one inside a national park. (Author's collection.)

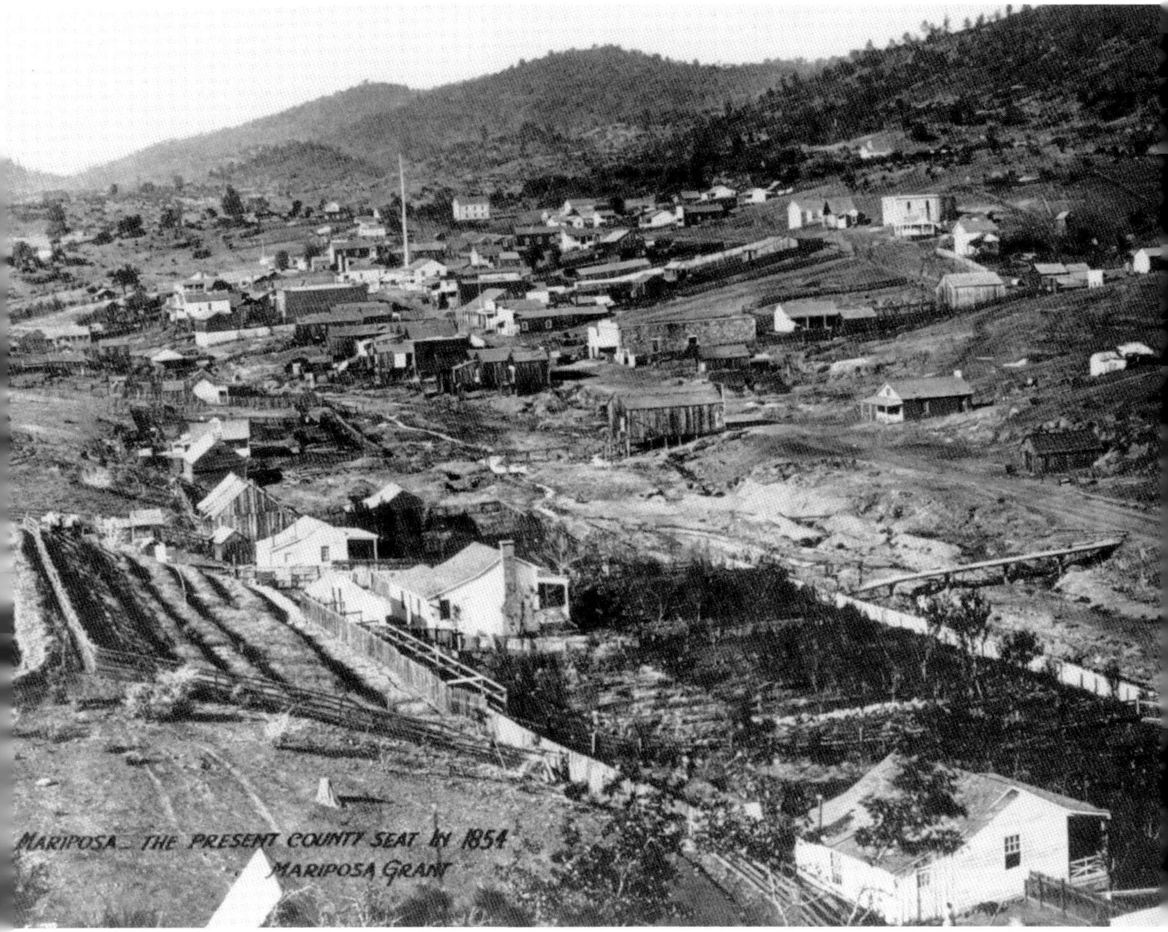

Mariposa, 1860

Knowledge of Yosemite Valley, the Mariposa Grove of Big Trees, and the high country spread rapidly as more and more newspaper articles and Hutchings's promotions generated more interest. But it was the early photographers who had the greatest impact. Carleton E. Watkins was one such photographer.

Watkins came West from New York with friend Collis P. Huntington to work in Huntington's Sacramento store. When the store burned, Watkins moved to San Francisco, where he went to work for R.H. Vance, owner of a daguerreotype studio. Vance sent him to his San Jose studio with instructions to hire a photographer. Instead, Watkins had seen enough to warrant his attempt at photography, which proved successful. Moving to Fords Studio and Ambrotype, Watkins began experimenting with glass-plate negatives and prints. His first commercial use of the process was to photograph the Almadin Mines near San Jose for a court case. Being able to reproduce a number of copies from one negative placed Watkins at the head of the class of California photographers. In late 1859, he was contacted by Trenor Park, Fremont's partner, to come to Mariposa and photograph the assets of the Fremont Grant in the year 1860.

Being in Mariposa put Watkins close enough to visit Yosemite with Trenor Park, and he returned in 1861 to extensively photograph the valley and surrounding area. His collection of mining photographs from the Mariposa Grant, taken in 1860, and his Yosemite scenes became the standard for landscape photography in the West.

This image (taken in 1860, not 1854 as noted) is one of more than 50 taken for Colonel Fremont as a commercial photographic process, providing Fremont with a tool to raise money or sell the grant. (Photograph by Carleton E. Watkins, author's collection.).

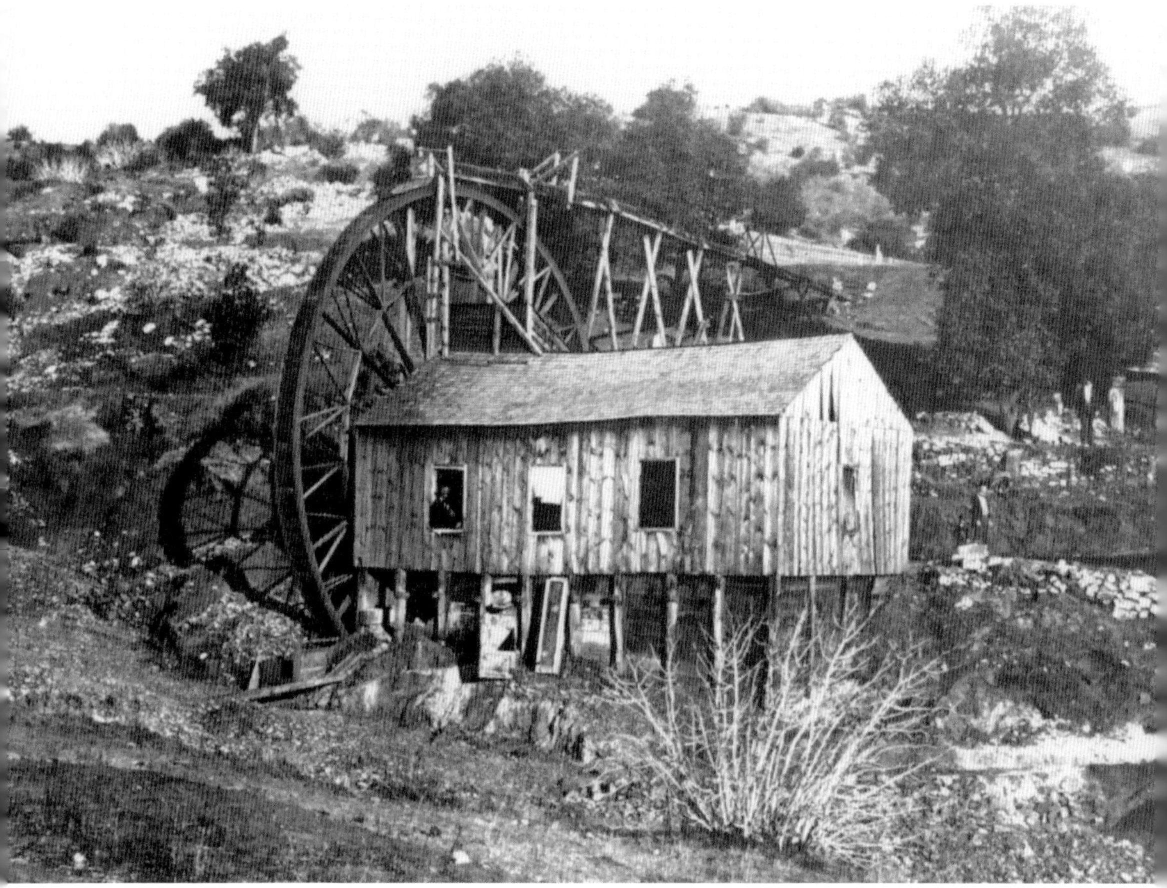

Mariposa Mine Mill, 1860

A set of Watkins's Yosemite photographs on display in New York was taken to Washington, DC, be shown to Pres. Abraham Lincoln. Although Lincoln was busy conducting a Civil War, what he saw in Watkins's prints convinced him of the desirability for the preservation of this Western wilderness. Thus, in 1864, at the height of the Civil War, President Lincoln caused the granting of Yosemite Valley and the Mariposa Grove of Big Trees to the State of California for the purpose of creating a state park. Shown here is the first quartz mill at Colonel Fremont's Mariposa Mine. (Photograph by Carleton E. Watkins, author's collection.)

Yosemite Cathedral Rocks

Watkins's photographs of Yosemite were important to the understanding of the unique nature of Yosemite. He returned and photographed in Yosemite a number of times later in life. Here, he captured Cathedral Rocks. (Photograph by Carleton E. Watkins, author's collection.)

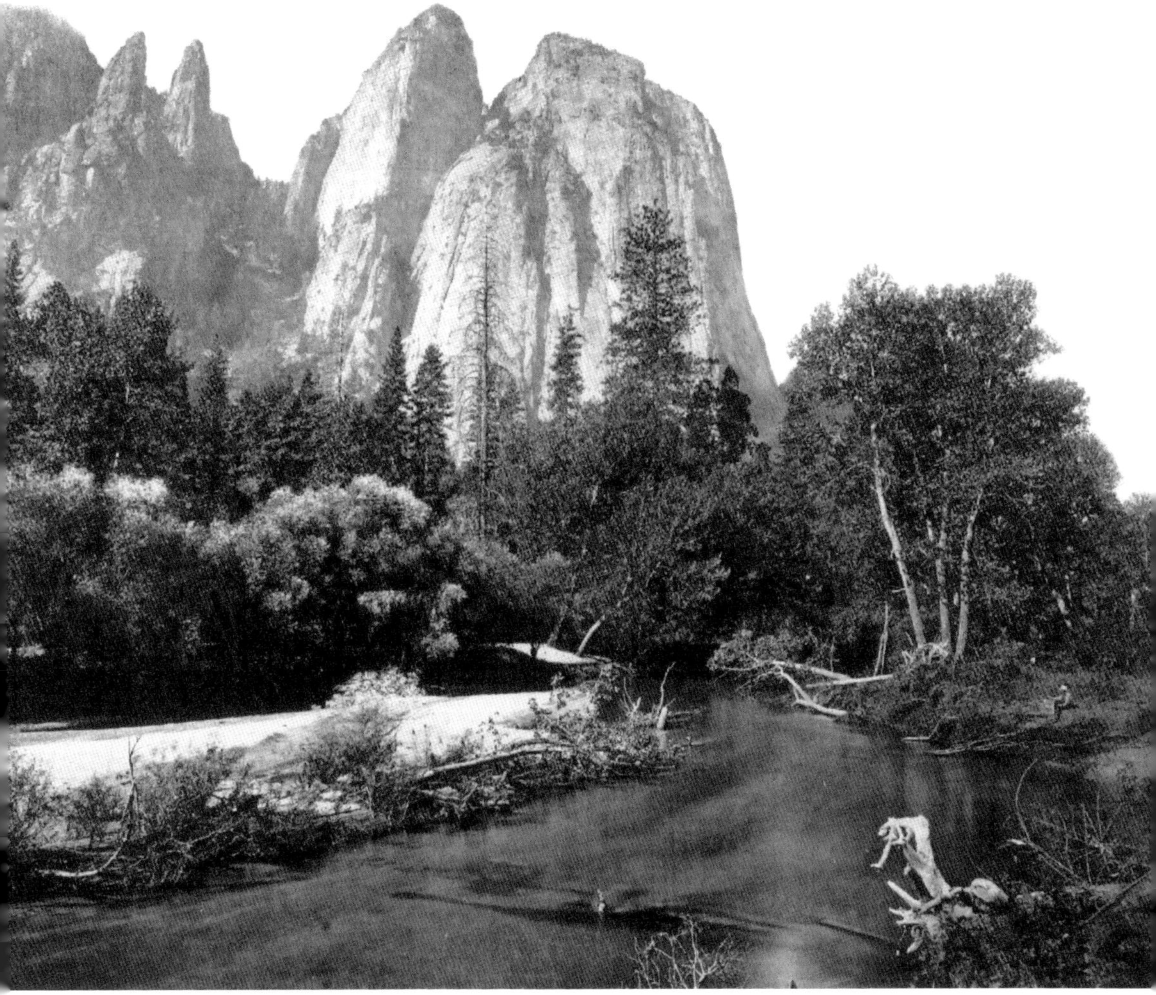

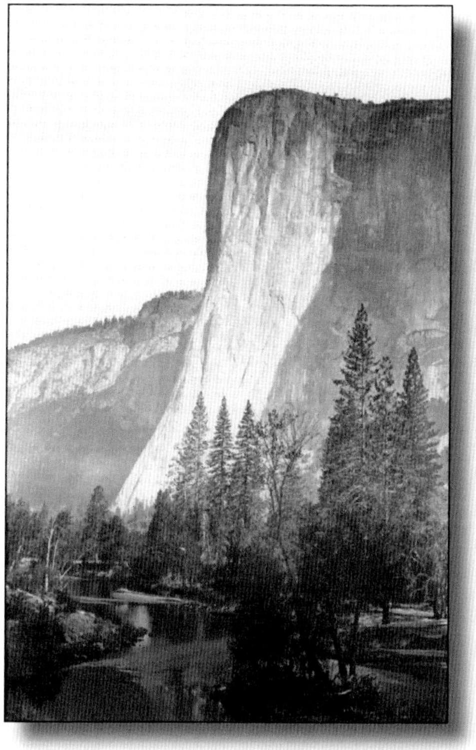

El Capitan and Yosemite Falls across valley from Glacier Point
These images, plus many others, were from the collection shown to Pres. Abraham Lincoln that contributed to the granting of Yosemite Valley and the Mariposa Grove of Big Trees to the State of California for purposes of forming a public park by 1864. (Photograph by Carleton E. Watkins, author's collection.)

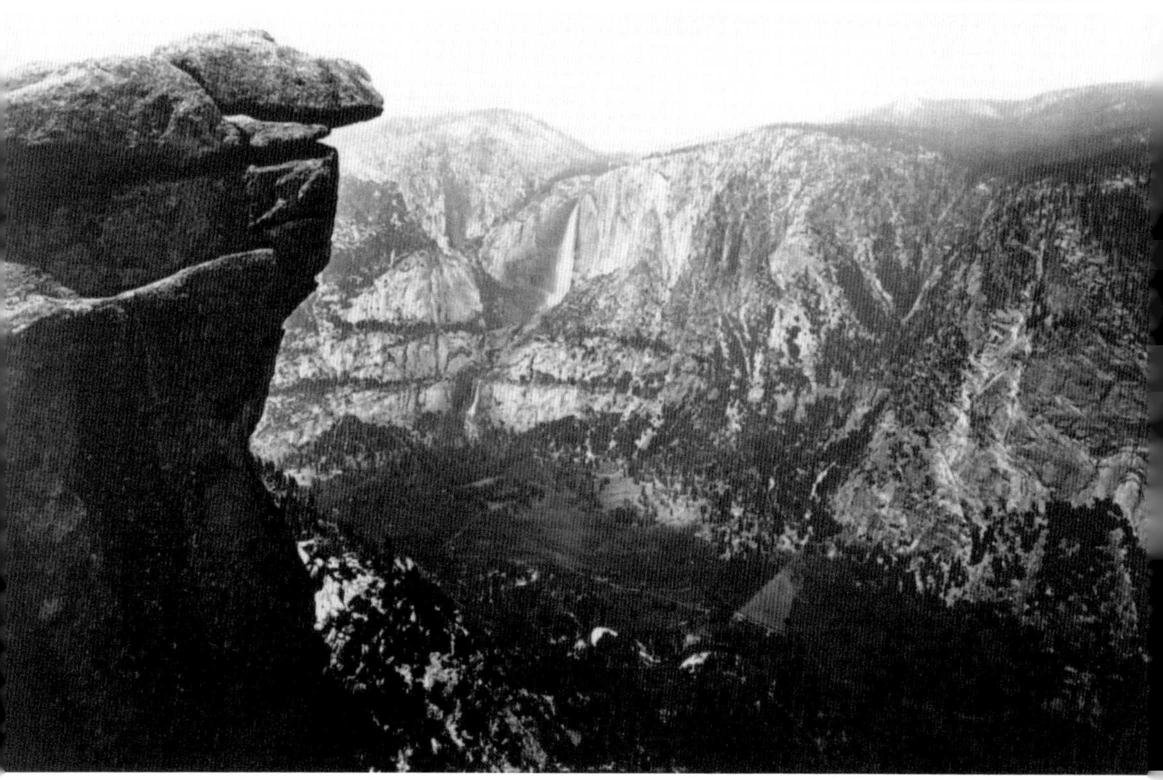

CHAPTER TWO

A Legendary Bandit and the Evolution of Mining

Even though a few determined individuals were visiting Yosemite and telling about its wonders, gold mining in the Mother Lode and Mariposa County continued to be of primary interest. It was the prospect of wealth that brought people from around the world—not the beauty of Yosemite. At first, gold was found mostly in the streams and stream banks where it was deposited millions of years before. But without water to wash the placer, no profitable work could be done until the fall or spring rains. It was quickly determined that tracing gold to its source, mining of the quartz containing the gold, and processing it was the way to go. No longer were the easy pickings of gold in the stream sustaining the farm boys who rushed from around the world. This change required many men with some expertise in the process, machines, and capital.

The lust for gold led to the long-lasting legend of Joaquin Murrieta in Mariposa County. He is counted as a citizen of Mariposa County because he was a part of the early history of bandits who roamed the foothills of California, and at the end of a short life, he became an attraction in the gold mining town of Hornitos. According to author J.C. Cunningham in his *Truth about Murrieta*, the famous marauder lived and worked for a time in Indian Gulch (Santa Cruz) when it was a mining camp. He later appeared in Hornitos to rescue his band of men from incarceration. The California Rangers eventually caught him and his band of men along Cantua Creek near Coalinga in the San Joaquin Valley.

Young Joaquin Murietta

When California became a state, Mariposa County covered the whole of the San Joaquin Valley. In early 1850, a young Mexican lad, his beautiful wife, her brother, and his wife left San Gabriel, Southern California, to move north into the gold-rush region near Murphys. There, while Joaquin was away from his claim to buy supplies, his camp was attacked by a group of Americans who killed his brother-in-law and abused his wife. Returning to camp, he found his unconscious wife and her brother. Americans attacked Joaquin Murietta, tied him to a tree, brutally beat him, and then left him for dead. When his young wife came to and saw Murietta seemingly dead and tied to a tree, she killed herself with her own knife. Joaquin revived and found his wife dead by her own hand. These brutal acts sent him into a frenzy requiring revenge. (Author's collection.)

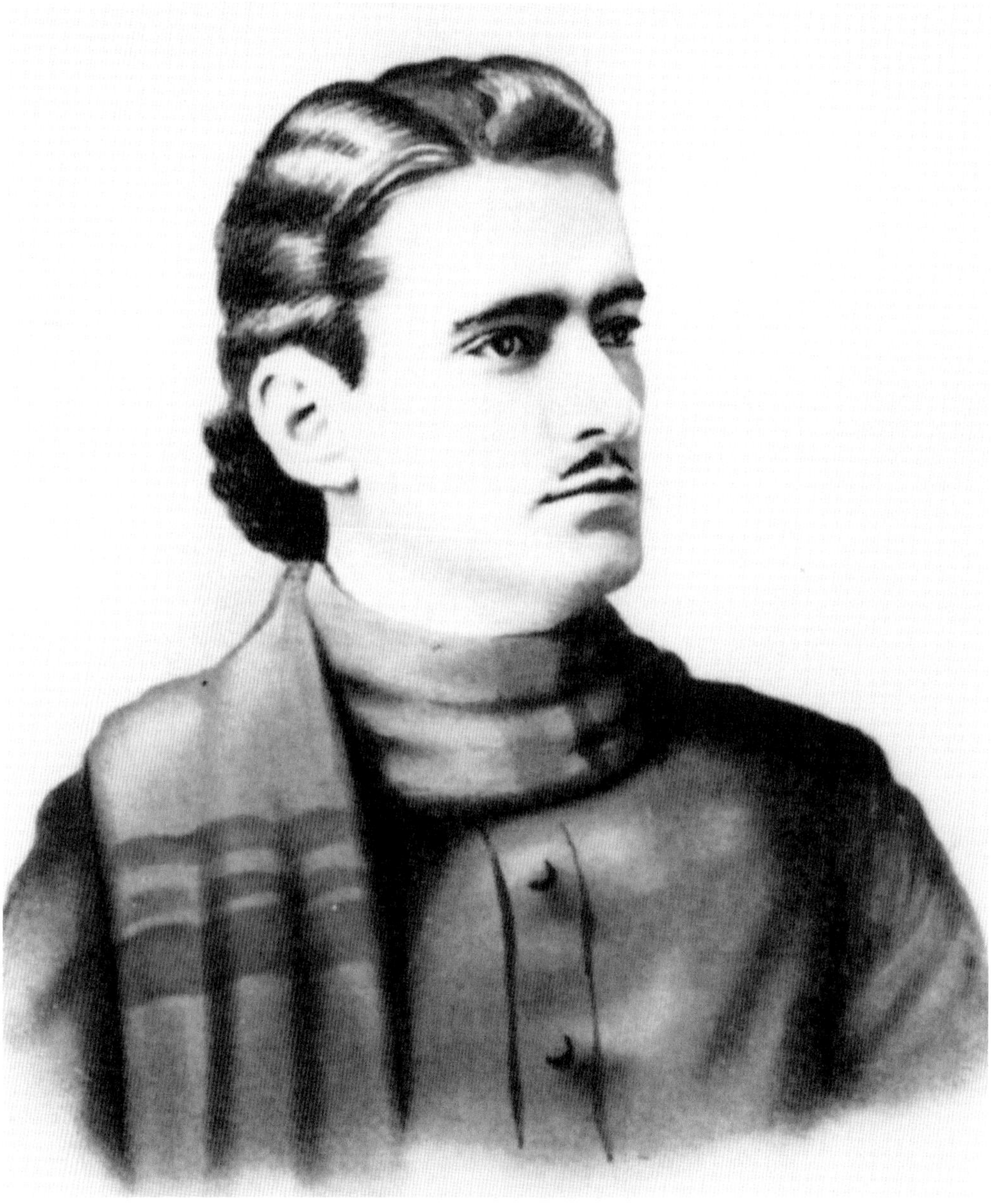

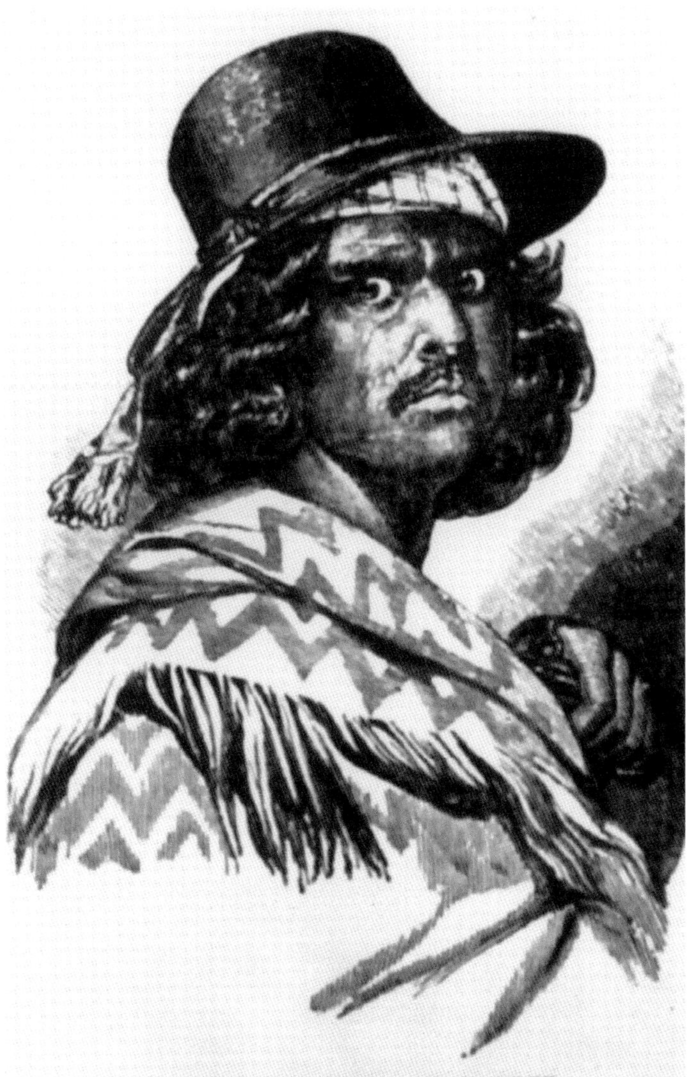

JOAQUIN, THE MOUNTAIN ROBBER.

Joaquin the Bandit Seeking Revenge
For the next two years, he moved from mining camp to mining camp carrying out the task of revenge. A group of young Mexican men joined him in the killing and robbing of the American miners responsible for his wife's death.

Once satisfied, he tried to resume a normal life, but by that time, the men who accompanied him had become despised bandits. At various times, he lived and worked in Mariposa County as a packer for a storekeeper in Indian Gulch. But his loyalty to the men who joined him in his revenge caused involvement in various acts around Hornitos. Other bandits in the state took the name Joaquin, thus making it became impossible for him to resume a normal life since he was sought in many areas of Northern and Central California.

A group of men formed by the governor as the California Rangers was charged with the task of capturing or killing the famous outlaw. The leader of the group was Harry Love of Quartzburg, Mariposa County. Also listed on the roster was Capt. William J. Howard of Bridgeport, Mariposa County, who was an acquaintance of Joaquin. (Author's collection.)

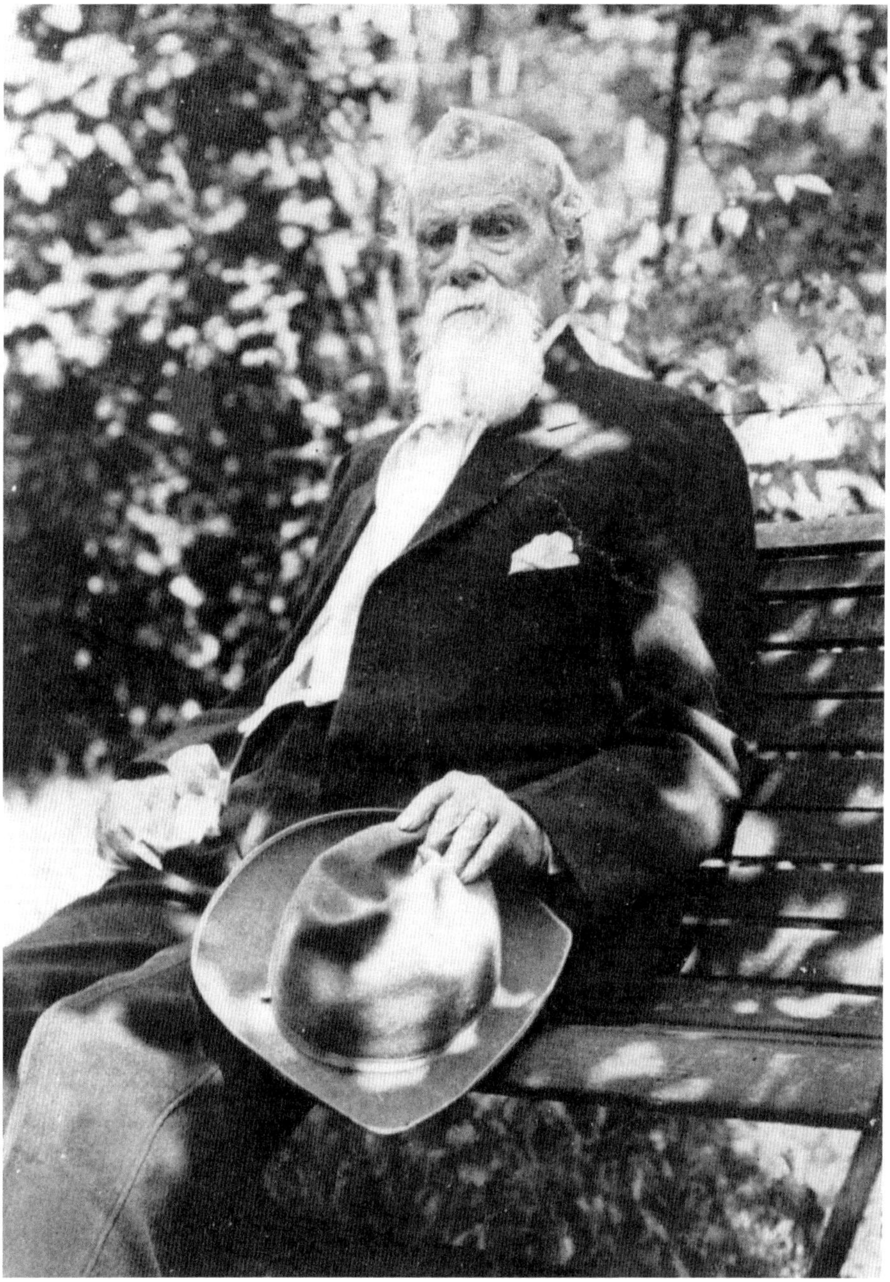

William J. Howard

Capt. William J. Howard, a member of the California Rangers, deputy sheriff, district attorney, and rancher near Hornitos, is pictured later in life. He was the first to identify the head of the bandit killed at Cantua Creek as Joaquin Murietta. He sent the head to Dr. Miller at Millerton for preserving.

While a member of the rangers, Howard was at home in Bridgeport on the day they captured and killed Murietta. He had important business to attend to at the ranch. The rangers captured Joaquin Murietta, and in the process, he was killed, and his head removed. At the same time, Joaquin's lieutenant, Three-Fingered Jack Garcia, was also killed, and his hand was removed for identification. (Author's collection.)

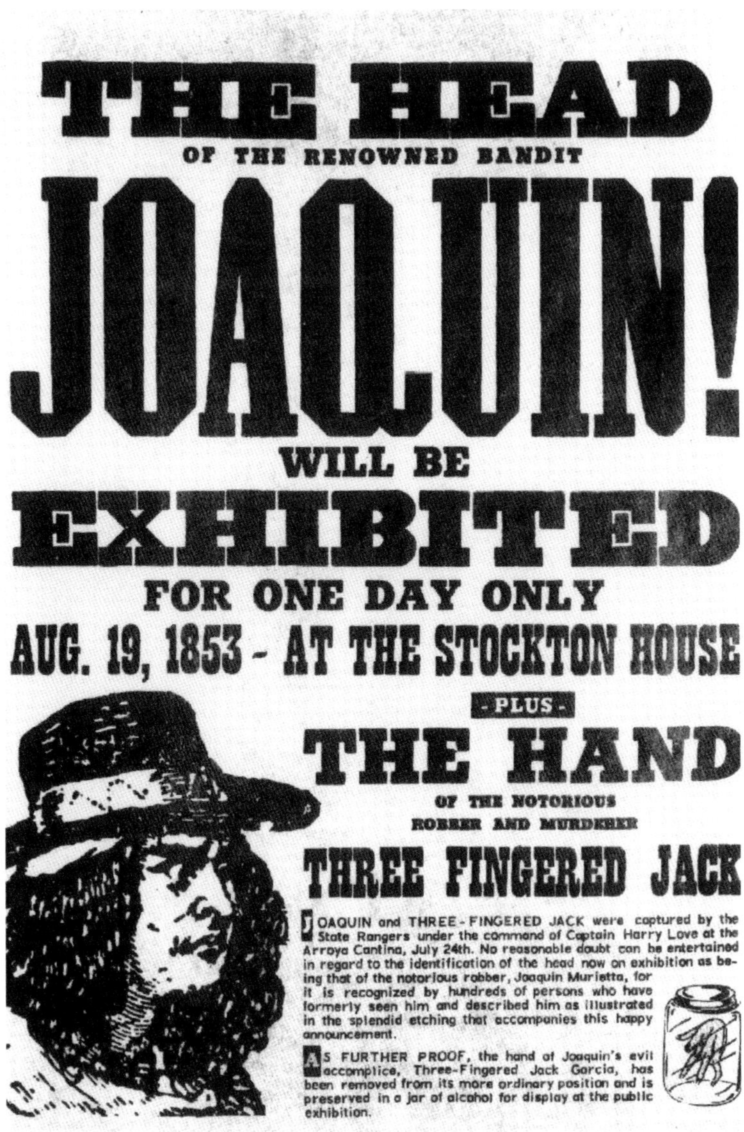

Playbill of the Exposition of Murietta's Head and the Hand of Three-Fingered Jack
The killing of Joaquin and many members of his band was celebrated throughout California. His head was brought first for positive identification to Capt. William J. Howard at his ranch in Mariposa County and then to Millerton for preservation in alcohol by Dr. Miller; the hand of Three-Fingered Jack was also preserved. The head and hand were returned to a Hornitos bar for exposition. Many who saw the head in the jar commented that it was Joaquin, but others disputed the claim.

Even today, there is disagreement about the identity of the head in the bottle. Some felt that it looked too much like a Mexican or an Indian. Others who thought they knew Murietta said that because he was half Virginian, because of his mother's ancestry, he should appear more like an Anglo. Many finally agreed that the head was that of an Indian. The facts of the death of Murietta were and are still in dispute. The controversy will continue, as the head in the bottle was on display at the end of a bar at the time of the in 1906 San Francisco earthquake and fire and was never recovered. Lost forever was the legendary Joaquin Murietta. (Author's collection.)

Mariposa Mine, 1890

The opening of the Mariposa Mine along the vein discovered by Fremont's Mexican miners began the era of underground hard-rock mining. The Gold Rush was over. Many men tried to sustain life from the creeks and rivers, but they lived difficult, lonely, and dangerous lives. There were just enough stories about the "big strike" to keep them trying, but few enjoyed success. Many of these gold-seekers were destitute men from foreign lands, such as Chile, Europe, China, and Mexico. Once here, it was difficult for them to return home. Added to that, the State of California imposed a "Foreign Miners Tax," which was directed at non-American prospectors. Whole settlements disappeared overnight. Some of these men went to work in the large mines, while others built railroads and rock fences. Their dreams of fabulous wealth faded.

Families, mostly from the Midwest, moved to the area, setting up small farms, many on land of the Fremont claim. These farms and ranches provided the labor for the mining operations usually on a seasonal basis. This was because even the large mills processing the ore from the underground mines needed water. So with many men to pay and no ability to operate year-round, the mining company depended on the miners providing their own living part of the year. The miners and their families welcomed the agricultural products from these small farms. Thus, sustainable agriculture was transferred to the gold region and became the basis of the local economy. (Author's collection.)

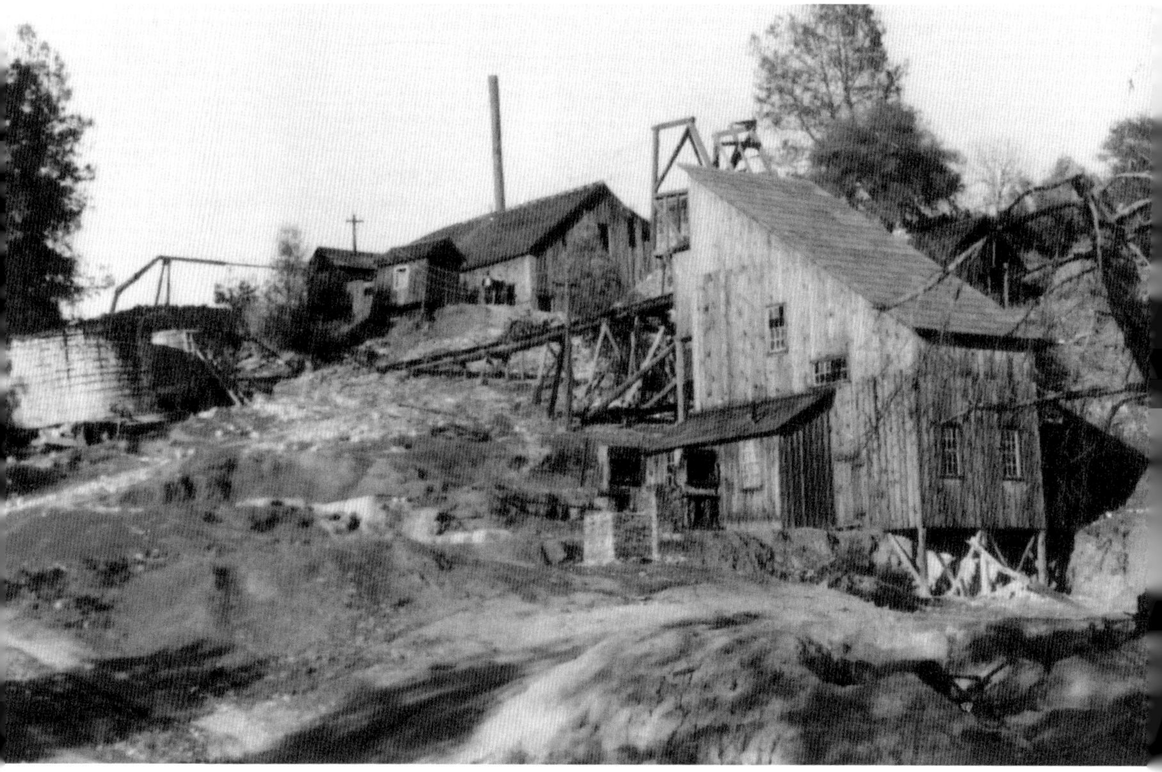

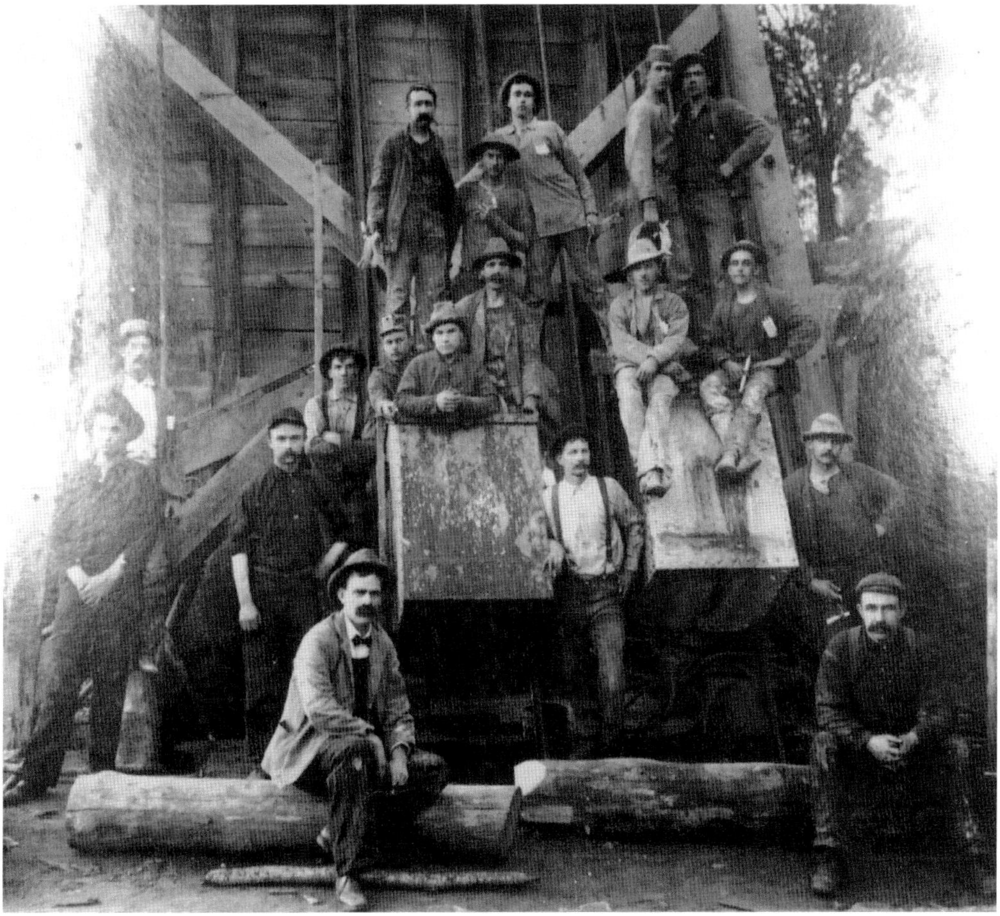

Joseph Lind at Mariposa Mine

In spite of these difficulties, towns near the main mines were founded and prospered. Mariposa, Mount Bullion, Bear Valley, Hornitos, and Coulterville were all founded or sustained by the proximity of employment for the men. The mines were sustained by the stock sales around the world. It was often said that it was not the gold that was being mined but the stockholders. Loss of one's investment became common, but the dream of wealth continued on. Crews were led by experienced mine superintendents, like Joseph Lind and Frank McGuire, seen here with their crew ready to descend into the shaft.

As time went on, the utilization of natural resources and seasonal employment in Yosemite became sources of income for those permanent residents. Once arrived, many of these men and families did not have the resources to return to their original homes. Conditions in the East, particularly, were not very good with the impending difficulties between the North and South. The new residents, bringing their families, came with the intention of making Mariposa and the Mother Lode their home. Many of the forty-niners were unable to return to their homes in the East and, consequently, lived lonely, unsatisfied lives to their end, frequently by accidents or at their own hands. The new families that came after the initial Gold Rush formed the basis of communities that exists today. (Author's collection.)

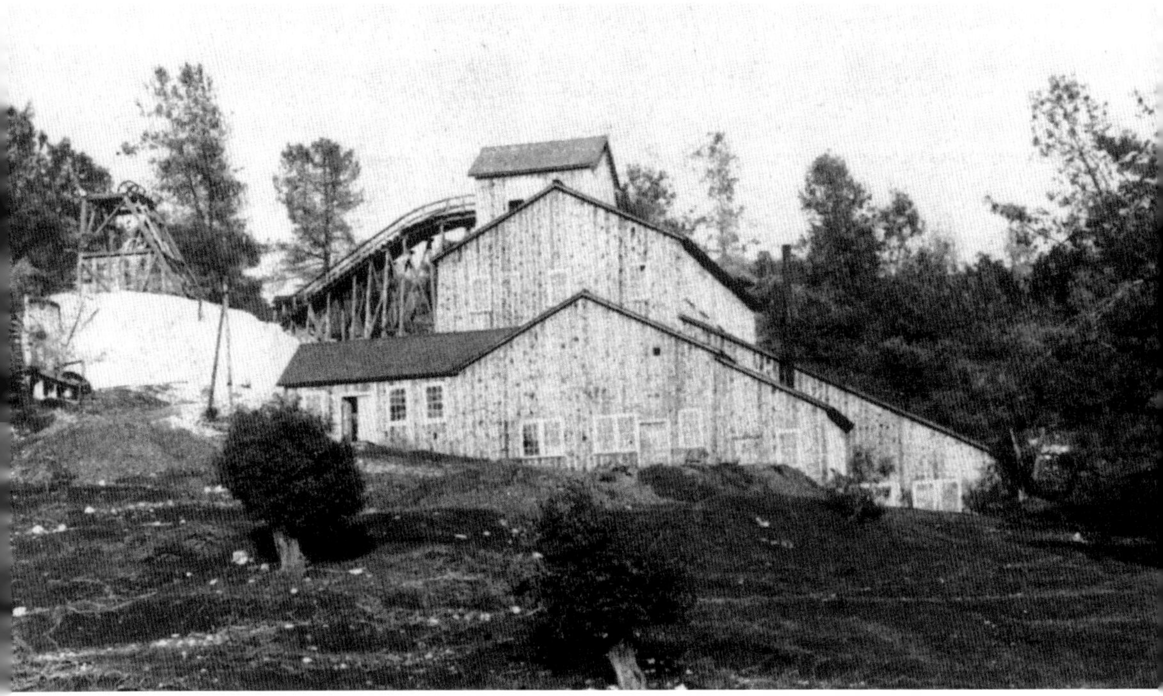

Mariposa Mine, 1904
Mariposa Mine is pictured at its most active around 1904. The main mill building fed from the head frame to the left. Even today, the dream of the forty-niner, with his gold pan and pick, still draws a crowd to the towns founded by adventure. (Author's collection.)

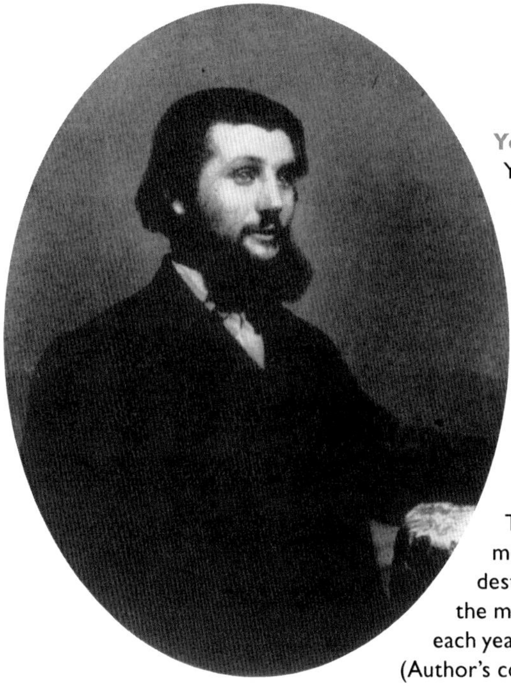

Young John Muir
Yosemite Valley and the Mariposa Grove suffered to some extent under the politically appointed state commission. Homesteads were applied for and claimed, orchards were planted, hay was raised in the meadows, and hotels and other commercial facilities were built and operated. James Mason Hutchings built a sawmill below Yosemite Falls to provide lumber for the projects. In 1869, while following a band of sheep, a Scottish immigrant came to the mountains examining the flora, fauna, and the natural environment and understanding the purpose of the various species to the scene. The sheep were intended to graze in the high meadows of the Sierra. John Muir understood the destructive nature of the clove-hoofed harvesters of the meadows and comprehended the short time period each year that the meadows had to regenerate themselves. (Author's collection.)

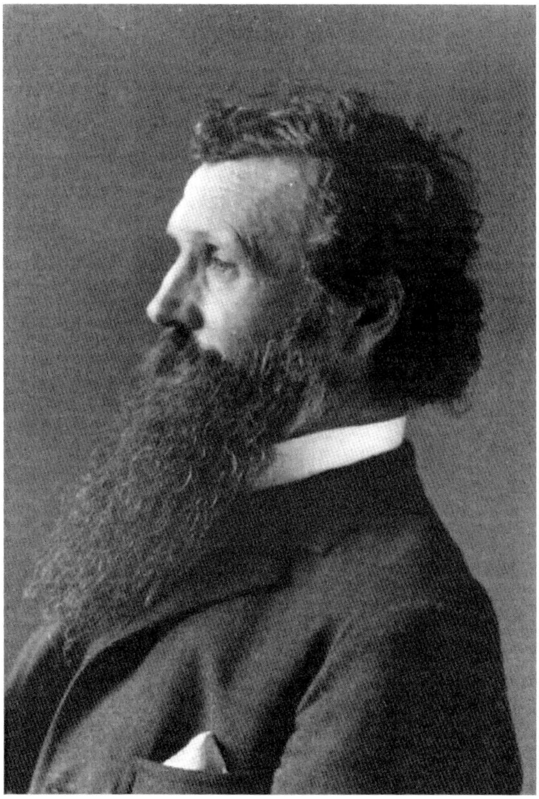

Muir's Early Days in Yosemite

When Muir arrived in Yosemite Valley, he went to work for James Mason Hutchings at his sawmill. These activities and the urbanization and development of agriculture within Yosemite Valley along with the grazing in the higher country disturbed him greatly. He advanced the concepts of conservation and preservation. He formed a small but active group, mostly from the University of California, called the Sierra Club. He developed an understanding of the formation of Yosemite Valley. Contrary to the positions of higher-placed well-known surveyors and geologists, he began to describe the nature of the formation of Yosemite Valley and other areas in the Sierra as being the result of glacier activity. By 1890, he convinced the federal government to form Yosemite and Sequoia National Parks. By late 1890, federal troops, including African American troops, were patrolling the park to evict sheep and cattle and other poachers of the environment. (Author's collection.)

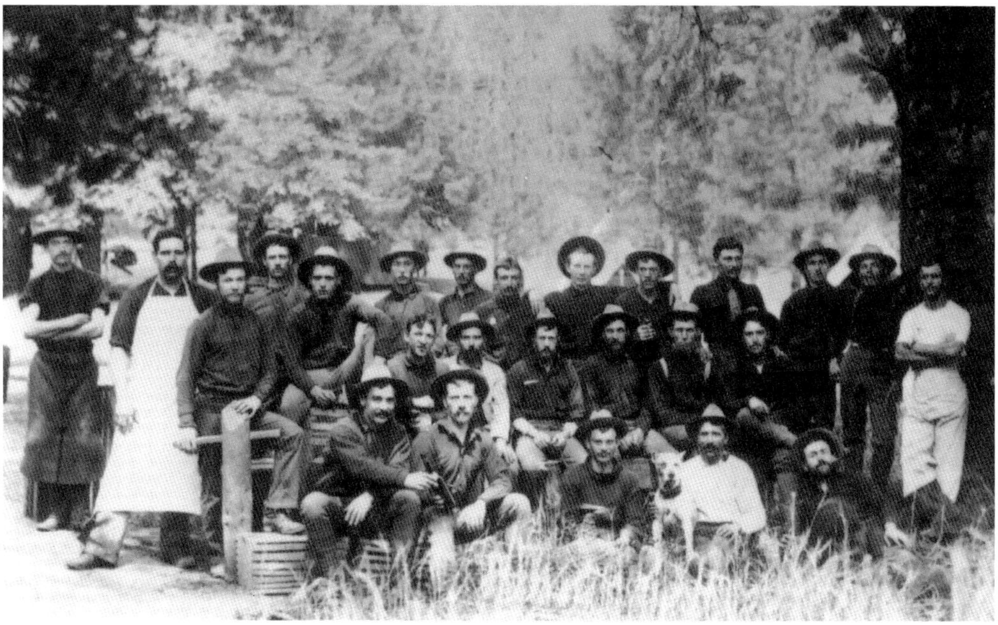

Army Troopers at Camp Hoyle in Wawona

Because Yosemite Valley was still under the control of the State of California, Army troops, such as those pictured here, were stationed outside the Valley. (Author's collection.)

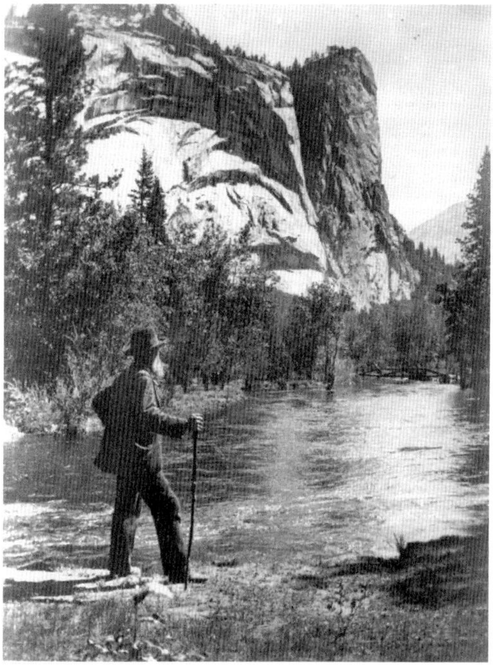

John Muir along Merced River, Washington Column ahead of Him

John Muir spent many days alone appreciating the grandeur of Yosemite Valley, wishing that the valley was part of Yosemite National Park. By 1903, he met Pres. Theodore Roosevelt and spent three days with him. The result of the visit was the retrocession of Yosemite Valley and the Mariposa Grove of Big Trees to the federal government for inclusion in the park.

Muir's activities as founder and leader of the Sierra Club made him the greatest advocate for preservation of the unique wild areas of our country. However, at the end of his life he stated that his greatest failure was his inability to prevent the building of the Hetch Hetchy project within the boundaries of Yosemite National Park, which provided water and power to the city of San Francisco. (Courtesy of Yosemite Museum Library.)

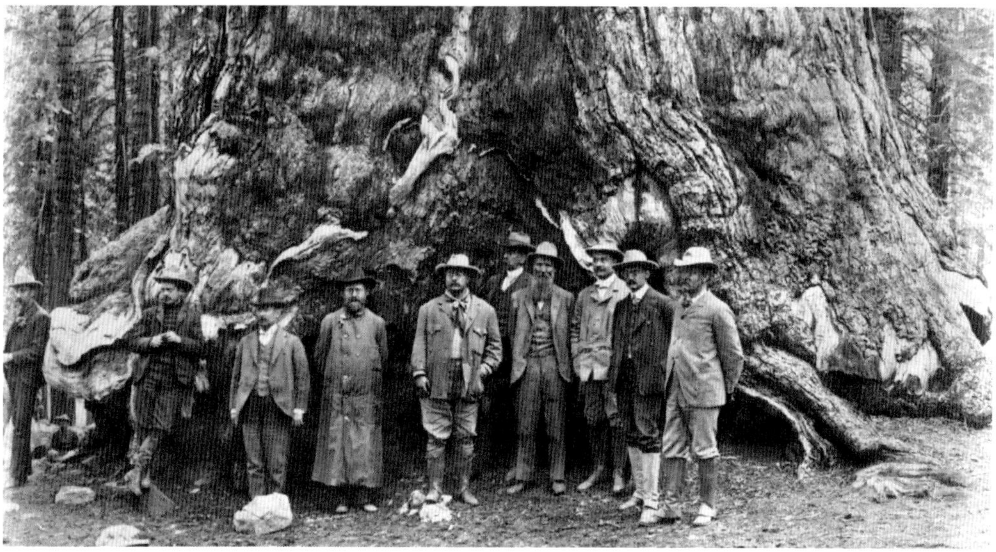

Muir, Roosevelt, and Dignitaries in Mariposa Grove

Muir and Roosevelt traveled around the park with only a guide and cook, sleeping on the ground and interacting with the environment. This couple of days with Muir influenced Roosevelt's thinking about preservation.

Muir's visit with President Roosevelt in 1903 was a singular occasion. Roosevelt already had some appreciation of nature but also loved to collect animal species by hunting. Whether or not Muir had any influence on Roosevelt in that regard is not completely known, but he certainly found an understanding ear. Roosevelt came to Yosemite with a large contingent, which he left behind at the Wawona Hotel while he toured the park with Muir. His experiences with Muir helped shape later decisions of many presidents, some not always positive but at least considered. (Courtesy of Yosemite Museum Library.)

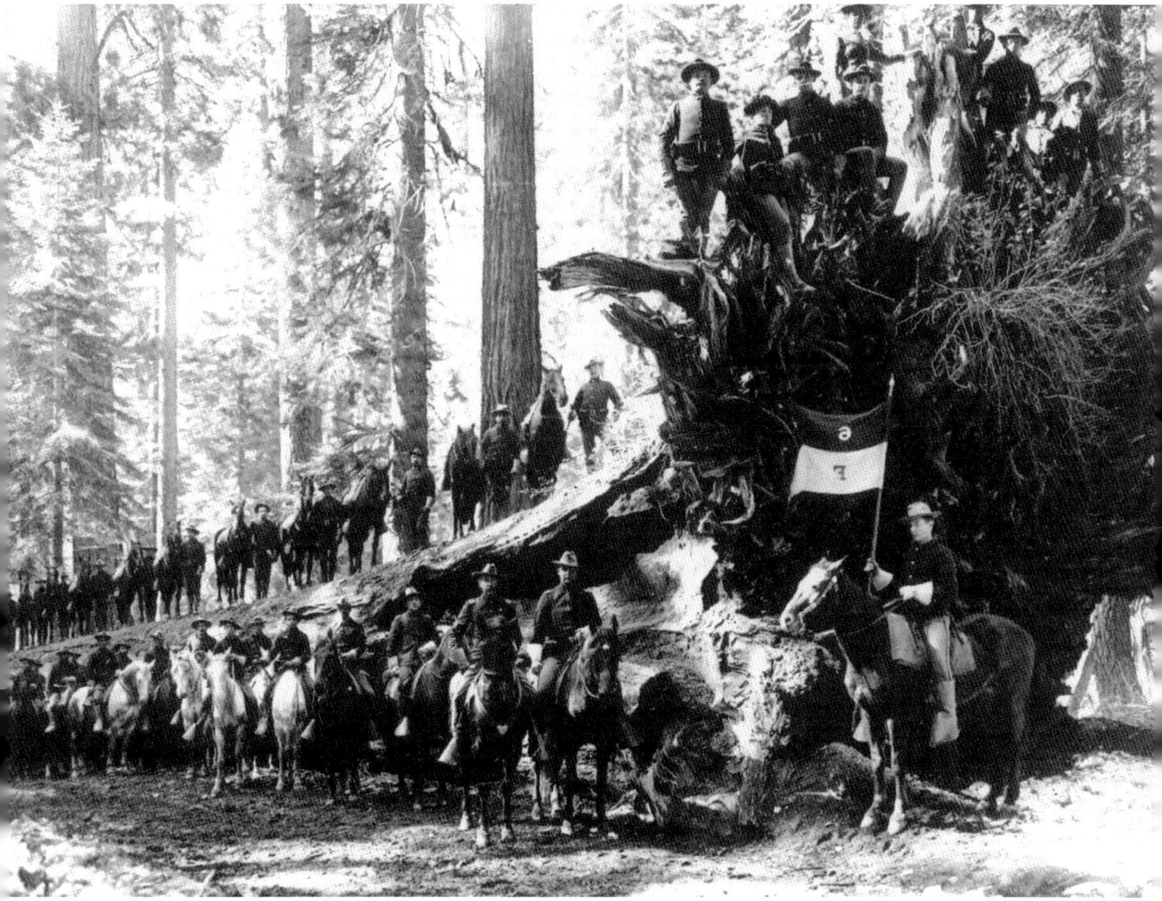

Yosemite National Park Army, 1899

Army units from the Presidio, San Francisco, were patrolling in Yosemite National Park during the summer. This group stationed at Camp Hoyle, near Wawona, were posed on the Fallen Monarch in the Mariposa Grove.

During the period before 1900 and a bit beyond, Yosemite was managed and protected by mounted Army units from the Presidio in San Francisco. Their main task was keeping the livestock operators, mainly from Mariposa County, from grazing in and damaging the fragile environment of the park. Sheep were the greatest problem because of the damage they caused in the wet meadows. Following Muir's meeting with Roosevelt, the federal government reacquired the Valley and Big Trees, which for a short time were managed by the military units. During the Spanish-American War, black troops replaced their white counterparts as they were needed in Cuba. The black troops gained the title of Buffalo Soldiers here and elsewhere serving many difficult and hazardless tasks following the Civil War.

By 1906, the fruits of Muir's labor began the process of returning Yosemite Valley and the Mariposa Grove to the federal government. The process took some time, and by 1915, a ranger unit was formed with the first members being local ranchers and mountain men who were especially valuable because of their knowledge of the park. They served until the establishment of the National Park Service. Their primary task was to prevent illegal livestock grazing within the park and to monitor fire within the reservation. (Courtesy of Yosemite Museum Library.)

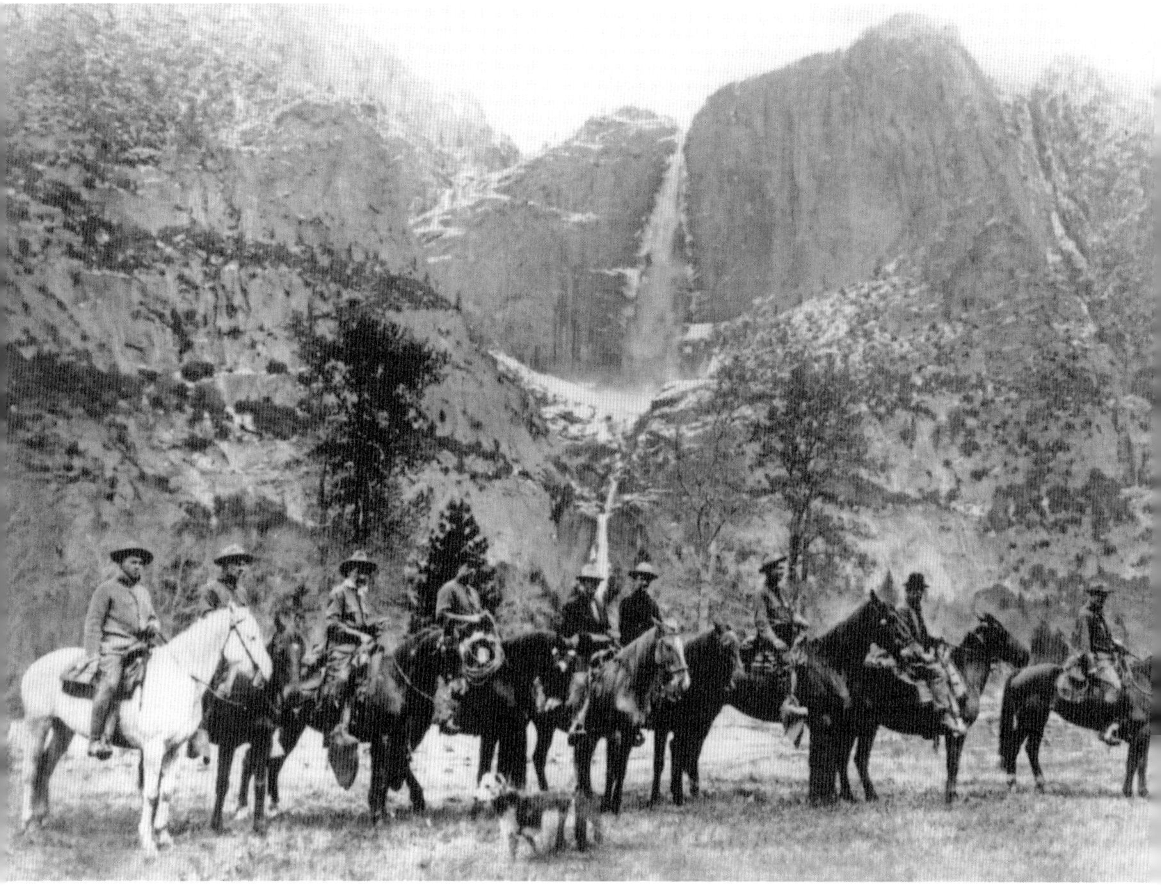

First Rangers

The first rangers in Yosemite, in 1915, were made up of local men who knew the park well. From left to right are Charles Bull, Oliver Prien, Jack Gaylor, Clyde Booth, George McNabb, Charlie Leidig, Charlie Adair, Archie Leonard, and Forest Townsley. (Courtesy of Yosemite Museum Library.)

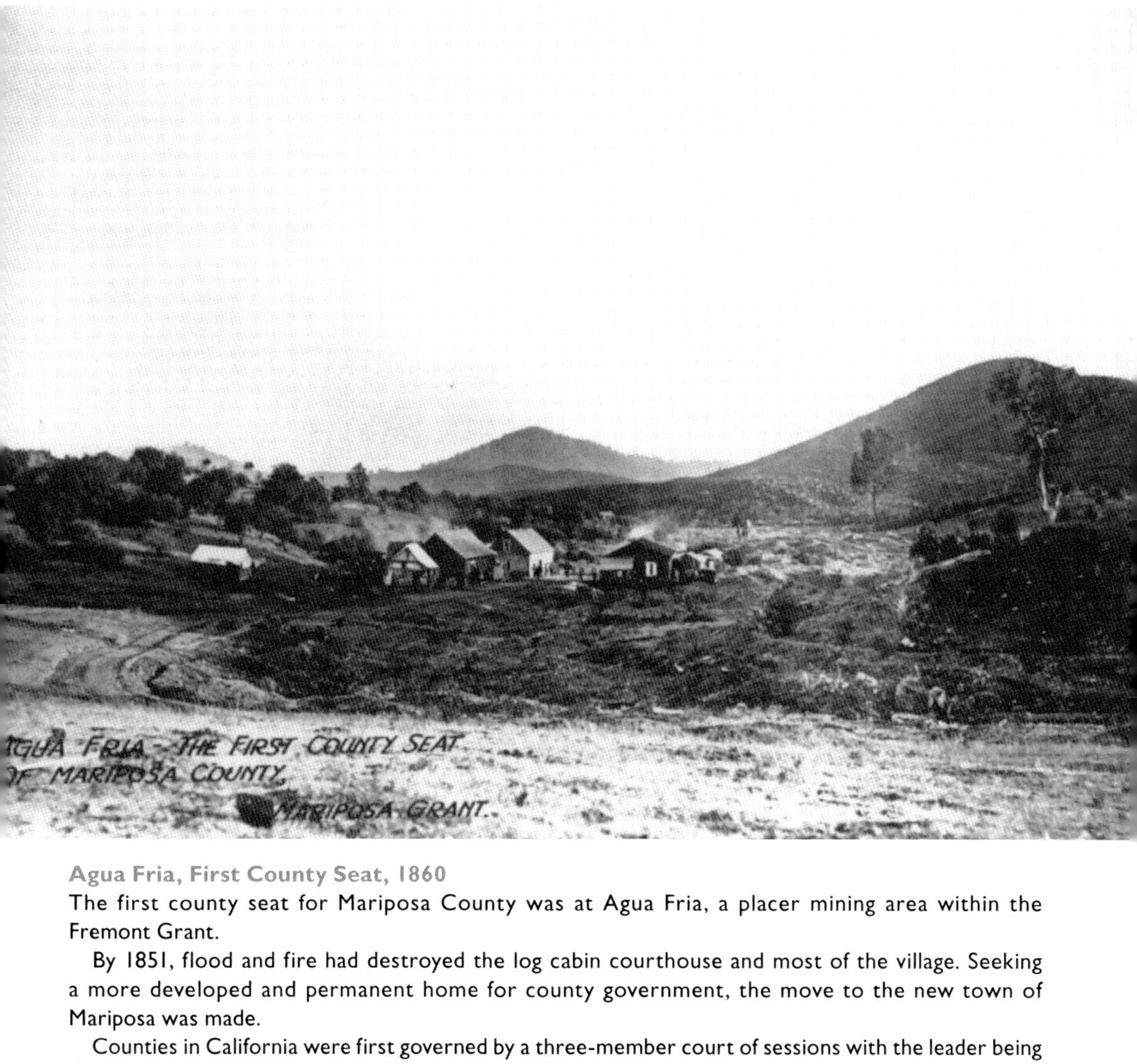

Agua Fria, First County Seat, 1860

The first county seat for Mariposa County was at Agua Fria, a placer mining area within the Fremont Grant.

By 1851, flood and fire had destroyed the log cabin courthouse and most of the village. Seeking a more developed and permanent home for county government, the move to the new town of Mariposa was made.

Counties in California were first governed by a three-member court of sessions with the leader being the presiding judge. This panel had both the criminal and civil responsibilities for the county. After moving the county seat to Mariposa, government took place in various locations, often in the parlor of county clerk Edward C. Bell, but then, it seemed desirable for the county to have a proper seat of justice. The court of sessions accepted the plan of Perrin V. Fox on June 21, 1854, and granted a contract to Fox and builder Augustus F. Shriver for the sum of $9,000 on July 21, 1854. The structure was to be 40.5 feet wide by 50.5 feet long, two stories tall, and on a site of "high eminence," donated to the county by William R. Owen. The land was part of the Las Mariposas Grant, which Fremont did not have title, and thus neither did Owen.

David Clark of Midpines was given the task of providing the lumber for the new building. Clark was a New Englander who knew the lumber business and sawmills. (Photograph by Carleton E. Watkins, author's collection.)

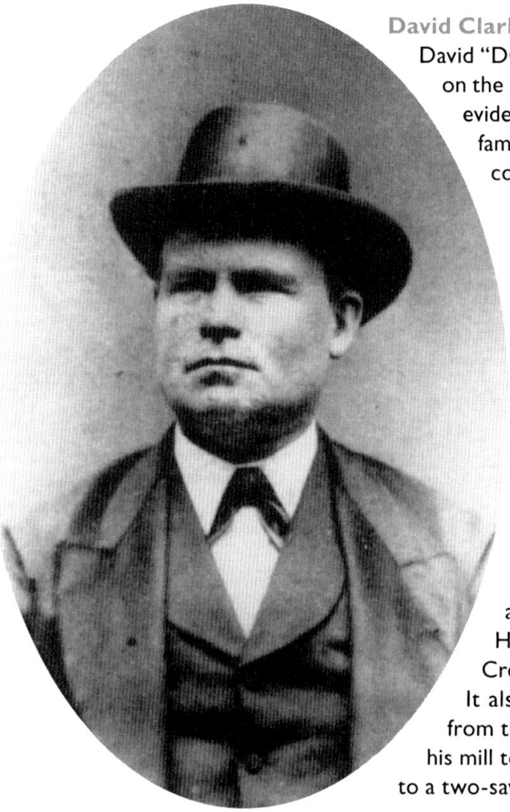

David Clark

David "DC" Clark came to California about 1852 perhaps on the hope of richness from gold, but it quite soon was evident that his trade as a lumberman would sustain his family. He prepared at least some of the lumber for the courthouse. (Courtesy of Roene Clark Wilson.)

Clark's Mill at Midpines

Clark returned East to acquire a sawmill and quickly returned to establish his mill and home in Midpines, at today's corner of Highway 140 and Triangle Road. His mill was steam operated with a vertical blade. A second steam mill, operated by Humphrey and Geiger, was located on Mariposa Creek near a stand of white pine just north of town. It also had a vertical blade, but how much lumber from this mill was used is not clear. Clark later moved his mill to Snow Creek, east of Mariposa, and converted to a two-saw circular mill. (Author's collection.)

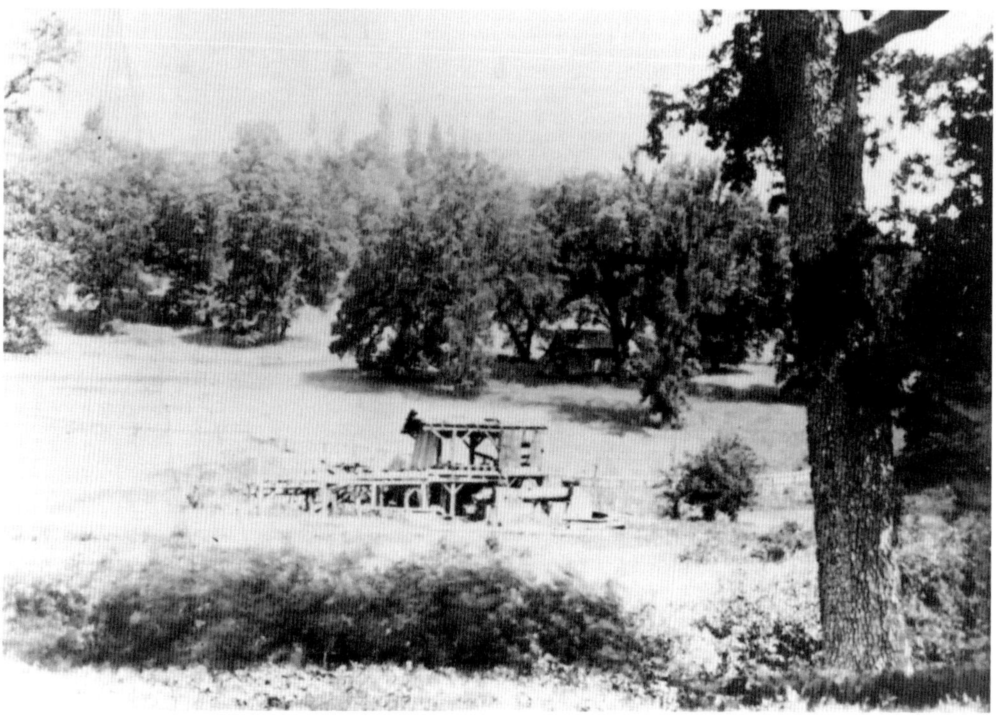

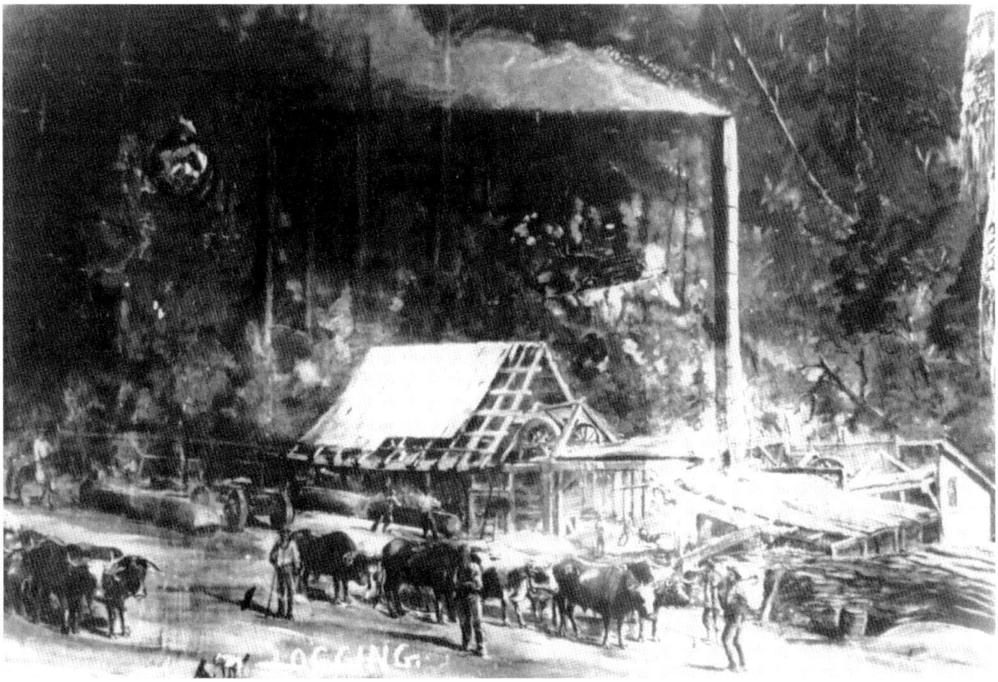

Swartz's Painting of Lumber Being Sawed for the Courthouse

The courthouse was built on land donated by William R. Owen, who essentially had squatter's rights to the property but not the title since Fremont also did not have title. A few years later, after gaining American title in 1856, Fremont was broke and needed to sell the grant. The county government became concerned about the ownership of the property under its courthouse and contacted Fremont. He gracefully transferred the title to the county for $1. This painting by Swartz shows lumber for the courthouse being sawed. This painting hung in various establishments in Mariposa for years before disappearing in one of the many fires. (Author's collection.)

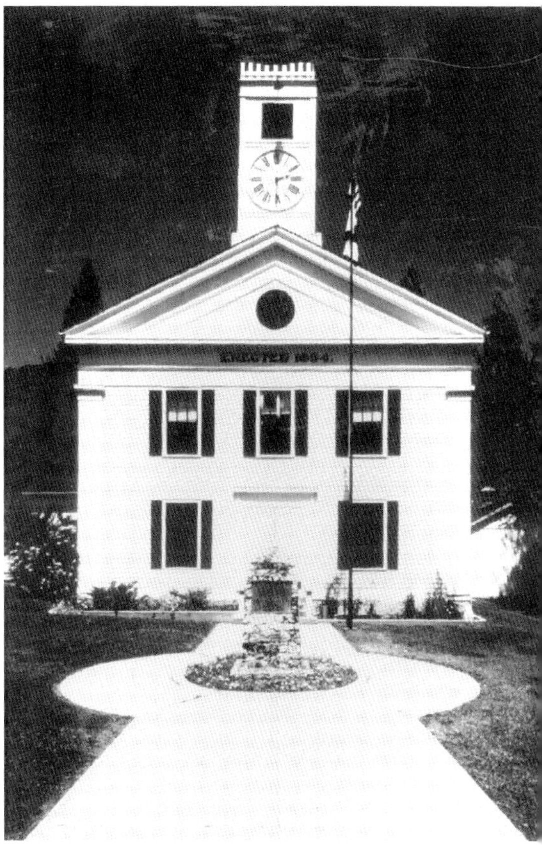

Mariposa County Courthouse, 1854

The structure is framed of whipsawed pine timbers, joined together with mortise and tenon cuts at points of contact. The joints and splices were secured with pine pegs. No nails were used in the substructure. However, square forged nails were used to secure the floors, wall, and ceiling boards to the structure. More details may be found in Pinkerton and Radanovich's *Mariposa County Courthouse, Shrine to Justice*, published by Mariposa Heritage Press. (Photograph by author.)

Angevine and Virginia Reynolds (OPPOSITE)
One of the greatest editor/publishers of the *Gazette* was Angevine Reynolds. About 1850, a young man named Reynolds arrived with a party from Texas, riding a white mule. The mule had the reputation of having been part of a Texas Ranger militia unit during the Mexican war. Reynolds and part of his party began mining at Chicken Gulch just a short distance down Mariposa Creek, south of Mariposa town.

Within a short time, he sought another profession, and with the white mule, he began transporting mail to the mines from Stockton. This turned into a freight business. Again he decided to move on to become a deputy county clerk and then county clerk for 14 years. In 1874, he purchased the *Mariposa Gazette* and began publishing on January 1, 1875. He was also admitted to the bar that same year. He fathered at least 15 children, many whom did not reach maturity. He lost his first wife, Virginia, mother of the 15, in childbirth. She is buried holding her last child in her arms in the IOOF cemetery north of town. Near her are a number of the other children, as well as Angevine.

Virginia was the great inspiration at the *Gazette*. Angevine did not live to the fullness of life and died leaving the *Gazette* to his second wife who left Mariposa with the printer after selling the paper.

Reynolds's writing was superb, and he was able to attract many of the pioneers to recall their exploits on a regular basis in the paper. Were it not for Reynolds, there would not be firsthand accounts from John Hite and Capt. John Diltz. He covered the local and national scene as well as any could and left an outstanding legacy of Mariposa history. (Both, author's collection.)

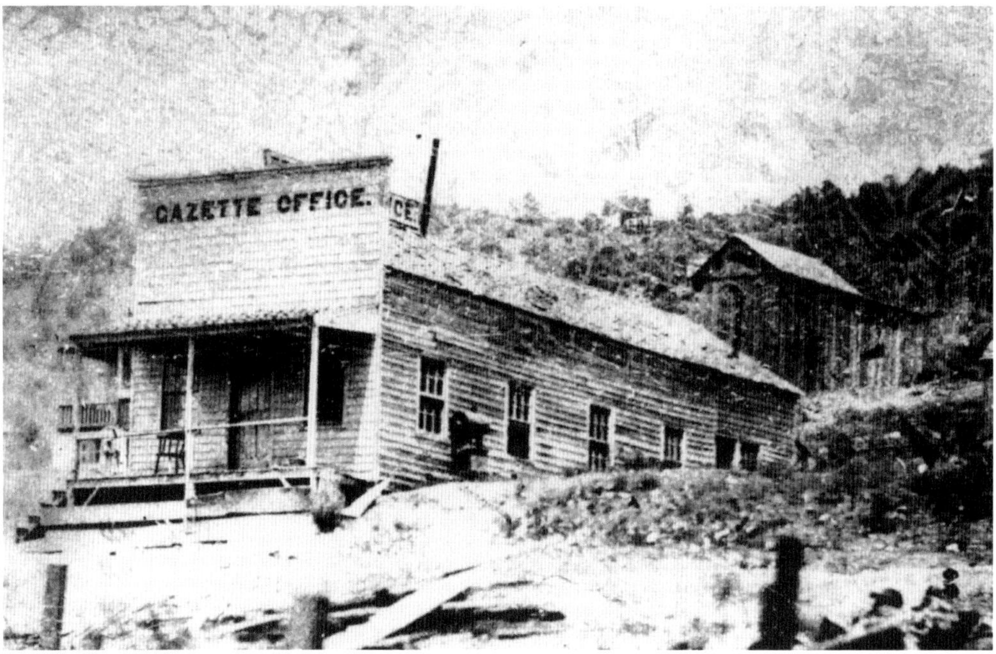

***Mariposa Gazette* on Bullion Street**
On January 20, 1854, the first issue of the *Mariposa Chronicle* appeared in the town of Mariposa. One and half years later, the name was changed to the *Mariposa Gazette*. This weekly newspaper has published continuously since and has become the repository of history for Mariposa County. Various editors and publishers have given direction to the *Mariposa Gazette* over the years, giving it a proper place in the history of California. (Author's collection.)

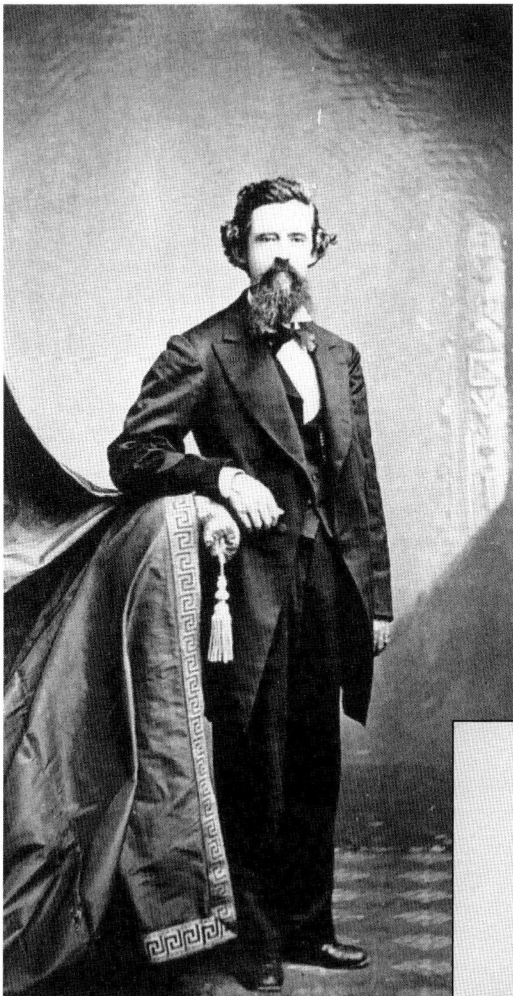

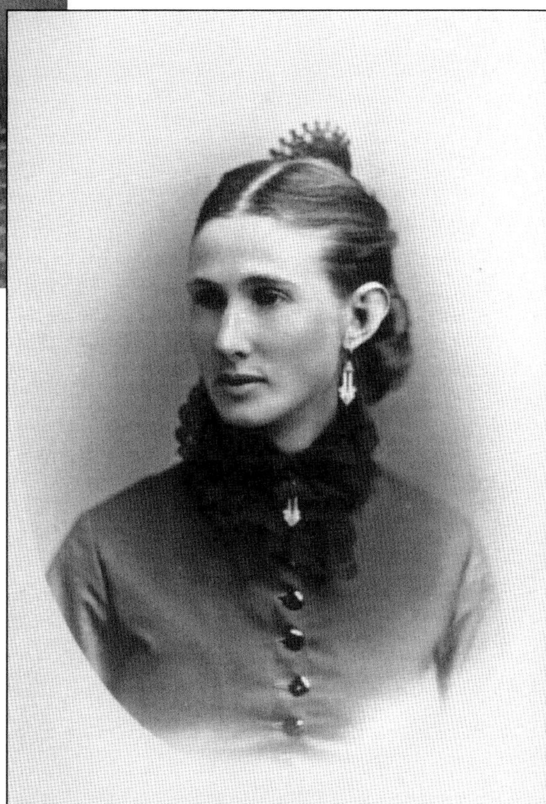

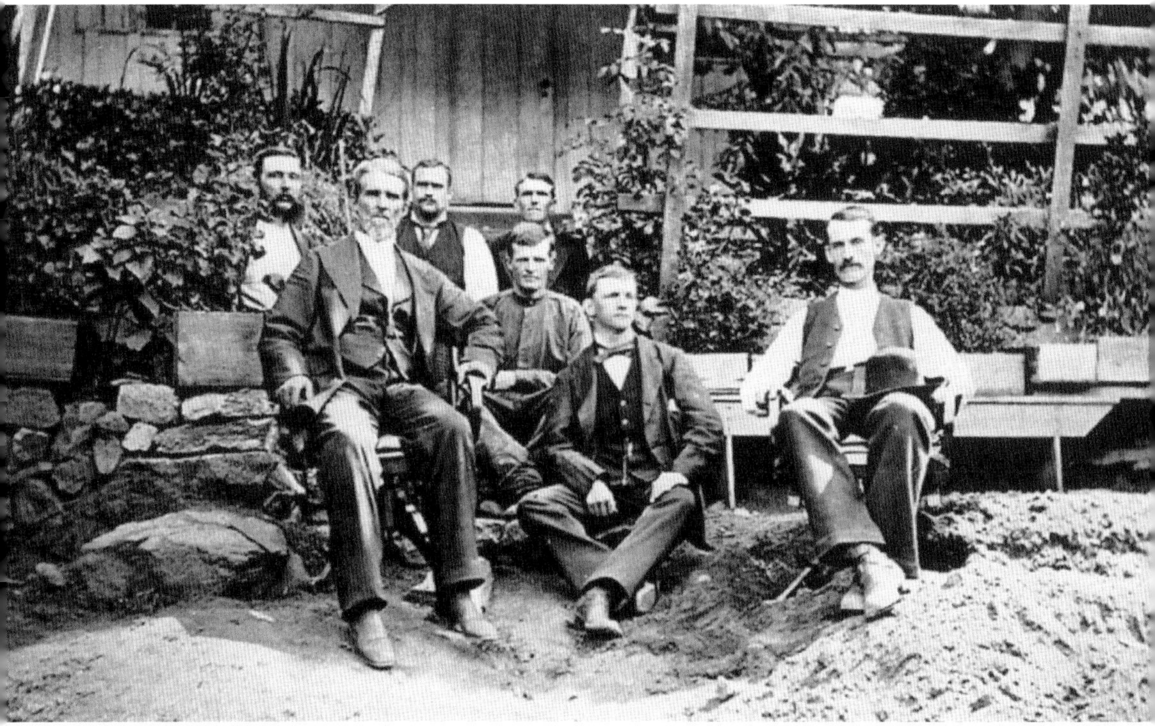

John Hite, Millionaire Miner

John Hite, left front, one of the most successful miners from 1850 to 1880, is pictured with his miners.

Hite came to Mariposa County early during the Gold Rush. He first mined at Ned's Gulch on the Merced River. Like Savage, he attracted Native Americans to work with him when a young Indian woman told him of a place where there was much gold located farther east up the South Fork of the Merced River. He prospected the area and found a very rich vein above the river at a place later named after him, Hite's Cove. He married the young woman's sister Lucy in a native ceremony. They lived as husband and wife for a number of years. He developed the rich mine, building a community of miners and their families. School was even held for the children. Hite set up a large mill run by electricity generated by a waterwheel in the river. He became quite wealthy and when he got into a water rights dispute, which made it difficult for him to run his mill, he decided to retire. (Author's collection.)

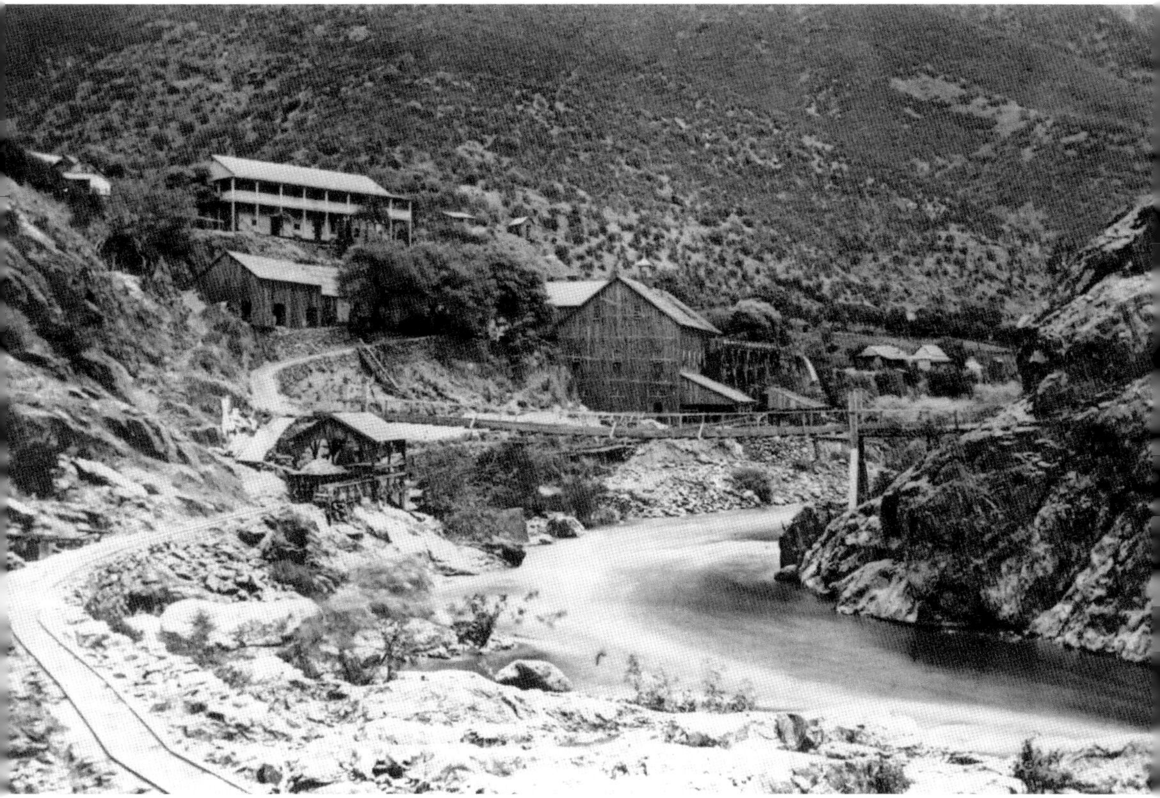

Hite Cove Mine

On the south fork of the Merced River, six miles east of the main river, John Hite established one of the richest mines in Mariposa County.

Hite then moved to San Francisco leaving everything, including Lucy, behind. She understood that is the way things were. Hite became sick, and while convalescing at a San Francisco hospital, he met and fell in love with his nurse. He married the nurse, and the San Francisco newspapers reported the marriage of the millionaire miner. A son of Lucy's, by a previous liaison, read the article and pointed out to his mother the fact that she is John Hite's wife and should sue for divorce and her share of the assets. Reluctantly, she files in the Court at Mariposa. Because Native Americans did not as of then have legal standing in American courts, she only had a common law Indian marriage and since she was an Indian, the court did not know what to do with the case. So the suit was transferred in some fashion to San Francisco where a judge agreed to take the case.

Lawyers all expecting to get a generous share of John Hite's wealth surrounded Lucy, and in fact, they did win the case. But the judge, knowing that he was establishing legal precedence, granted the divorce, awarding her roughly $27,000 from which she had to pay the lawyers. He did, however, protect Lucy by limiting the fees to the lawyers, leaving her a small trunk of money to take home. Within two days after arrival at her home near Mariposa, the trunk was found in a nearby field, empty and upside down. The son was nowhere to be found. (Author's collection.)

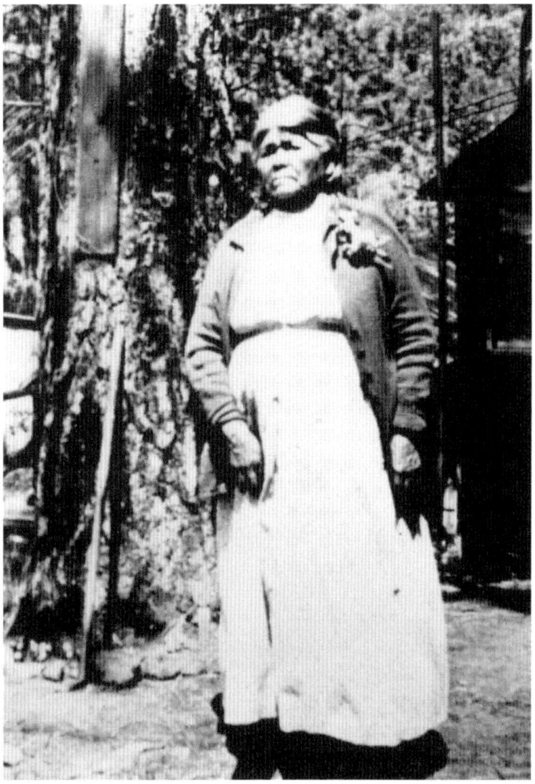

Lucy Hite

Lucy Hite lived out her life on a small ranch on Indian allotment land near Indian Peak, making a living serving as a cleaning lady for the ranchers' wives nearby. However, her case did some things. First, it was the first time in US history that a Native American was given standing in an American court of law, and secondly, her common law Indian marriage was recognized, and she was granted a divorce with distribution of assets. (Author's collection.)

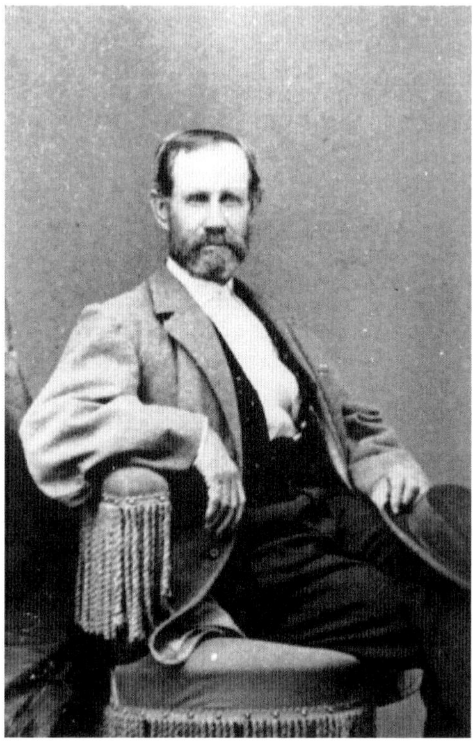

Capt. John Diltz

A sickly Indiana boy whose father had died when he was 12 years old, John Diltz was taken by an uncle to Georgia to learn gold mining. In Georgia, his health improved until he was old enough to start his own mining operation. Unlike most of the forty-niners, he came to California and Mariposa County with the knowledge and understanding of the art of mining and processing of the ore. At first, he worked on Agua Fria Creek, using an old steam mill, and then he moved to a Mariposa Creek building, a large mill that was water driven. (Author's collection.)

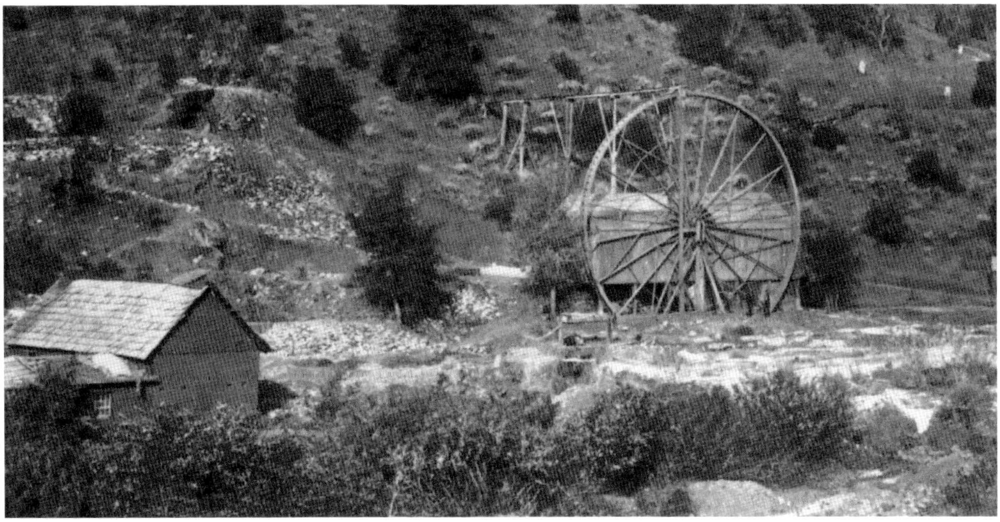

Diltz Mill at Agua Fria Creek

Diltz and a partner established this steam mill on land claimed by Col. John C. Fremont. Because Diltz's mill was located on the Fremont Grant, when Fremont gained clear title, it became necessary for Diltz to search elsewhere off the grant for his future activities. He began mining on Whitlock Creek and developing the Spencer Vein. Being successful for the most part with various partnerships, he developed what was to become the Diltz Mine just off Whitlock Road. This area proved to be as rich as many other mines developed nearby. His skill as a mechanic and designer of mills resulted in his being invited to work at the Mount Ophur mine by Fremont's partner, Trenor Park. (Photograph by Carleton E. Watkins.)

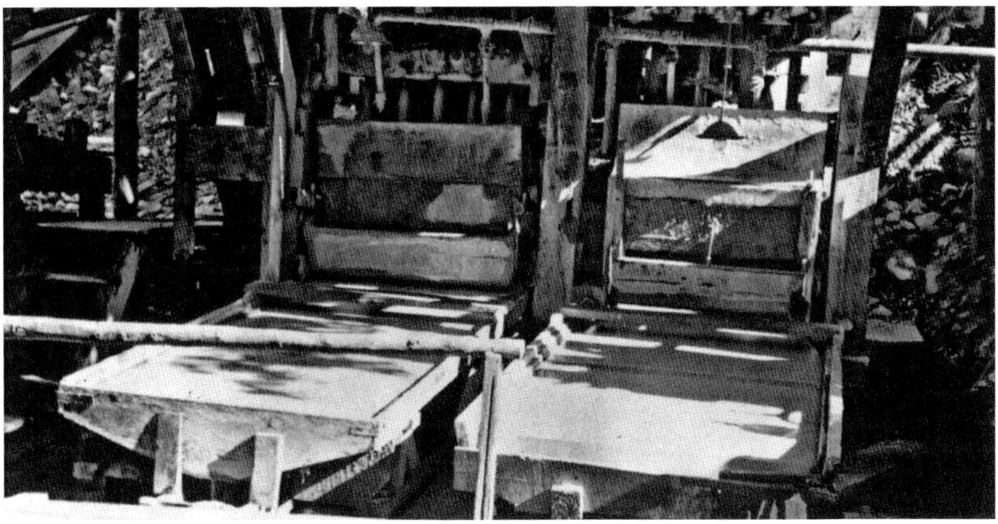

Two Banks of Stamps and Flotation Tables at Diltz Mine Mill

Diltz became known as a successful and generous person. He frequently took friends with him to San Francisco, where they would return to Mariposa with items for their businesses and personal lives. He finally passed away in a state hospital in 1897, but not before Angevine Reynolds invited him to write of his adventures. Following his death, his mine was idle for more than 35 years. When reopened, it became successful using modern techniques and equipment. The mine paid handsomely for a time. (Author's collection.)

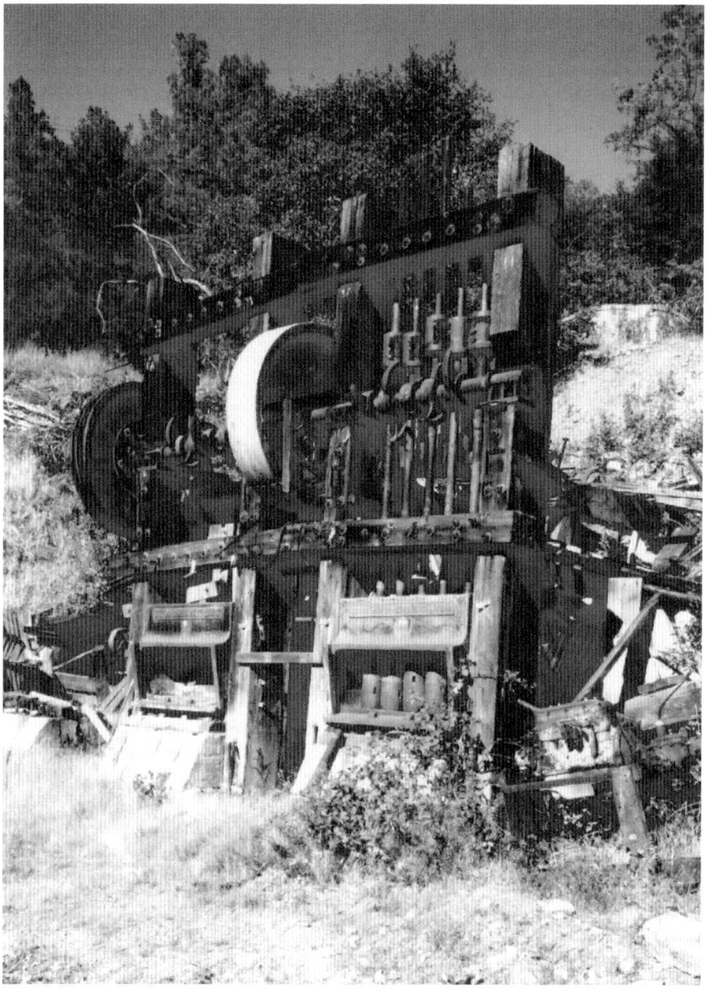

Abandoned Five Stamp Mills at Diltz Mine

Mining became a sporadic activity. Lack of water, and in the case of hard-rock mining, capital, or the scarcity of it, became the major issue. The gold was there but while it was finite, it also cost a great deal to recover. There was the lack of expertise in hard-rock mining. Most of the forty-niners were farmers or shopkeepers, but if they succeeded, it was because placer gold was plentiful in the creeks, and in some instances, the streets of the Gold Rush towns and over the counter or bar. Farmers knew how to move dirt and gravel, but to trace a vein through a prehistoric coarse was another matter.

They learned, but it was expensive and difficult. The greatest source of capital was the selling of stock in the mines in Europe, mainly England. The British Empire had a lot of experience in mining and perhaps the stockholders could be mined also. Primarily it was coal that they mined in England, but this was running out. Thus, many investors looked elsewhere for a return on their investment.

When Fremont became desperate for capital, he headed for Europe. Finding no investors, by 1863, he sold the grant to a group of Eastern investors who knew little about mining and California. The new Mariposa Mining Company did not do well in spite of hiring Frederick Law Olmsted as manager. They did not provide him with capital to restock the stores and develop the property and could not even pay him more than one year's salary. Olmsted stayed on the property one more year but then moved on to other projects while the company went into bankruptcy. Subsequent owners did not do well. (Photograph by author.)

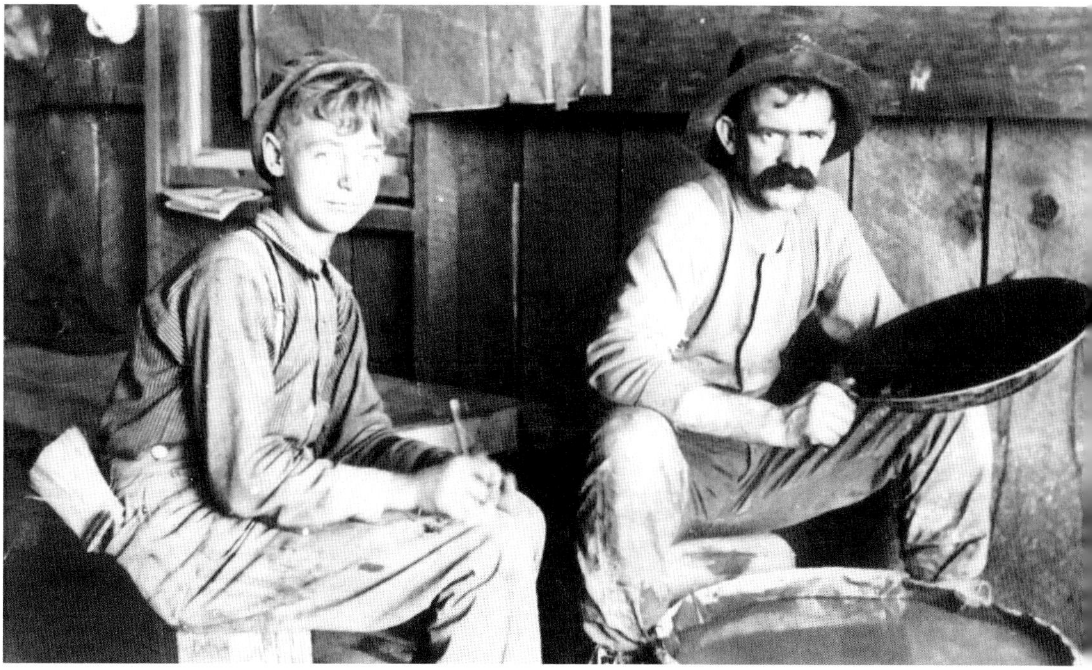

Frank McGuire

In the early 1880s, the Mariposa Commercial and Mining Company was formed in England and purchased the assets of the Fremont Grant. The last superintendent of the new company was Frank McGuire. A mining man from Grass Valley, California, he knew California mining, geology, and the business from top to bottom. At the turn of the century, he was managing the mining operations as well as the real estate of the grant company. He crafted a method for the company to show a profit on its holdings and was more than likely the first to do so. He continued to operate and sell the milling of the ore but leased out the mines, often even various levels of the same mine. Others gathered the ore. He processed the ore and separated the gold. Milling was always profitable because it was contracted in advance based on tonnage. Frank McGuire (above, right) and a young Alan Shira are pictured at the Mariposa Mine "doing clean up." They are washing the gold and sand left over on the flotation table at the end of the stamp mill operation. (Courtesy of Linda Milburn Parsons.)

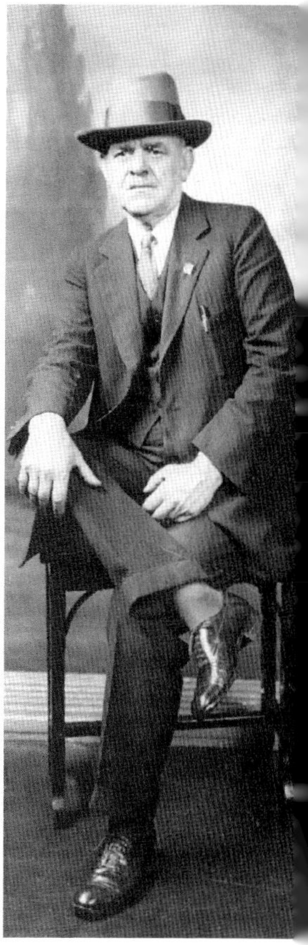

Superintendent of Mariposa Commercial and Mining Company

While the milling was profitable, not always was the mining. In a report to his stockholders early in the 1900s, McGuire told them perhaps the reason that their mines have not been as profitable as those farther north on the Mother Lode, in which he had experience, is that they have not invested enough capital to mine deep enough in the earth. Such mines as the Kennedy in Jackson and the Empire in Grass Valley had done very well because they were extending their mining below the 1,200-foot level. No mine in Mariposa County had ever tried to do so. The limitation to the Mariposa Mines was usually the lack of capital and excess water below 900 feet. The irony, of course, was that the lack of surface water in Mariposa County drove the miners underground to begin with. McGuire served as the superintendent of the Mariposa Commercial and Mining Company until his death in 1939. (Courtesy of Linda Milburn Parsons.)

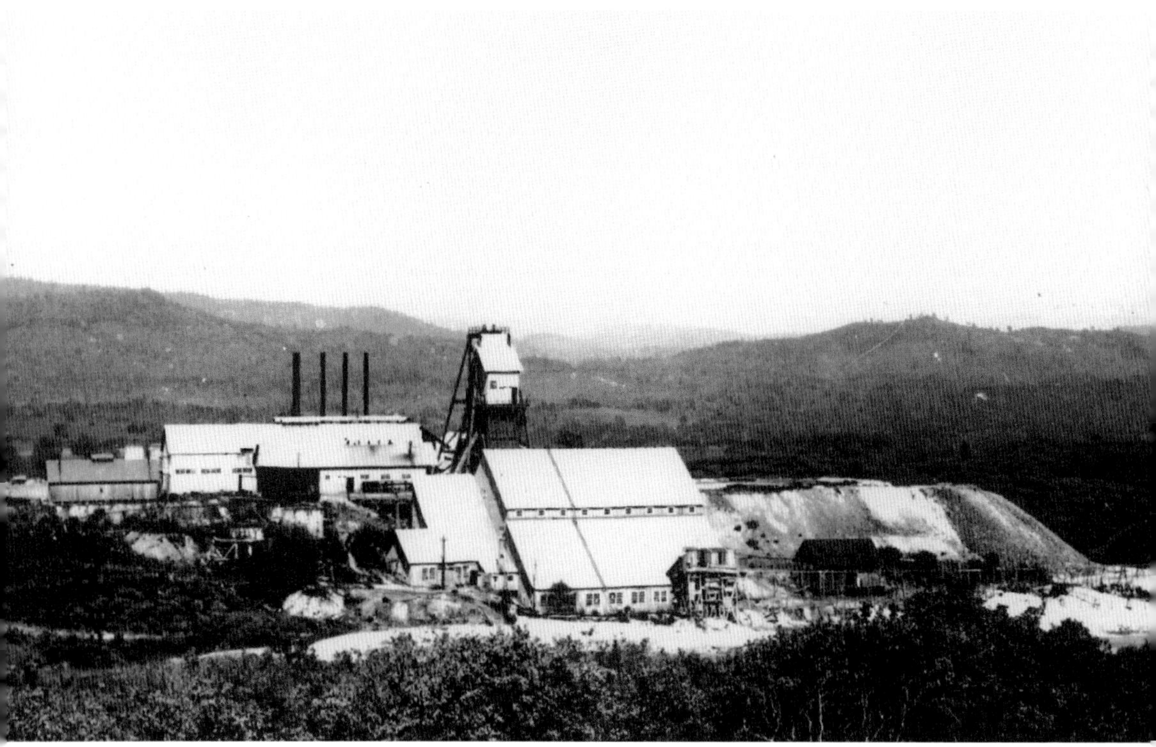

McGuire's Princeton Mine

Most active in terms of total production, this mine in Mount Bullion, just north of Mariposa, was managed by Frank McGuire.

The main mine on the grant owned and/or leased to others by the Mariposa Commercial and Mining Company was the Princeton in Mount Bullion. Until its closing in 1913, this mine produced approximately $5 million in value of gold at that time. Other mines were the Mariposa, Pine Tree, Mount Ophur, Josephine, and Black Drift.

In 1913, two fires on the grant closed the era of large industrial mining. The Princeton Mine in Mount Bullion was closed due to a fire in the engine house that also captured the head frame. At the Mariposa Mine, the mill building itself burned. It required additional capital to reopen the mines, and World War I was impending. Europe being the larger source of investment capital was under the pressure of war. With the mines went the jobs. With the jobs went the businesses, creating a major decline in the economic prospects of the county. Yosemite National Park was yet to develop as an economic asset for the county. (Author's collection.)

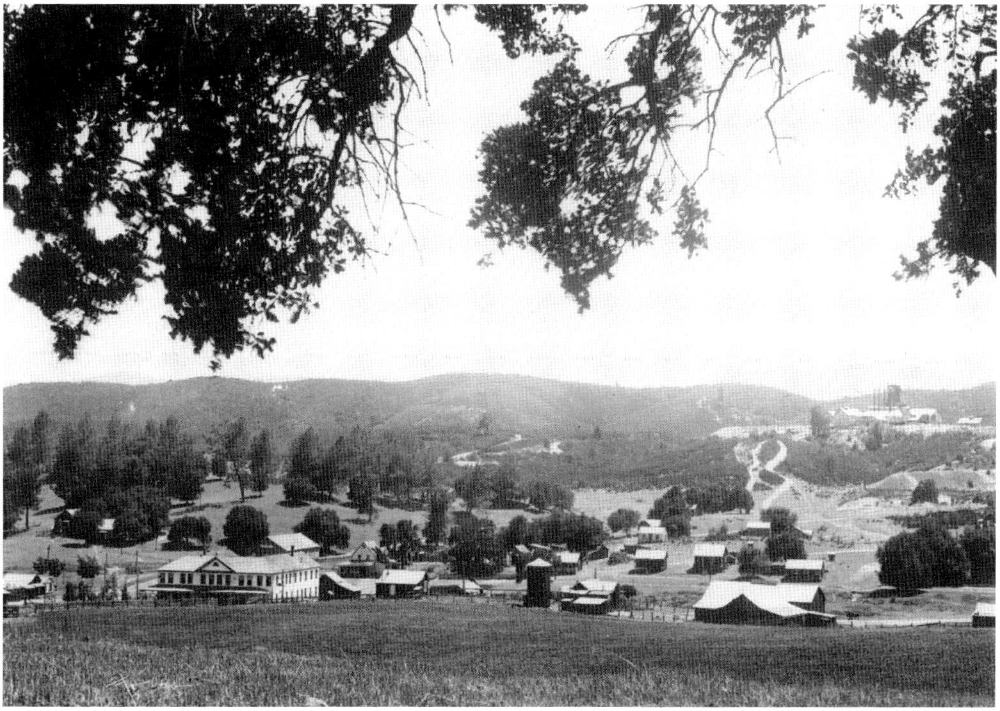

Mount Bullion
Mount Bullion served as the headquarters for Princeton Mine. The large building to the left was the Princeton Hotel, which was really a residence for many of the miners at the Princeton Mine, which can be seen to far right. (Author's collection.)

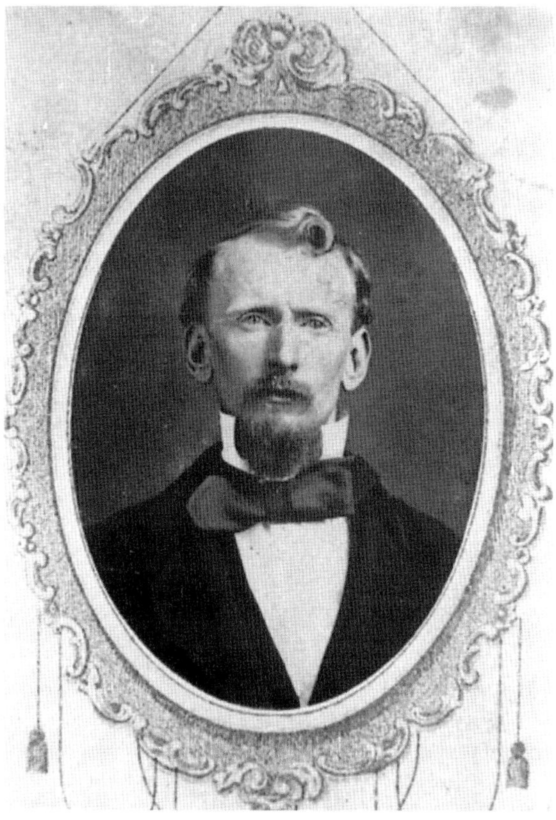

John "Quartz" Johnson
John "Quartz" Johnson, while a partner in the early development of mining properties south of the Merced River, also filed claims on the North Side of the river outside Fremont Grant. The group of mines associated with the Mary Harrison was the result. (Author's collection.)

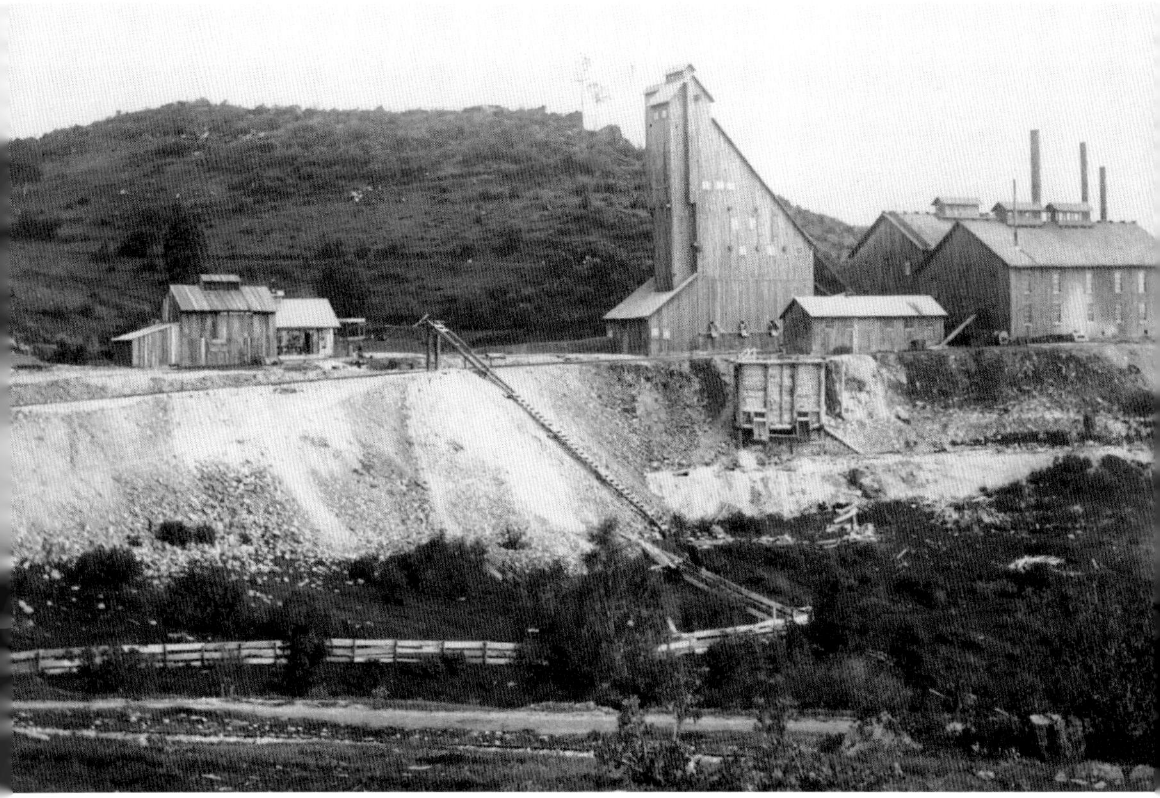

Mary Harrison Mine

This was the principal mine in the Coulterville area. The little steam engine, *Whistling Billy*, which is still on display in the town of Coulterville, carried ore to the mill from other nearby mines. Gold mining, especially for little pay, was hardly a pleasant venture. Men worked in damp, dusty air with only a single candle for light. They were always risking the opportunity for a cave in or an errant charge that goes off prematurely or fails to discharge and does only after the miners reenter the face on a daily basis. It took tough, hardworking men to engage in the search for gold. (Author's collection.)

The Saga of the *Whistling Billy* (OPPOSITE)

The Oliver Fiske Freighting Company of Greeley Hill delivered the little engine to Coulterville in 1894. When a forest fire destroyed the Mary Harrison, it caught the *Whistling Billy* also, destroying the trestle from the mine to the mill, dumping the whole train into the soft dirt bottom of a nearby canyon. It was some years before the engine and tender were rescued, refurbished, and put on display in Coulterville under the Hang Mans Tree. (Above, photograph by Roy A. Radanovich, below, both, author's collection.)

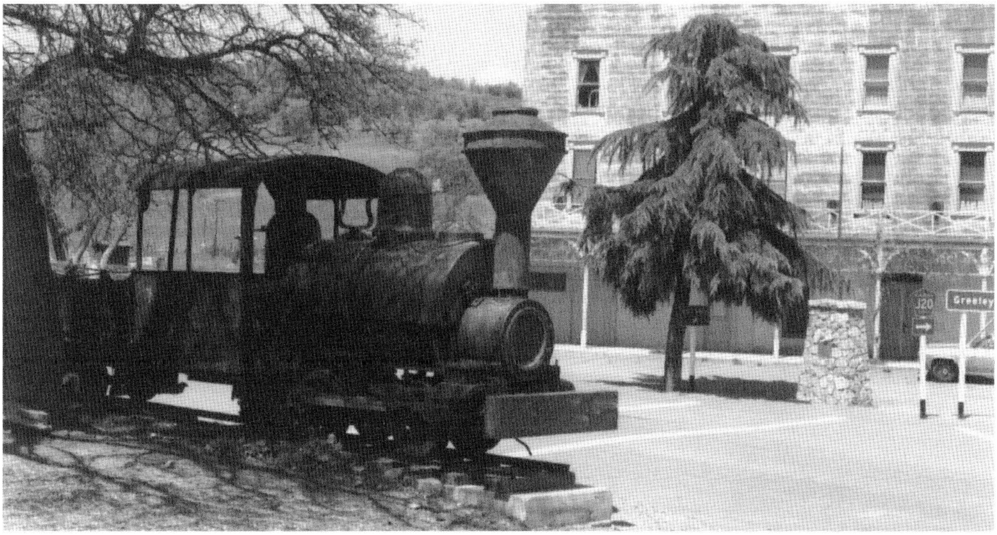
J20
Greeley

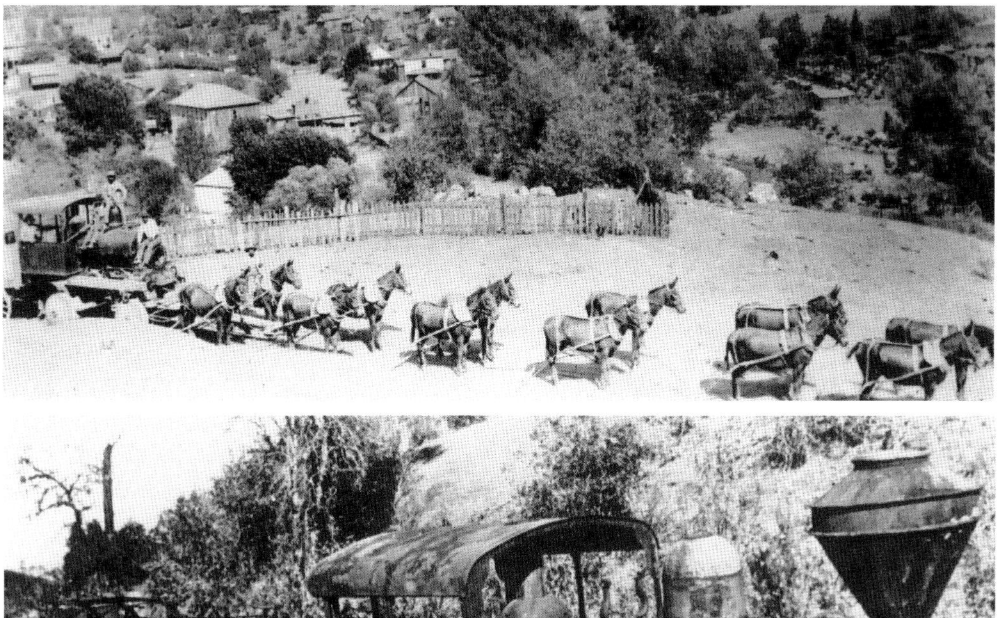

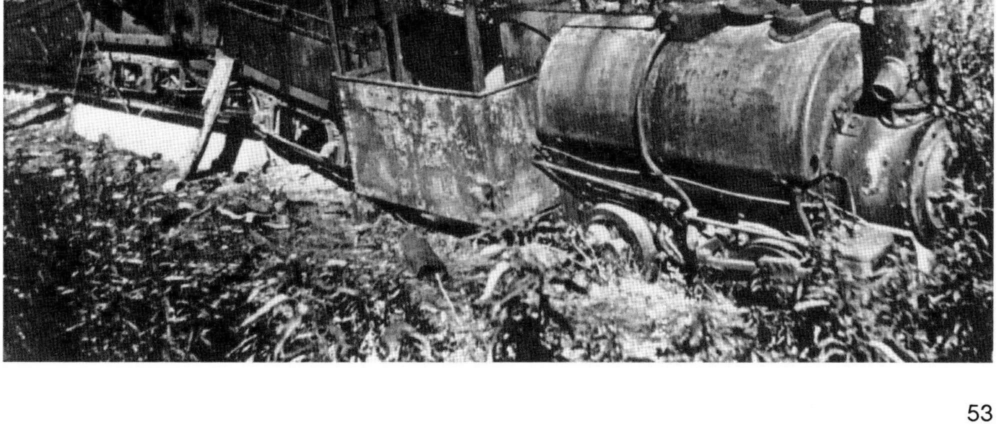

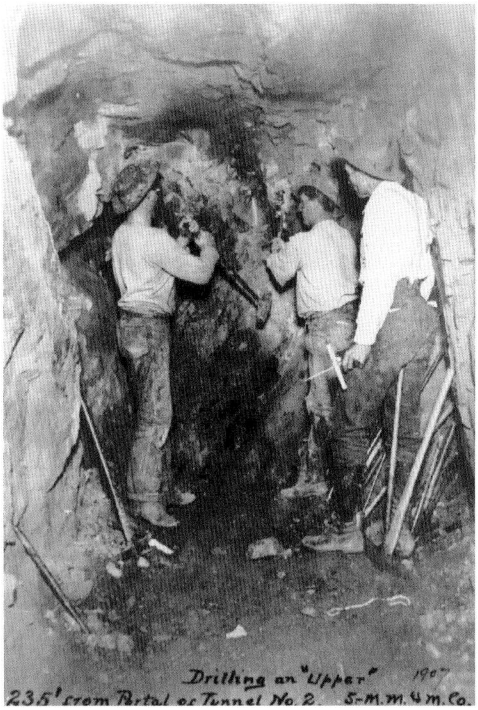

James Treidder and Miners

Cornish Miner James Tresidder at the Whitlock Mine exemplifies the tough, no-nonsense stance of a man who works underground. During the 1880s, out-of-work Cornish coal miners were recruited by the California mine industry for their skill and expertise in ridding deep mines of water using a devise they brought with them called the Cornish pump. They saved the industry in California. (Both, author's collection.)

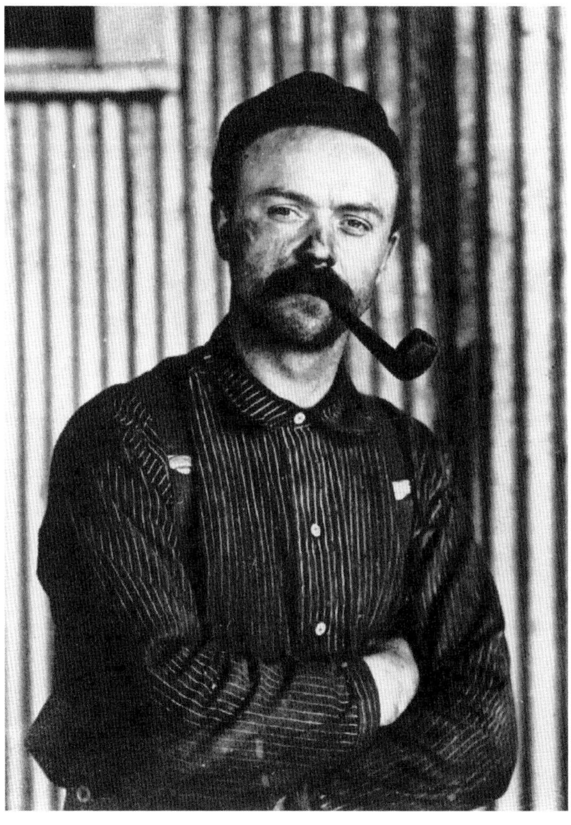

CHAPTER THREE

Legends Following the Gold Rush

Mariposa County, of which Yosemite National Park and other federal holdings occupies about 50 percent of the total area, has never been wealthy or heavily populated. Yet, because of the unique nature of its geography, climate, and the specialized activities having taken place, this county in the center of California has a diverse history. The purchase of a Mexican land grant, even before California was owned by the United States, the ambition of John C. Fremont, the Gold Rush, and the designation of Yosemite Valley and the Mariposa Grove of Big Trees as the first place set aside for rest and recreation as a national park, all created a county of incredibly diverse history. That diversity attracted people from all over the world, not in large numbers, but with special needs and desires. Almost always the capital for the development and growth of the county came from outside its borders.

It was the desire to become rich that drove early development. Then, it was the beginning of recognition that this was not only a land to be exploited but to be preserved. The confusion created by opposing ideals of manifest destiny and preservation influences, even to this day, the social and political ideals of Mariposa County. Out of this environment came the creation of the ever-present Sierra Club, as well the demands of success of the profit-driven economic system to fund the public use of these lands.

From the beginning of the 20th century, no longer was it gold that drove the interest in the physical environment, but it was the scenery. Thus, hotels with beds and baths became necessary to attract the public to Yosemite. To have the general public be exposed to and enjoy this environment was necessary to convince the federal government that this park and other parks had value to the public, primarily for recreation.

While there have always been some who can sleep on the ground and bathe in the streams, of the more than four million who visit every year, most prefer a bed indoors, meals prepared, and transportation via roads to special overlooks that can be visited in rapid succession.

The next few chapters introduces the reader to the individuals and groups of people who, in one way or another, influenced the quality of life in Mariposa County and Yosemite.

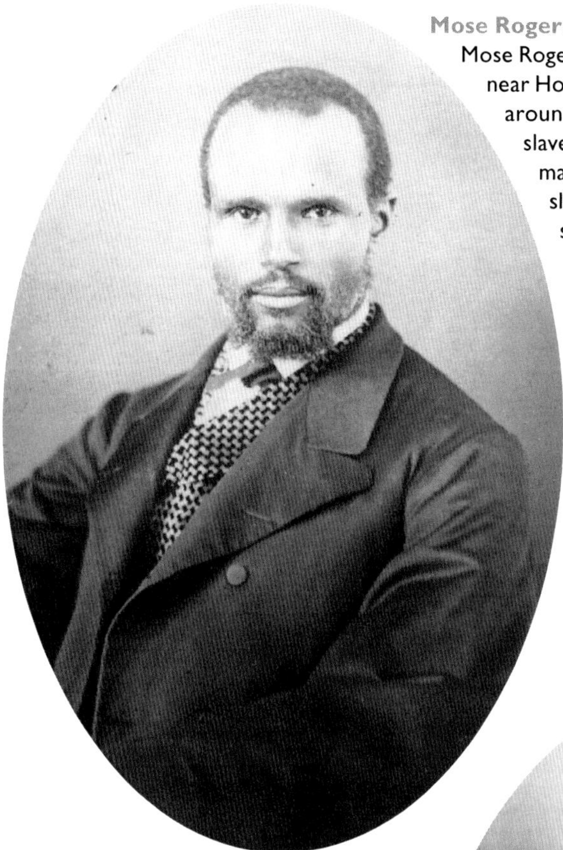

Mose Rogers
Mose Rogers and his wife, Lorella, came to Quartzburg, near Hornitos, from Texas with Col. Thomas J. Thorn around 1850. The discussion continues as to the slave status of the Rogers. Soon, however, Rogers managed the Washington Mine. It is thought that a slave would not have the mining and engineering skill that Rogers possessed. The best research in Texas where the group came from indicates that Thorn's slaves were released before he left Texas, but Rogers and his wife are not mentioned. (Author's collection.)

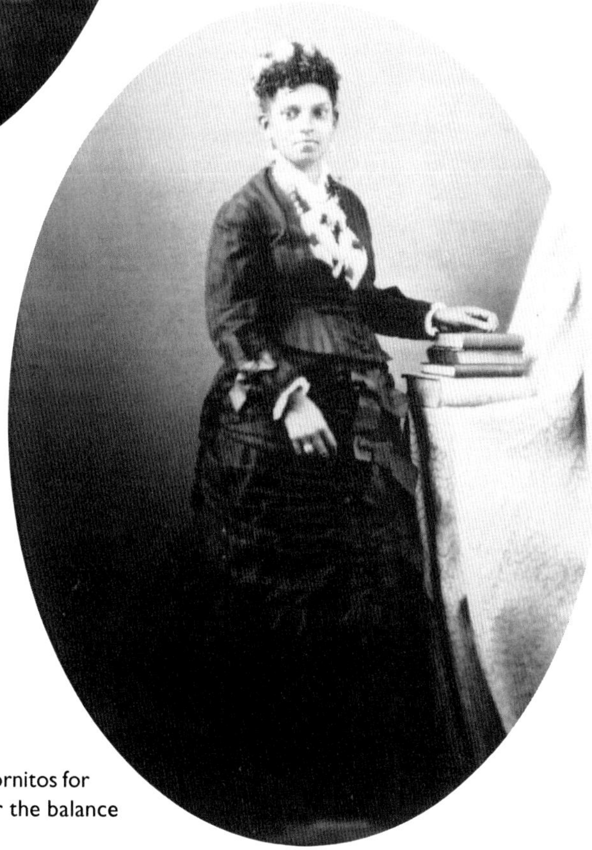

Lorella Rogers
The wife of Mose Rogers, Lorella, lived in Hornitos for a number of years, moving to Stockton for the balance of her life. (Author's collection.)

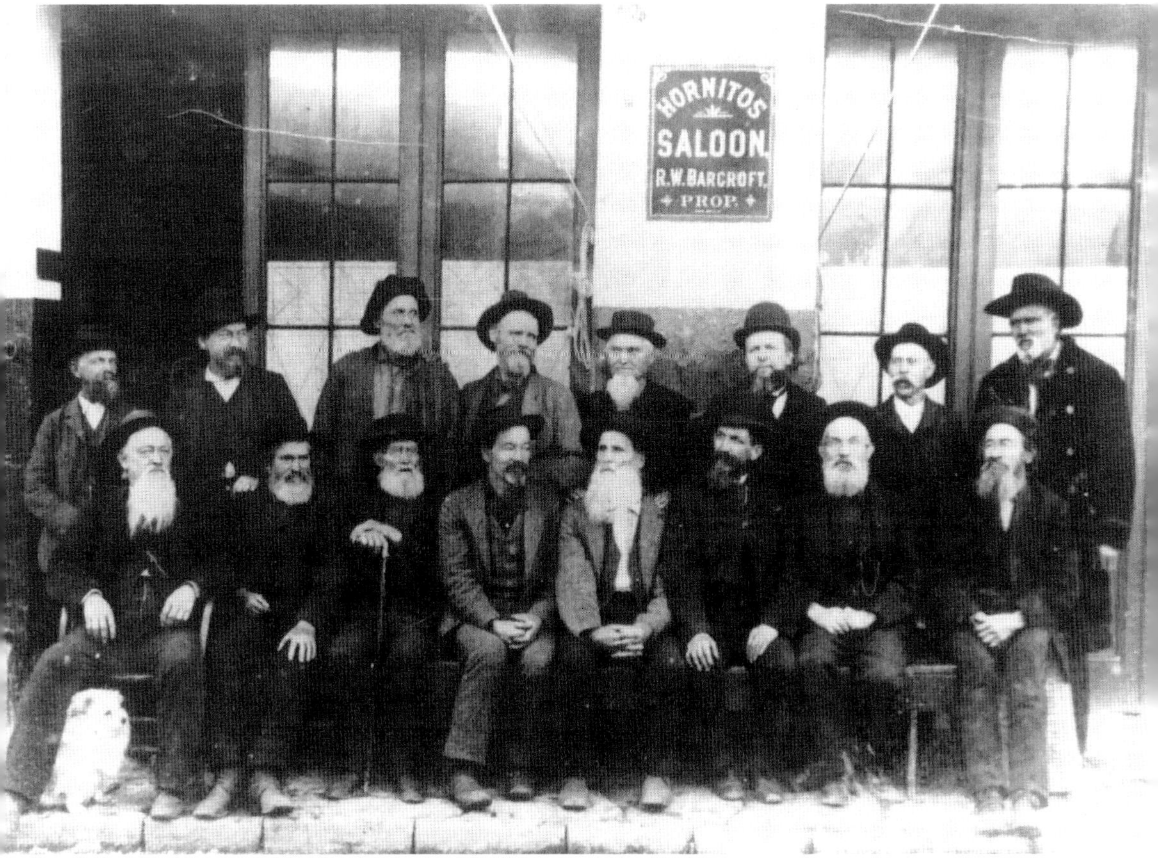

Old-Timers Reunion, Hornitos

Rogers not only ran the principal mine in the Hornitos area but also was involved in building roads. When the first road to Yosemite from Mariposa was proposed, he was a bidder for the project. The project was never accomplished. Bonds were sold by the State of California but later canceled. The above photograph is of the pioneers around Hornitos at a late-19th-century reunion. Mose Rogers is at the far right in the second row; Thomas Thorn is third from the right in the first row. (Author's collection.)

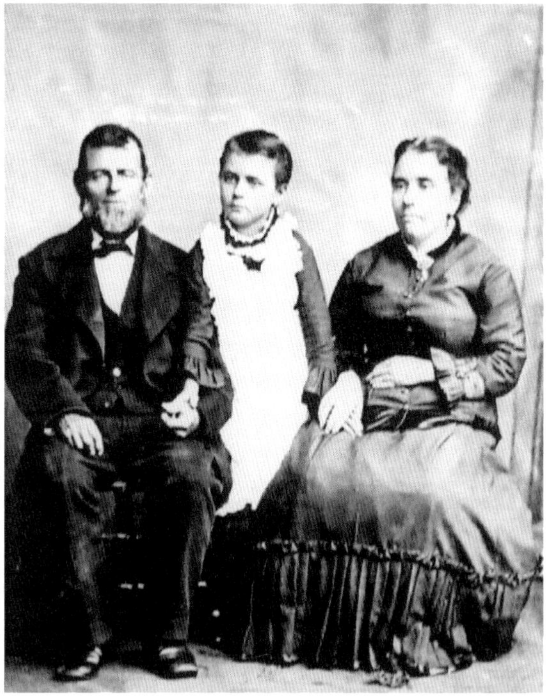

Louis and Eleanor Trabucco, Merchants in Bear Valley
Louis (Luigi) Trabucco came to California from Italy about 1850, working his way down the Mother Lode until settling in Bear Valley. He placer mined for a time but discovered that the task of growing and selling vegetables was more to his liking. Soon he added a store to his activities. He had left a young woman in Italy who was his intended. After some delay, he returned to northern Italy to find that the young lady had grown tired waiting and had married, and in fact, she already had children. Not wanting to come back to Bear Valley empty handed, he married one of the young lady's relatives, Eleanor, who was 20 years his junior. (Author's collection.)

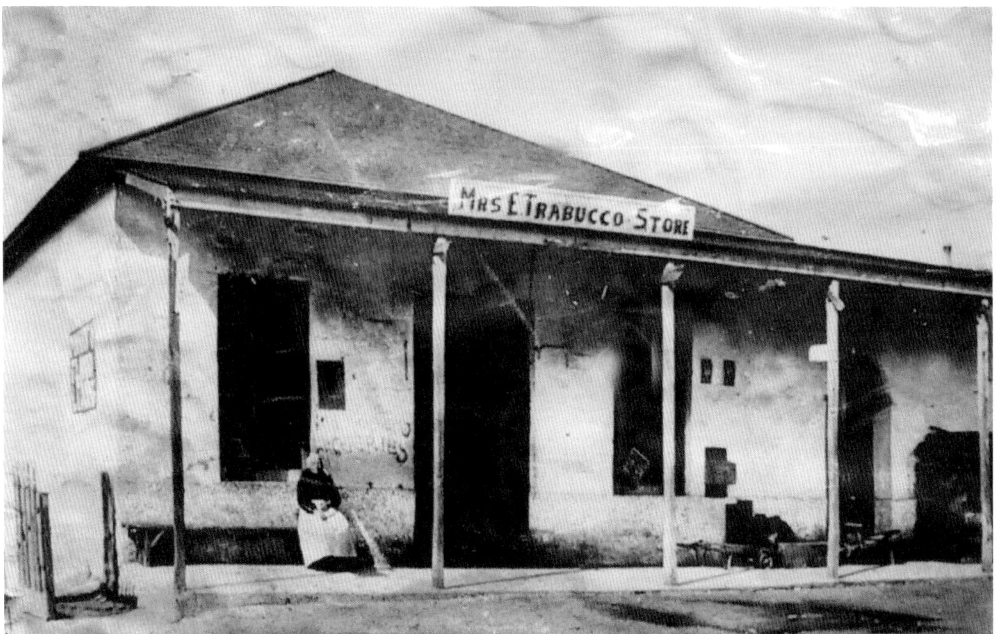

Eleanor Trabucco Groceries in Bear Valley
They returned to Bear Valley to start a family and purchased a store building. Eleanor bore five children, and when, in 1883, Louis passed away, she undertook successfully running the store, which she did for more than 20 years. When she closed the store, she built homes for her children in Bear Valley and Mariposa, including one for son Judge Joseph J. Trabucco. She died in 1923. (Courtesy of Mariposa Museum.)

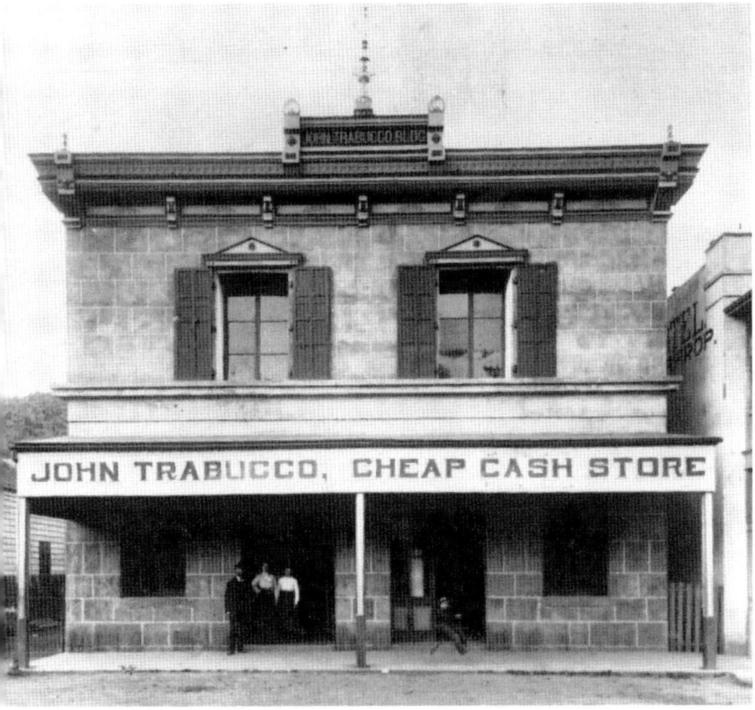

John, Katie, and Emile Trabucco at Cheap Cash Store, Mariposa
On a trip back from Italy, Louis and Eleanor Trabucco brought young relative John Trabucco with them. At first, he was brought to raise the vegetables and garden for the Bear Valley store. Then, he began delivering merchandise and groceries to the mines and ranches. John went to work on the Casaccia Ranch at French Camp; after a few years, he leased the Black Ranch in Hornitos. By 1892, he met and married Catherine Razzetto in San Francisco who was a very skilled milliner. John, Katie (in white shirt in center), and their son Emile (on the tricycle) are pictured at their Cheap Cash Store in Mariposa. This was John Trabucco's second store in Mariposa. Their first was destroyed by fire.

Together they opened a store in the old Fremont Company building, eventually buying the structure, moving it north on Charles Street, and reconstructing the present historic building. They incorporated an embossed tin ceiling and walls and a four-ton cast-iron stairway to the second floor, which was shipped from the East around the tip of South America. Merchandise for the shopping center included groceries, clothing, hardware, mining supplies, including dynamite, and building materials. (Author's collection.)

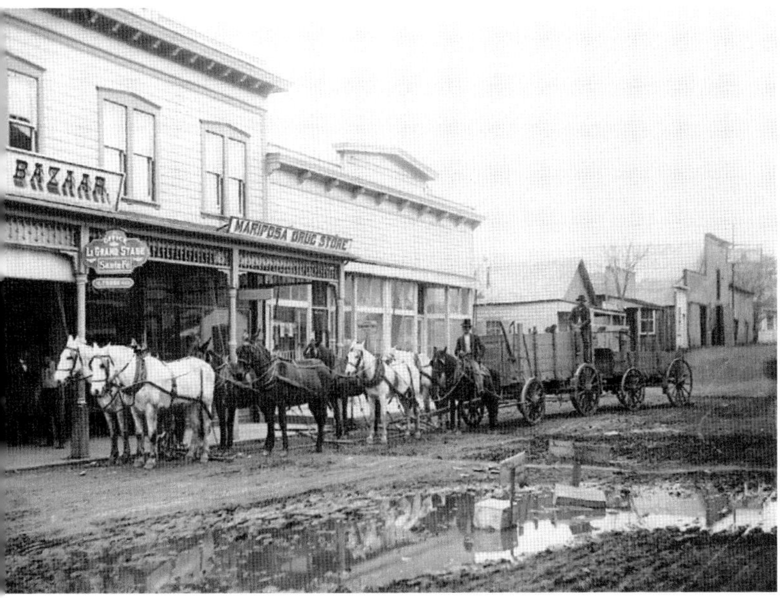

Victor Trabucco with Freight Wagons
Everything imaginable came from Merced in a two-freight wagon train driven by John's bachelor brother Victor. It took two days to arrive in Mariposa via La Paloma Road and Hornitos. (Author's collection.)

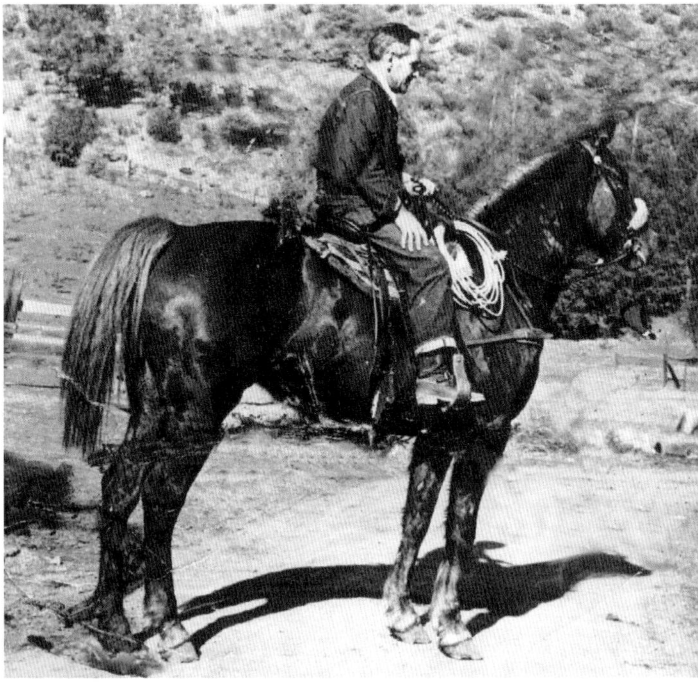

Emile and Horse

John and Katie had one son, Emile, who was educated in San Francisco, being guided by his mother's sisters. This handsome young man returned to Mariposa to work with his parents in the store, having his own delivery route via horses and wagon. They also installed a water system for downtown Mariposa, sourcing water from springs near Stockton Creek. By 1922, Emile was running the grocery and hardware side in an addition to the rear of the original building, while his wife, Leslie, and mother, Katie, were in charge of the dry goods and clothing. Leslie and Emile had four children who all took turns working in the store. (Author's collection.)

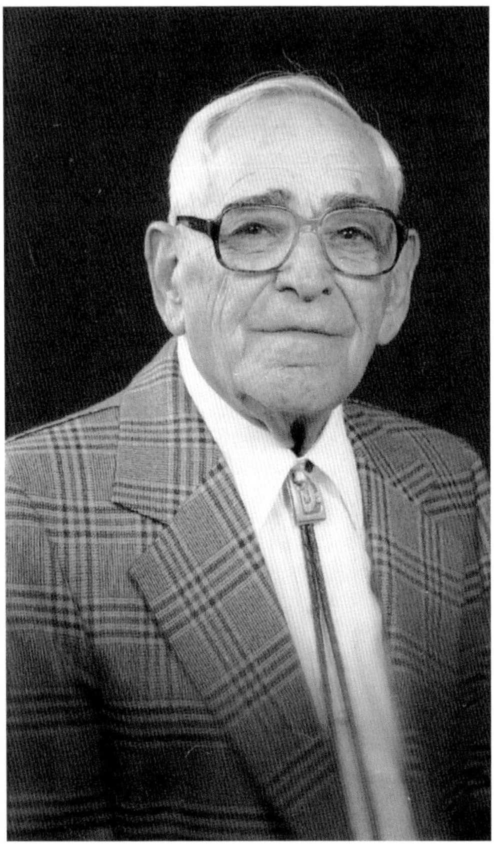

Emile Trabucco

For more than 60 years Emile was the leading merchant in Mariposa. He gradually took over the operations of the various investments, but in such a way, that it benefited the town of Mariposa and its inhabitants. During the 1930s, Emile became the dealer for White trucks and buses, and many of the high school buses were purchased through him. He also converted the freight system to Mariposa from wagons to trucks, causing Uncle Victor to have to learn to drive.

Emile was instrumental in bringing the Bank of America, the California Department of Motor Vehicles, and the California Highway Patrol to Mariposa. Following World War II, he built and opened for his son-in-law a laundry operation. Emile was family orientated and very supportive of local providers such as the tradition of buying and selling local produce. He provided an appliance, plumbing, and hardware section in his store and also sold water to the community. He raised cattle, wore Levi's and boots, sold dynamite for the mines, and was a friend to everyone. A major fire in 1950 destroyed the grocery department of the main Cash store, but Emile quickly rebuilt to also include the post office for Mariposa. (Photograph by author.)

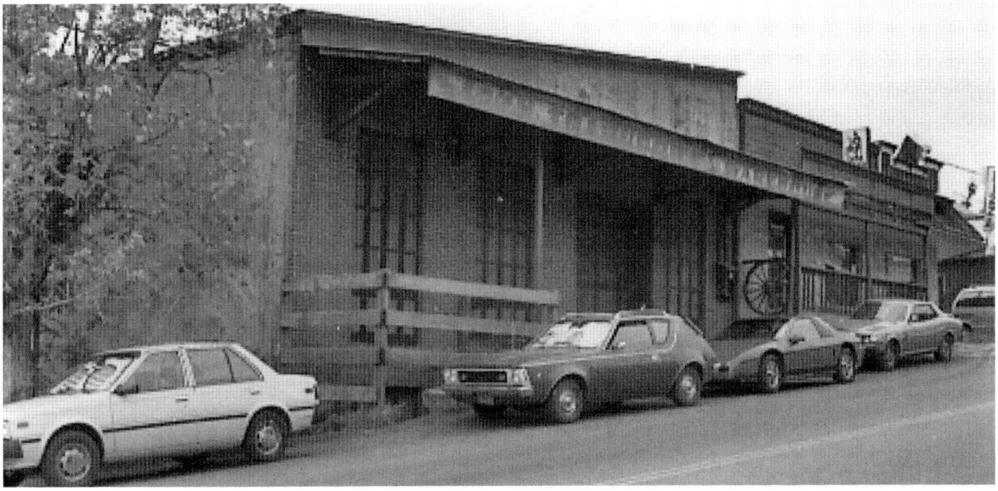

Trabucco's Warehouse

Early in the 20th century, John acquired a number of the historic buildings in downtown Mariposa. Along with the Fremont Adobe, the oldest in town, which is now the Bett's Gold Coin Club Tavern, he also bought the Bogan Building, the Mac Dermott Company, and Kerrins Livery Stable building, which he converted into a warehouse for his growing business, as well as other properties, including over 2,000 acres east of the town of Mariposa. The lower-floor livery stable was used to house the fright wagons and animals. (Author's collection.)

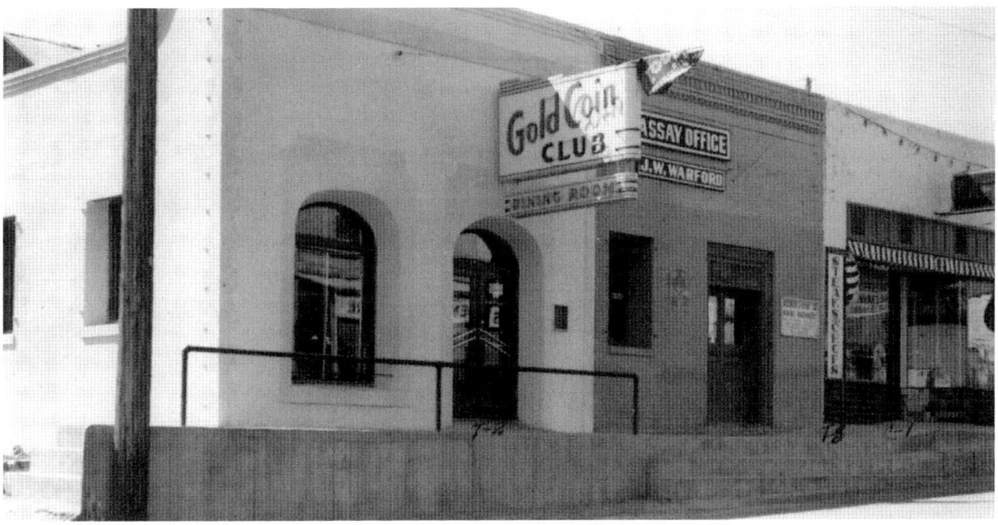

Fremont Adobe (Gold Coin)

John C. Fremont constructed the Fremont Adobe to house his agents, Palmer Cook and Company, in 1850. After a major fire in 1866 that destroyed 63 buildings downtown, the adobe badly was damaged. It was restored by replacing or covering the damaged adobe sections with brick. This remains the oldest building in Mariposa County. Upon restoration, among other uses, Gordon's Hotel and Saloon occupied the site. Located behind the adobe on Fifth Street was the Union Hotel, which was incorporated into the Gordon operation. The back portion of the building was destroyed in a fire in 1950. Today, the building houses Bett's Gold Coin Sports Tavern, a historic use dating to 1937 when the Gold Coin Club was opened by Charles Greenamyer and Don Turner. (Author's collection.)

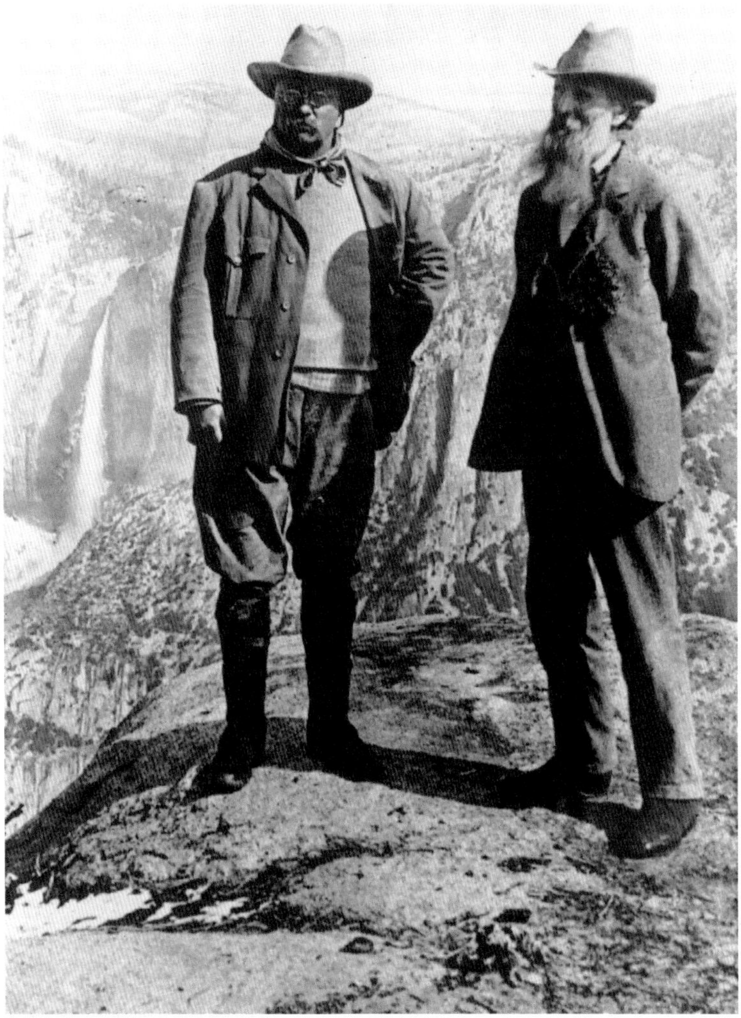

Muir and Roosevelt

The progression of development of Yosemite moved from the presence of Olmsted and his ignored plan of its preservation and use to the arrival of John Muir with ideas only understood and supported by a handful. These concerns led to the granting of Yosemite Valley and the Mariposa Grove of Big Trees to the State of California for purpose of creating a park in 1864. This event was aided by early photography by Carleton E. Watkins, which was shown to Pres. Abraham Lincoln.

The grant to the state was followed by confused management by commissioners politically appointed by the governor of the State of California under the direction of the legislature. For the next roughly 50 years, preservation and development were all political issues leading to great disagreement and even farming in the valley floor. The area surrounding the valley and big trees was unmanaged federal land that was utilized by ranchers and loggers. By 1890, through the efforts of John Muir, Yosemite National Park is formed and brought under federal management. But Yosemite Valley and Mariposa Grove of Big Trees were not included. The 1903 meeting of John Muir and Pres. Theodore Roosevelt began the process of returning both to the federal government. Thus, the 20th century began the slow process of recognizing of the true value of this pristine environment.

Pictured here, John Muir and Pres. Theodore Roosevelt toured Yosemite Valley and the National Park with only two assistants. (Author's collection.)

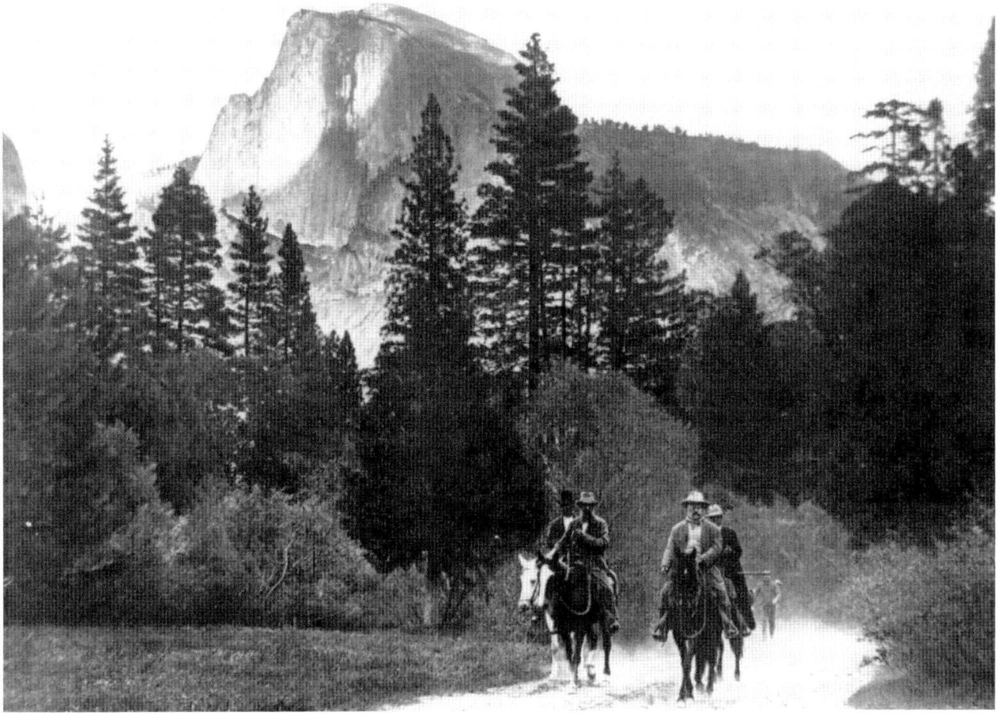

John Muir
Muir moved on to broadening the impact of his philosophies. Three personalities dominated Yosemite history for the next few years. First there was the unsatisfied figure of John Muir and his Sierra Club who wished for minimal development of Yosemite. Poorly funded management by the federal government, guided by political imperatives, called for a strong advocate for the National Park System. This was provided by Stephen T. Mather. (Author's collection.)

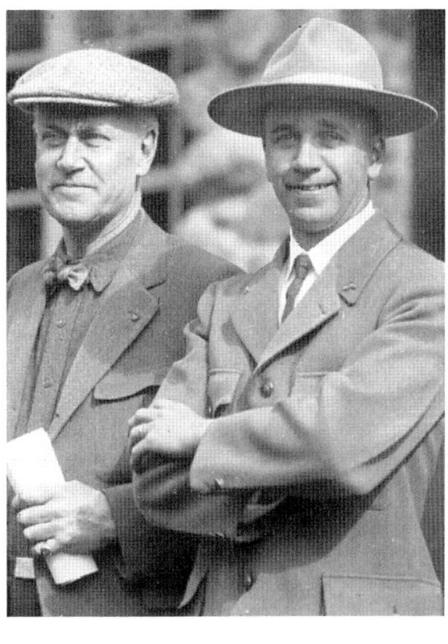

Stephen T. Mather and Ansel Hall
Stephen T. Mather was a wealthy mineral developer who had a clear idea of the future of the National Park System. He was in a position to influence the wealthy captains of industry, finance, and politics. He approached Secretary of Interior Franklin K. Lane, complaining about how the federal lands were being managed. Lane's replied that if Mather did not like the way things were, he should join Lane in Washington to fix the problems himself. He accepted the challenge, and thus began the park system. Museums and a naturalist program were established in each park, the first being under Ansel Hall in Yosemite. (Author's collection.)

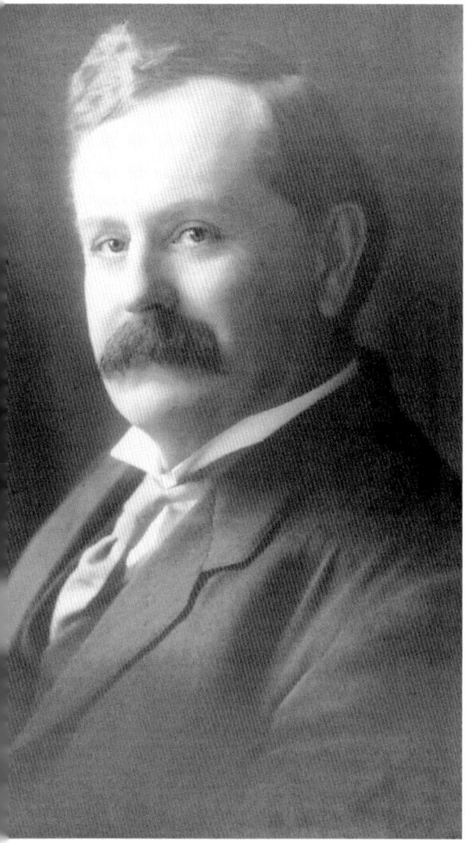

David Curry

In 1899, David Curry and his wife, Jennie, both schoolteachers, started Camp Sequoia in the shadow of Glacier Point. By 1900, Camp Sequoia's name was changed to Camp Curry. The Curry Camping Company had a major impact on the human history of Yosemite. David Curry saw Yosemite as needing development along the lines of a place of "rest and recreation," as outlined in the legislative document that created the grant to the state. As Palo Alto teachers David and his wife Jennie, appealed first to their educated colleagues and teachers seeking summer recreation in a cool environment from their schools and universities, they recruited summer employees from Stanford University and other students seeking summer jobs. (Courtesy of Yosemite Park and Curry Company.)

Early Camp Curry

Most of the guests were housed in tents and ate communally in a cafeteria. Asian cooks prepared the food. Each evening, the guests were entertained by lectures extolling the uniqueness of the Sierra environment or by musicians. (Author's collection.)

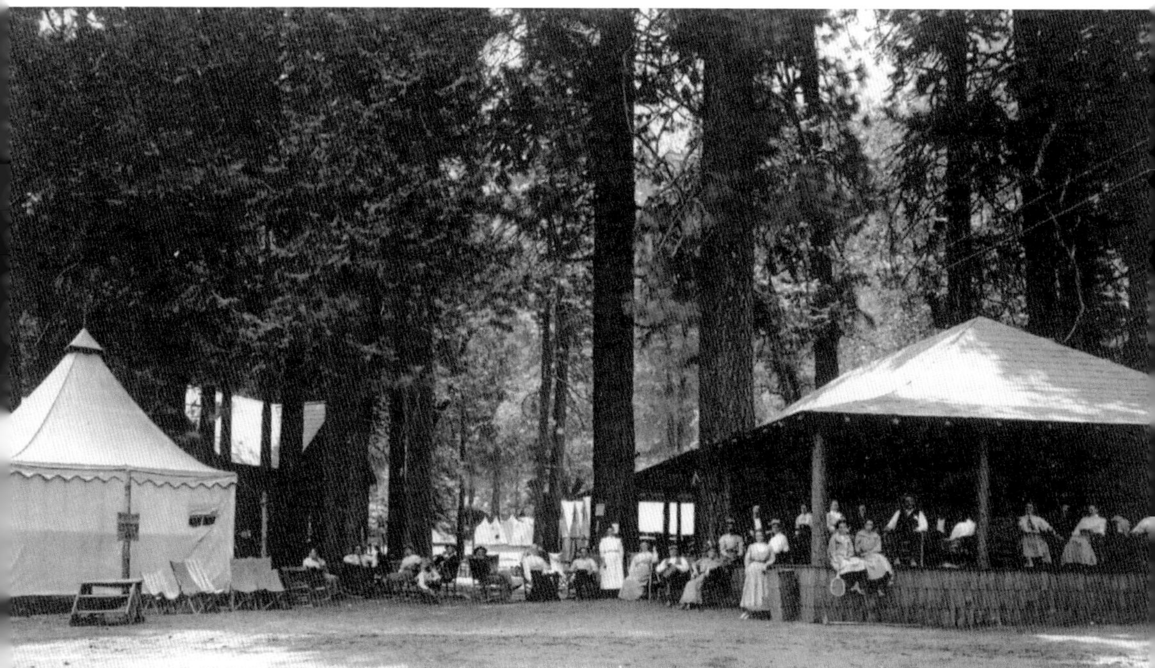

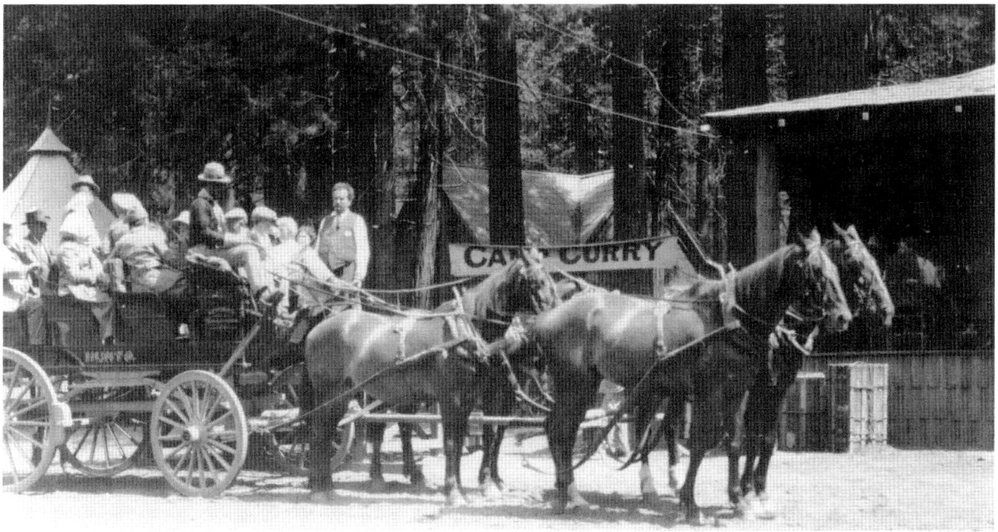

David Curry Welcomes Guests
David Curry's bombastic welcoming and farewell became an established tradition. Camp Curry developed under the negligent eye of the state commissioners and the park service. It had a petting zoo, bowling alley, pool hall, swim tank, a kitchen housed in a concrete structure with a ice plant in the basement, gas station and garage, fixed hard-sided structures, a dance pavilion, its own sawmill, toboggan runs, outdoor entertainment pavilion, cocktail lounge, gift and clothing stores, a miniature steam train, guided tours, bathhouses, and all the comforts of home for a more sophisticated class of guest who do not mind sleeping in a tent on a platform as long as it is in Yosemite Valley. Of course, many of these improvements came even after the death of David Curry, but Jennie and her daughter Mary proceeded with the development of Camp Curry. (Courtesy of Yosemite Park and Curry Company.)

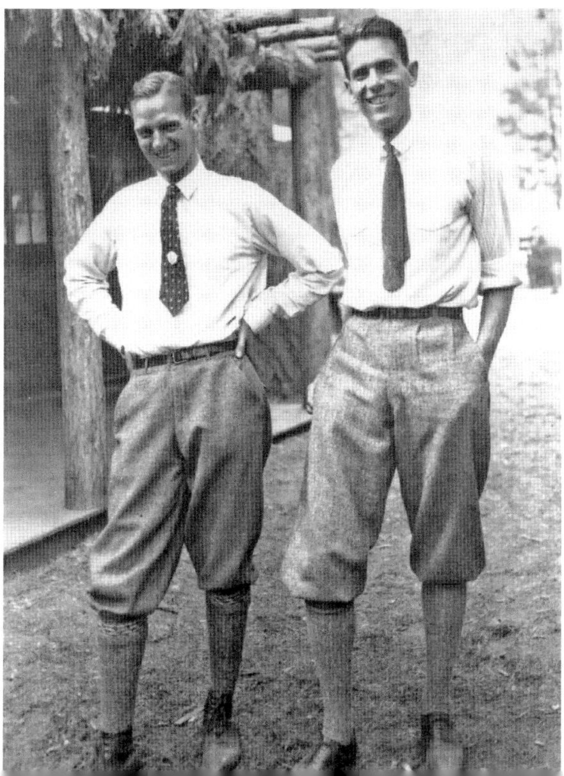

Donald Tresidder
Mary Curry married Donald Tresidder, who first came to Camp Curry as a "house boy," moving up to the front desk and then suitor for the boss's daughter. All this almost did not happen, for he was first fired by David Curry for taking his daughter Mary for a hike on the forbidden Ledge Trail. But the pleading of wife and daughter reinstated the future husband.

Donald is pictured on the right with Robert T. Williams. The two were young assistant managers at Camp Curry, and one rose to become president of the company. (Author's collection.)

James McCauley, the Four-Mile Trail, and the Mountain House

James McCauley completed the Four-Mile Trail in 1872 and built Mountain House at Glacier Point soon after. In 1899, David Curry started Camp Sequoia, which became Camp Curry in 1900. Trail builder John Conway and his crew are pictured on a lunch break during the trail's construction. (Both, courtesy of Yosemite Museum.)

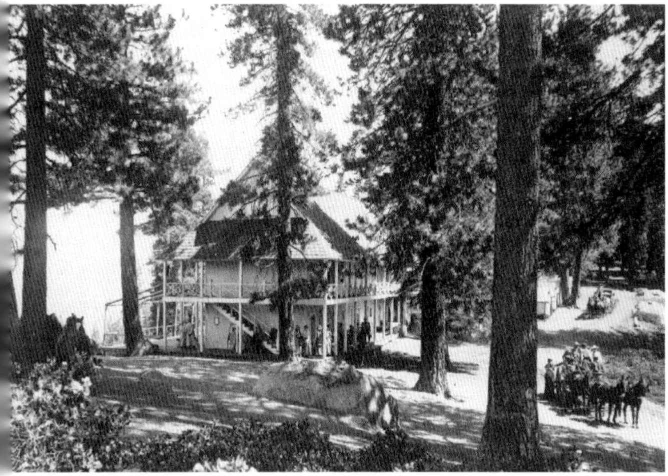

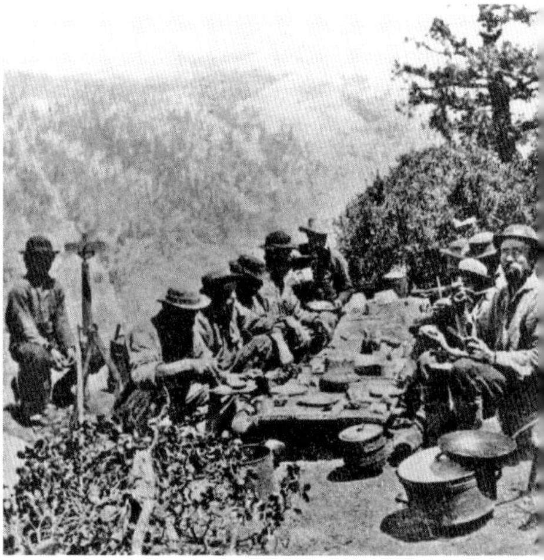

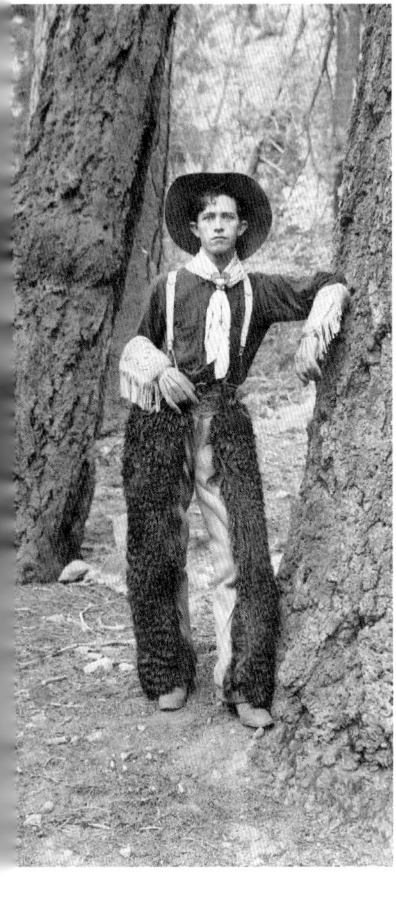

Jim Helm (LEFT)

Jim Helm was, even at a young age, head wrangler at Kinney Coffman Stables in Yosemite Valley. He later became treasurer of Mariposa County. (Author's collection.)

David Curry (RIGHT)

At Glacier Point, McCauley began a Fire Fall, which continued as for the duration of McCauley's operation. The Fire Fall was discontinued until David Curry reestablished the attraction and attention was called to the event by the stentor voice of David Curry calling, "Let the Fire Fall," from Camp Curry to Glacier Point. The tradition continued long beyond his death in 1917 until 1969, when it was discontinued by the park service. (Courtesy of Yosemite Park and Curry Company.)

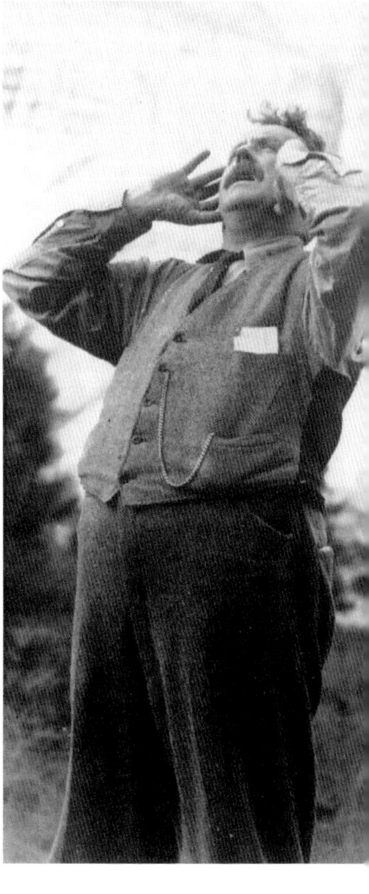

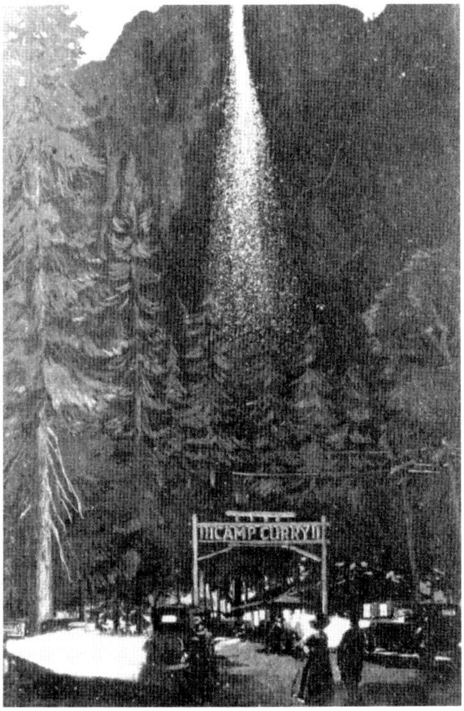

New Leadership

After the death of David Curry in 1917, Jennie and Mary Curry assumed leadership. Donald Tresidder became a physician, and following his marriage to Mary, he assumed the presidency of Curry Company. (Author's collection.)

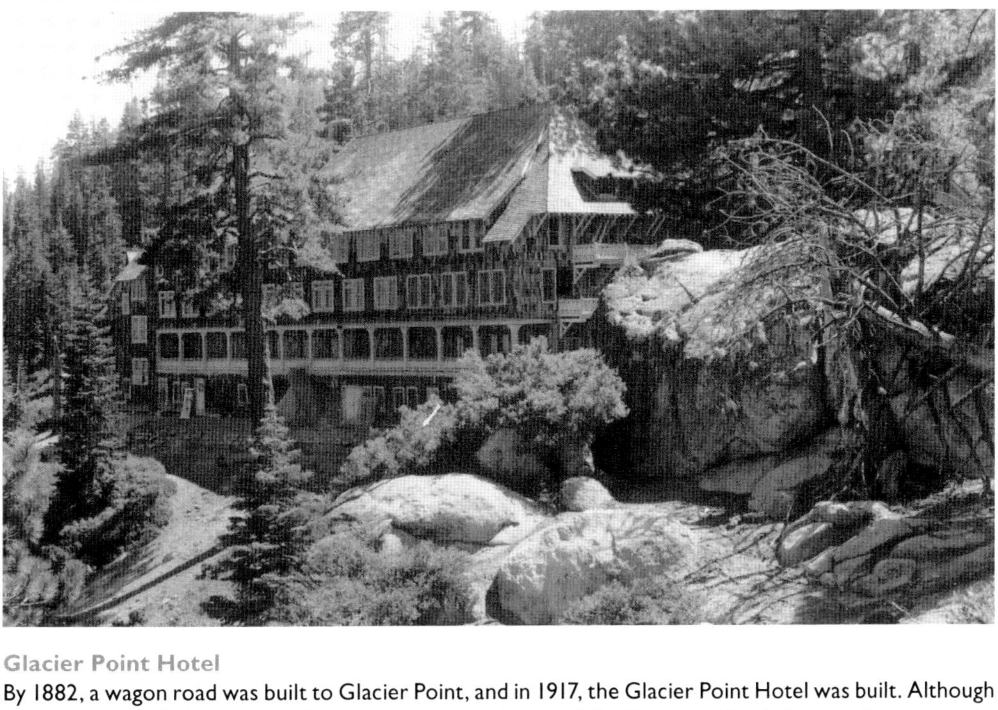

Glacier Point Hotel

By 1882, a wagon road was built to Glacier Point, and in 1917, the Glacier Point Hotel was built. Although it was a lovely Alpine design, the hotel almost bankrupted the Desmond Park Service Company, the investor. Lightly constructed to save costs, the structure was a concern based on the winter snow load. It was taken over by the Curry Company in the consolidation of concessionaires and burned down in 1969, having seldom been successful. (Photograph by Ralph Anderson, Park Service photographer.)

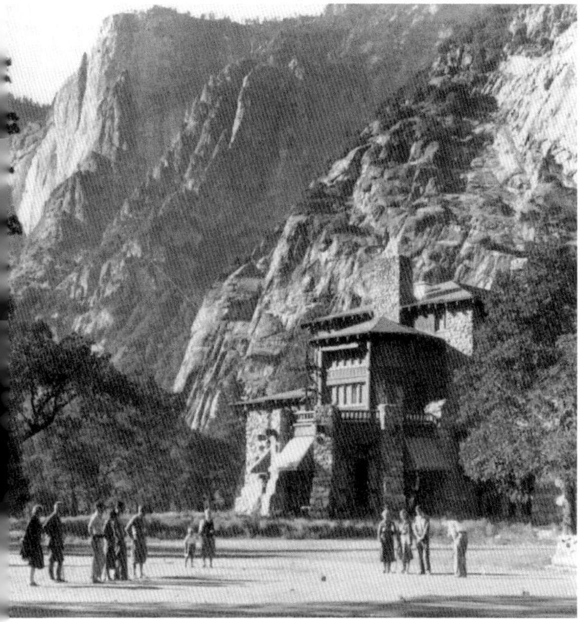

Ahwahnee Hotel
In 1924, Stephen Mather, director of the National Park Service, desired the consolidation of the many concessions in Yosemite Valley, as well as the building of a first-class hotel. The major concession was the Curry Company. The other major concession had recently built the Glacier Point Hotel, but its operations were bankrupt. With Donald Tresidder now president of Curry Company and Stanford University, Mather felt that he had a concessionaire that he could deal with without having to negotiate with the bombastic David Curry. Working with Tresidder, the Ahwahnee Hotel was built, giving Mather the first-class hotel he desired. Most of the concessionaires were absorbed by Curry Company, making the Yosemite Park and Curry Company with Tresidder at the helm. (Courtesy of Yosemite Park and Curry Company.)

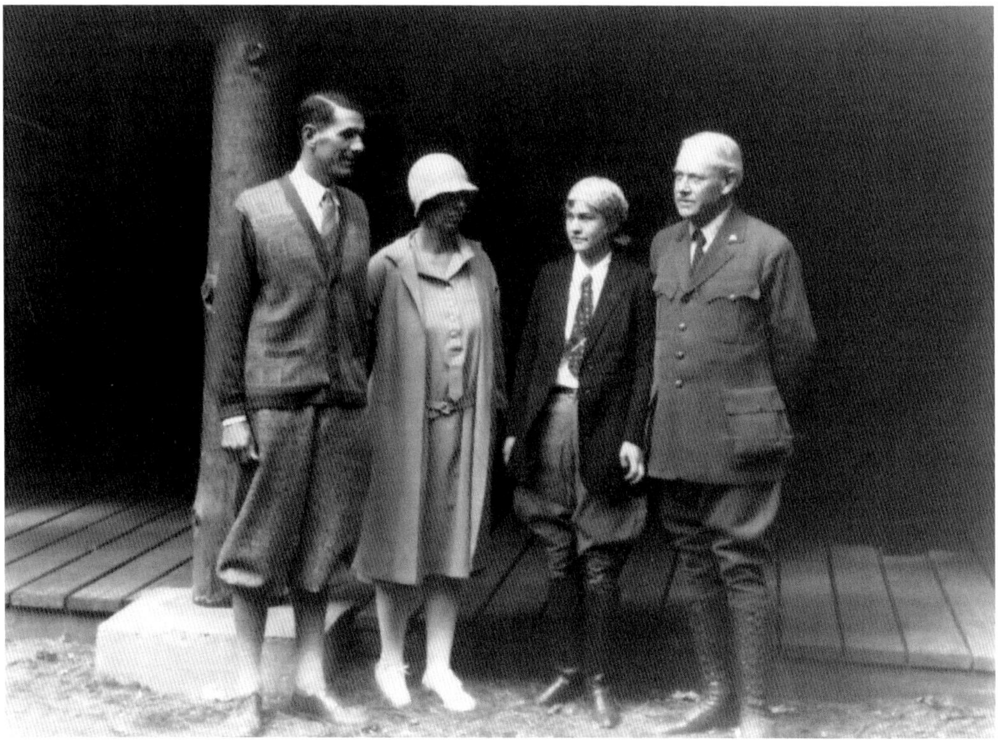

Mather and Daughter (right) and Don and Mary Curry Tresidder
The years-long goal for a first-class hotel was reached just in time for the Depression. The opening of the All-Year Highway through Mariposa in 1926 helped, but it was not until after World War II that the public began to use Yosemite National Park in the manner envisioned. (Courtesy of Yosemite Park and Curry Company.)

CHAPTER FOUR

A Few Legends of Impact

Following the end of industrial gold mining about 1913, the population of Mariposa County declined as families moved away looking for a source of income. Following World War I, the citizens of the county were sustained by subsistence farming and working in logging, mining, and railroad operations in the Merced River Canyon. Tourism to Yosemite was aided by the opening of State Highway 140 through Mariposa in 1926 but was limited by the Depression, beginning in 1929. World War II effectively closed Yosemite National Park due to wartime rationing, and working-age men and their families left the county to serve in the war effort. By 1960, the population of the county was still a meager 5,056. In 2015, the population is near 18,000, and the main industries are related to retirement, tourism, and government.

Based on slow growth, most residents know their neighbors and participate with them in business, civic, and social activities. This chapter features some of the legends that have participated in the growth and creating the quality of life.

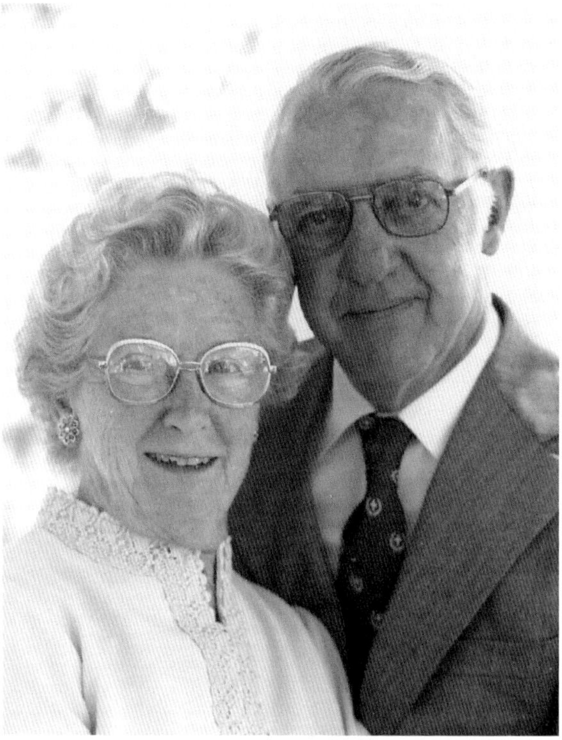

Andy and Betty Cummings
Early in the 1970s, retired professional portrait photographer Andy Cummings and his wife, Betty, from Whittier, California, moved to Mariposa to be closer to their daughter and son-in-law, Adele and Reid Marks. Andy built a darkroom in his new home off Silva Road but began missing photographing people. Slowly, he began to capture an eclectic group of Mariposa citizens to preserve their stories for the future. Unfortunately, Andy was never able to finish the project, but what he did accomplish was significant. (Photograph by author.)

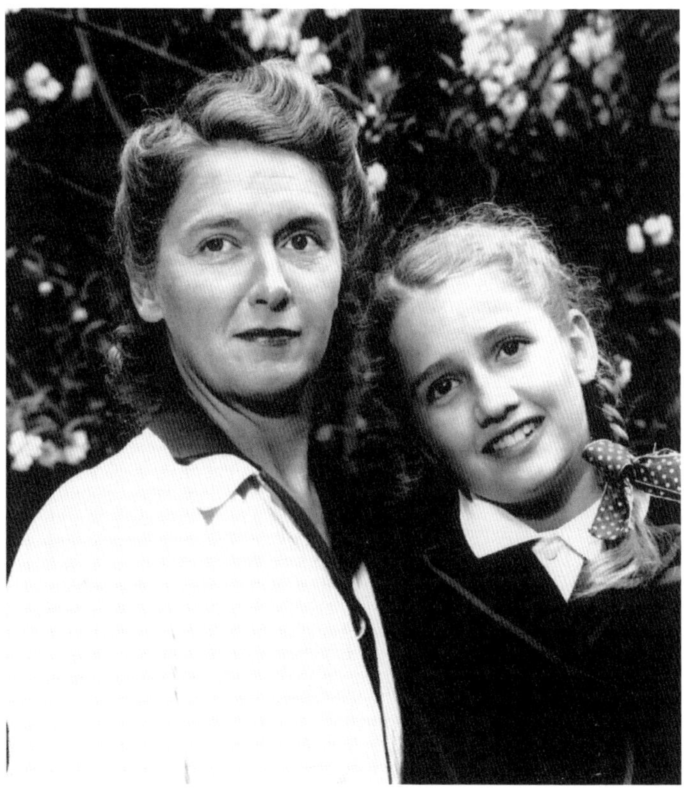

Betty Cummings and Adele Marks, 1944
After Andy passed away, daughter Adele gave the author Andy's negatives and prints from the effort, as well as a few from his earlier vocation. What follows is a collection of the casual portraits of Mariposa citizens taken by Andy or the author. Some other pictures were taken by unidentified photographers. (Author's collection.)

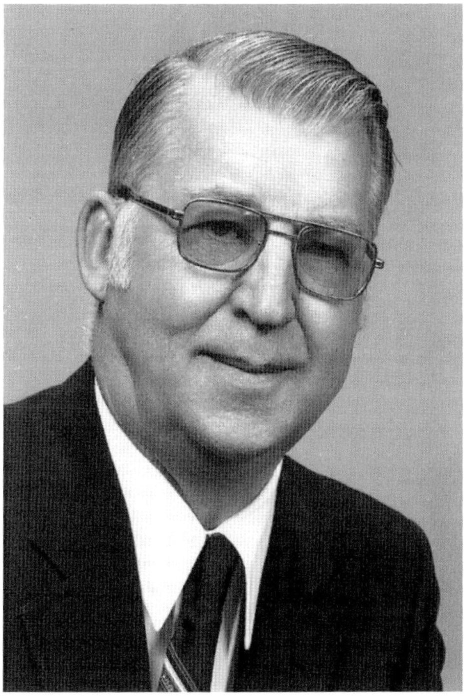

Superior Court Judge Dean C. Lauritzen
Dean Lauritzen served Mariposa County as district attorney from the late 1950s, and in 1969, he was elevated to judge of the superior court, Mariposa County, retiring in 1987. Most significantly though, during his early tenure as district attorney, he successfully negotiated a contract with the Merced Irrigation District providing Mariposa County with 50-plus years of revenue for water and utility development, probably the most important instrument ever concluded in Mariposa County history. It was from this source that a large portion of the Saxon Creek Project, bringing domestic water to the town of Mariposa, was concluded. (Photograph by author.)

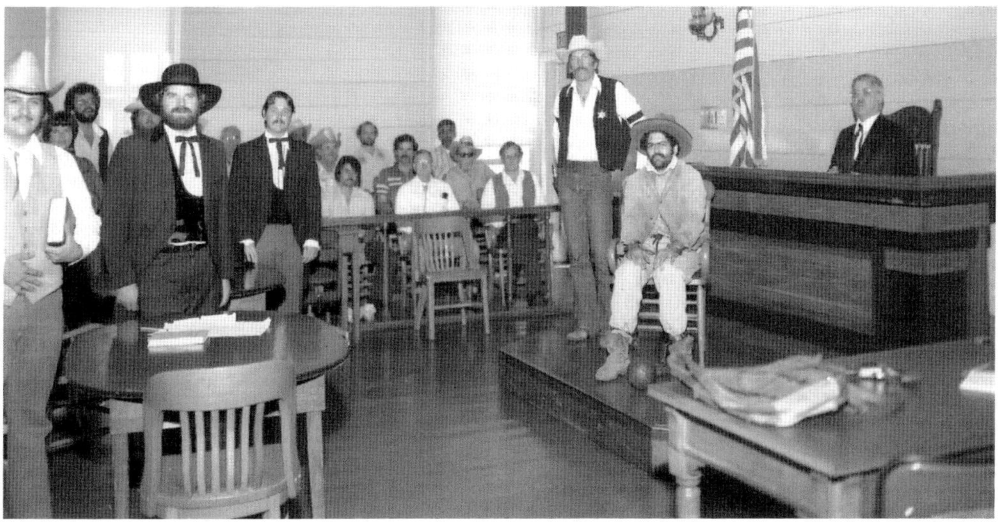

Trial of Young Mexican Miner, Judge Lauritzen Presiding
In 1979, Mariposa County celebrated the 125th anniversary of the building of the Mariposa County Courthouse and first publication of the *Mariposa Gazette.* Along with the usual parades, barbecues, and beard-growing contests, Judge Lauritzen arranged for the San Joaquin College of Law to come to Mariposa and reenact one of its most famous murder trials. A young Mexican miner was accused of murdering and robbing the Mariposa tax collector. The trial was held in full costume and beard in the historic courtroom, still in use, with Judge Lauritzen presiding. He was in full regalia with hair parted down the middle. The photographer, properly attired with ancient equipment, took a proper record of the event. The law students provided the lawyers for both sides, the townspeople were the jury, and the young Mexican, also a student, although convicted, was spirited away by his colleagues. (Photograph by author.)

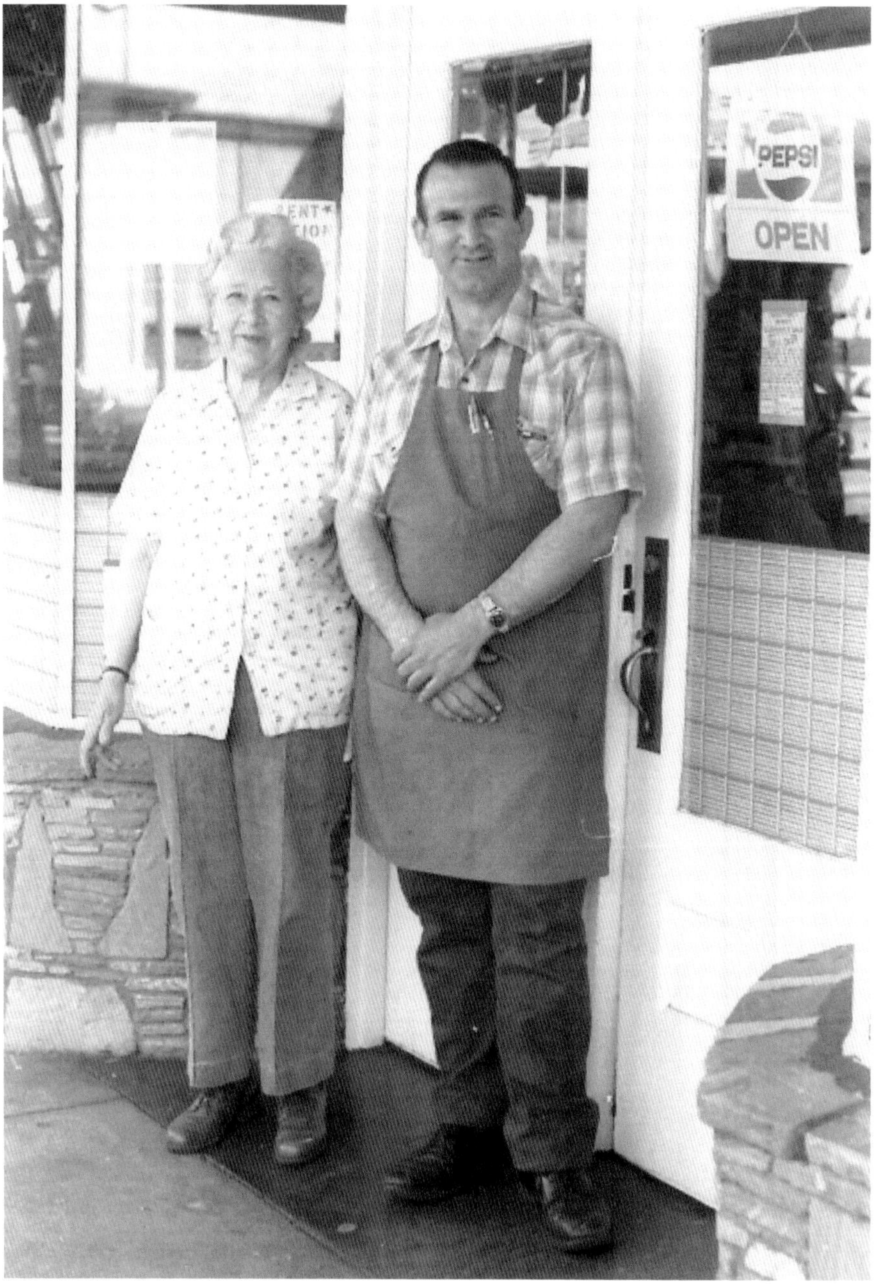

Jim and Marjorie Dulcich

Mother and son are shown on the occasion of converting the Butterfly Market into the Coast Hardware. Jim's father, also named Jim, started the Butterfly Soda Fountain and Telephone Company early in the 1930s when he purchased Gann's Soda Fountain and Telephone Company. It was located on the west side of Charles Street in the Grosjean Building. He then married Marjorie Walker and moved the business from its original location to a new location on the east side of Charles Street. He began an expansion program lasting many years, adding a meat market, grocery store, coffee shop, beer garden, and frozen food lockers; he also expanded the telephone company for a time before selling it. (Photograph by author.)

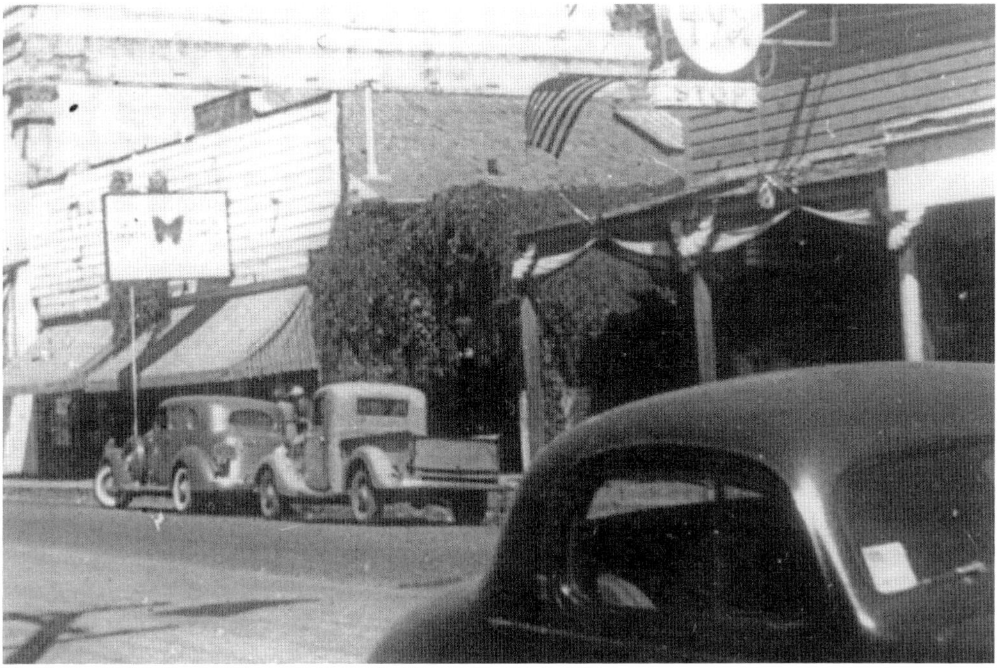

Butterfly Market and Telephone Company, 1937
As time went on, young Jim joined the operation, but after 1970 it became apparent that a larger competitor with more parking was to spell the end of the Butterfly Market and many other small markets in town. Father Jim, well past 90, agreed and supported the reconfiguring of the market into a hardware store, which was more in keeping with changing times. He did not live to see the success that the hardware store has become; nonetheless, he had a great deal of influence in the restructuring of the business. At the far right is the beer garden covered with hops. (Author's collection.)

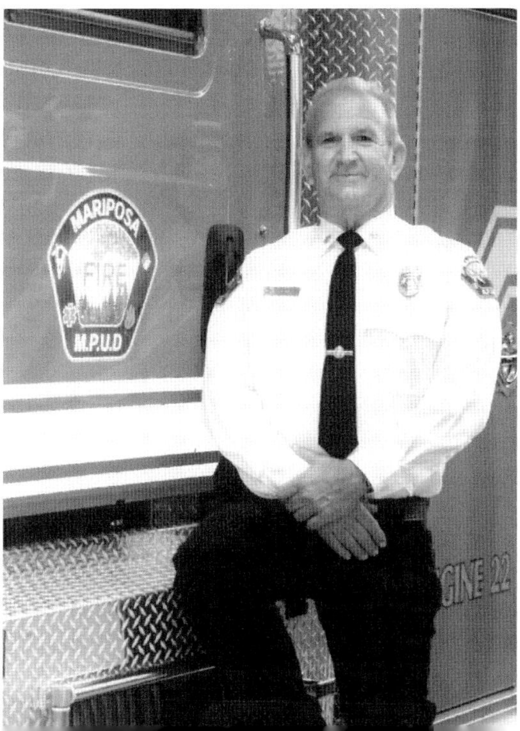

MPUD Fire Department
Chief Jim Dulcich
Young Jim was really the force behind that success. Outside of the business, Jim demonstrated great character and love for his community by serving as the fire chief of the Mariposa Public Utility District (MPUD) Volunteer Fire Department for roughly four decades. (Author's collection.)

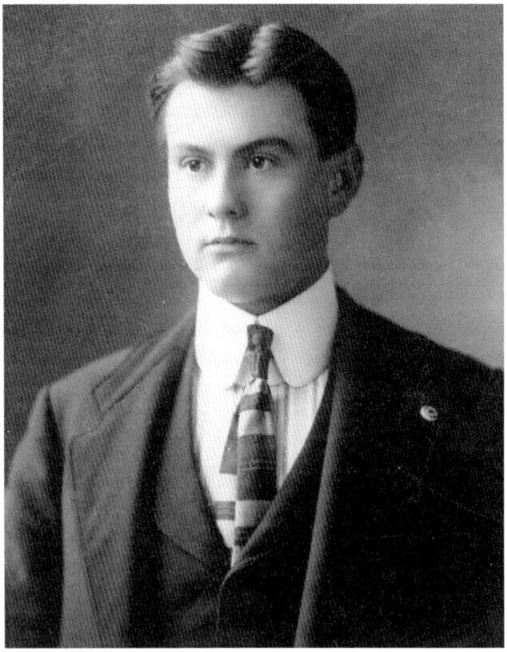

James P. McElligott

J.P. McElligott was one of four brothers born to Patrick and Lucy McElligott. Lucy was born in Bear Valley, California, in 1862. Patrick and brother Thomas had come to Mariposa in the 1880s, bringing a specialized piece of mining equipment to work on the mines on the grant. James "Jim" P. McElligott had three siblings: Maynard H., Charles F., and Mervin T. McElligott. (Author's collection.)

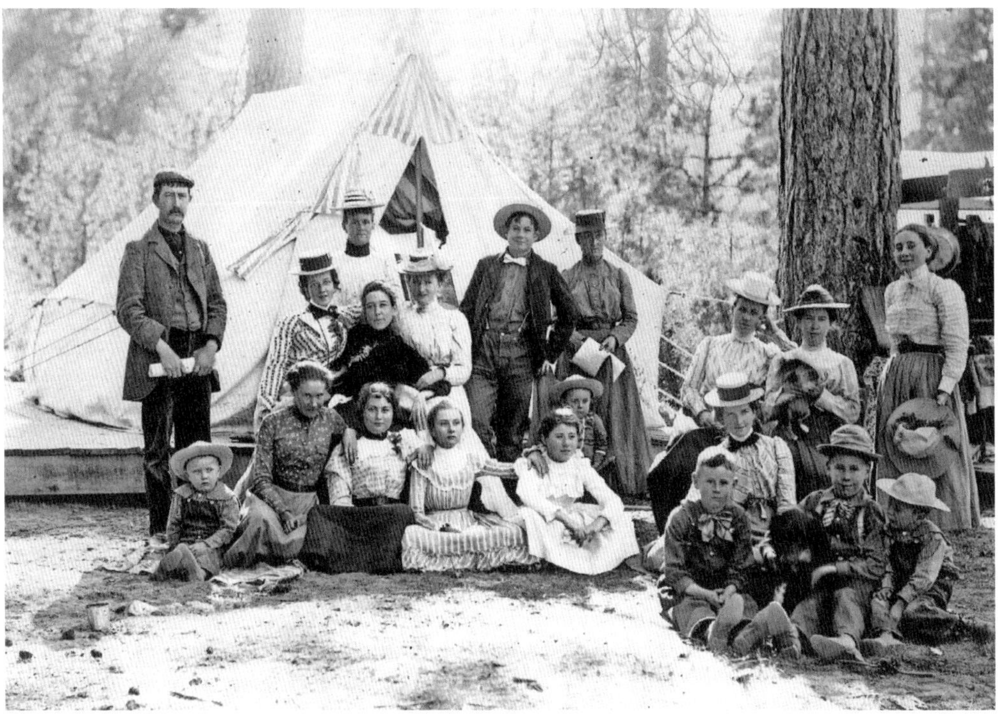

Mariposa Families in Wawona

The four McElligott brothers are included in this group shot. Jim is standing with the round hat, and the three little boys sitting are, from left to right, Charles, Maynard, and Mervin. During the summer, many of Mariposa's leading families spent the warmest period in Wawona, in the south end of today's Yosemite National Park. (Author's collection.)

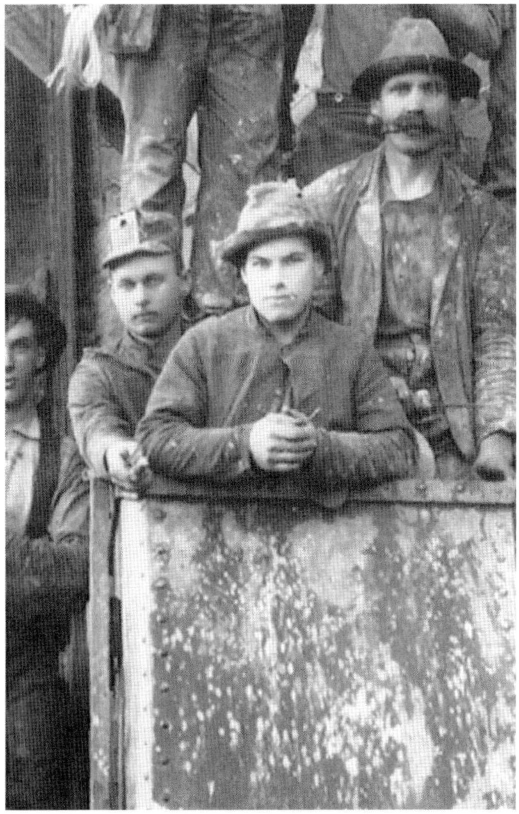

Jim McElligott at the Mariposa Mine
Jim, pictured in the center in the ore car looking at the camera, began his work life at the Mariposa Mine as a lift operator, working for Frank McGuire. He met and married Bessie Thorne, and from this union one daughter, May, was born. (Author's collection.)

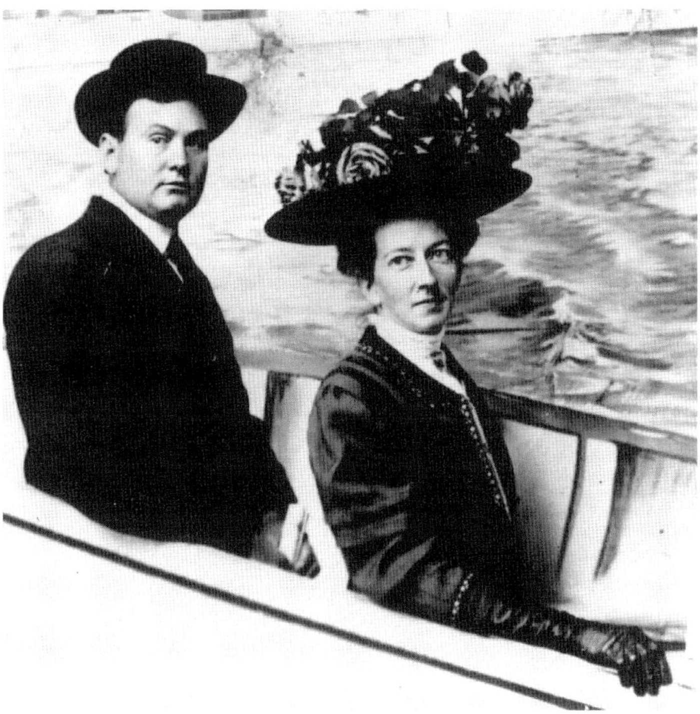

J.P. and Bessie on their Honeymoon
Around 1918, Jim and brother Charles became Ford dealers in Mariposa. They met with Henry Ford in San Francisco at a time when Ford was setting up dealerships in towns large and small. The Model T Ford was bringing a manufacturing revolution to the world, and Henry Ford needed people to sell the "Peoples Car." Brother Maynard worked as a mechanic in the garage while brother Mervin became an engineer working eventually for California Department of Highways. (Author's collection.)

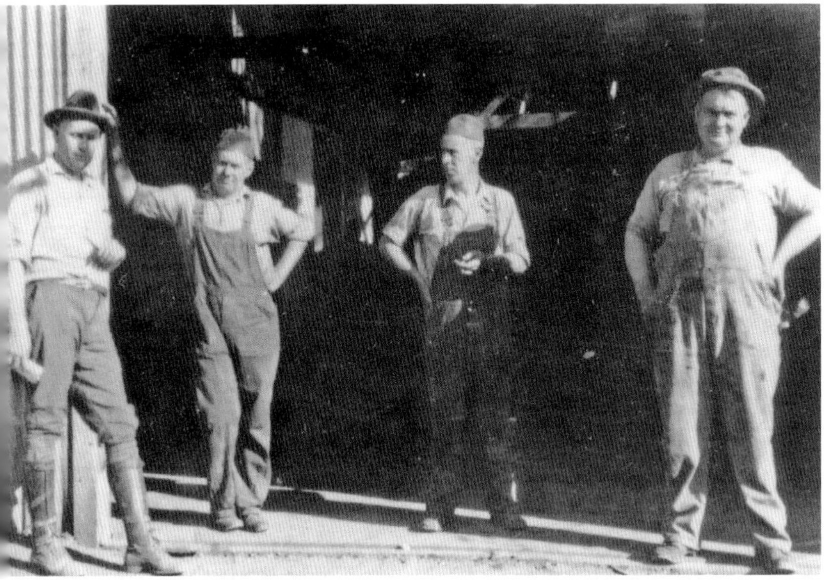

McElligott Brothers at Garage

J.P. served Mariposa in many capacities over the years as selective service, probation officer, and rationing board coordinator. Jim, Maynard, and Charles all created their family homes on the same block in Mariposa, which had been owned by the previous generation. Pictured from left to right are Mervin, Maynard, Charles, and Jim. (Author's collection.)

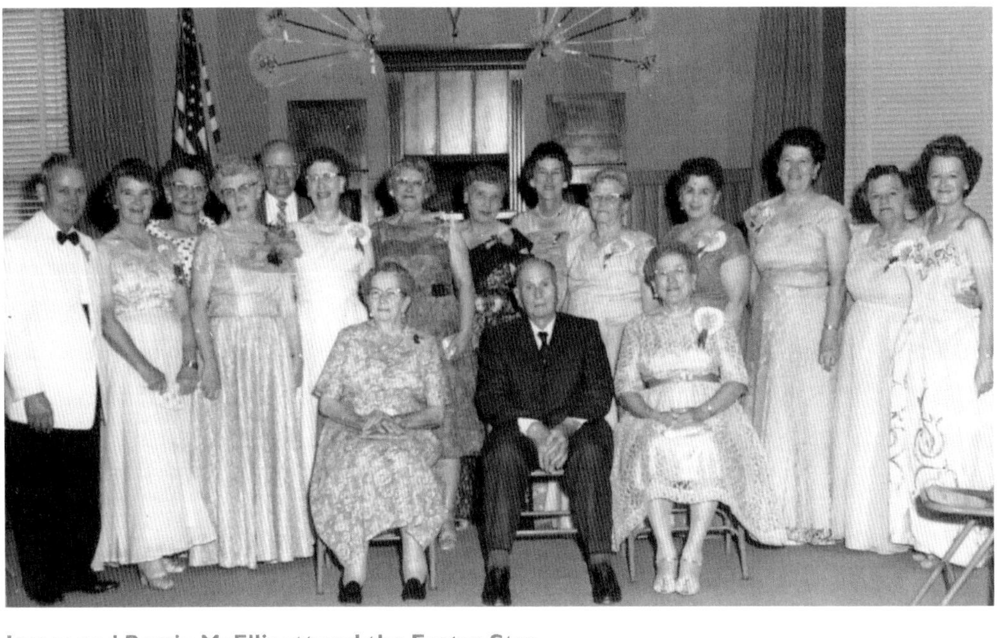

James and Bessie McElligott and the Easter Star

James P. McElligott (sitting) was involved in Easter Star with wife, Bessie (sitting to his right). Pictured around 1960, these citizens were all important in Mariposa. From left to right are Ansel Michael, theater owner and businessman; Winifred Bagby Freschlag, member of a pioneer family; Myrtle Schlageter McSwain, market and dress shop owner and once manager of Tenaya Lake High Sierra Camp; Ellen McElligott, wife of owner of Mariposa Garage Ford dealership; superintendent of schools George and teacher Lucille Fellows; unidentified; Vesta Spriggs, wife of high school principal; Beverly Pinkerton, wife of assistant road commissioner; Gladys Northrup, wife of pharmacist at Mariposa Drug Co.; Beth Hatcher, restaurant owner and artist; Ruth Womack, co-owner with husband of Fort Sumter Garage; Jane Sharp, political activist; and Virginia Michael, wife of Ansel Michael, of Bank of America. All of these folks made a significant impact on life in Mariposa. (Author's collection.)

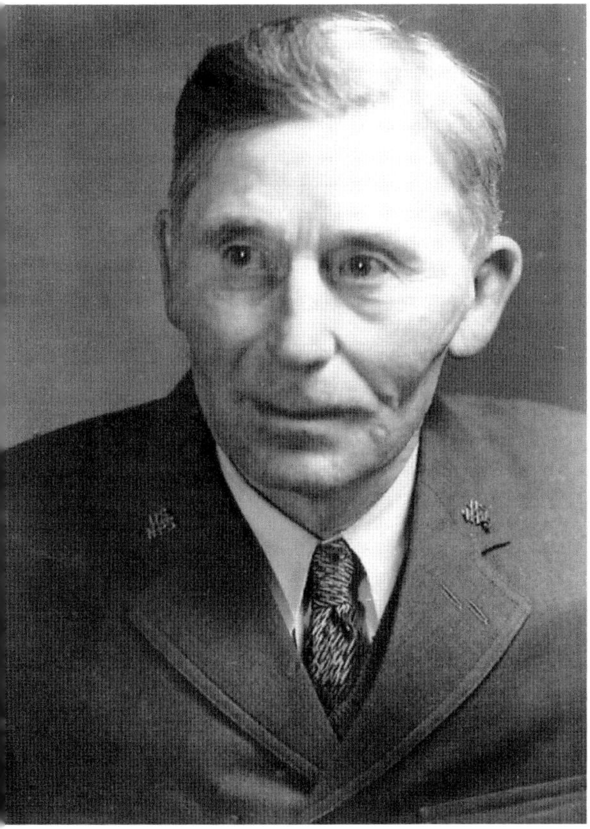

Gabriel Sovlewski

Born in Poland in 1866, Gabe immigrated to the United States and joined the Army. The assignment was the protection of the new Yosemite National Park. When Yosemite Valley was added to the federal park and temporary supervision was needed, Gabriel Sovlewski was appointed acting superintendent until the National Park Service was formed. For more than 30 years, he supervised the construction and maintenance of the trails in the park, and his last major task was overseeing the construction of the Wawona Tunnel in the 1930s. He also served on the board of education for Mariposa County and was instrumental in the construction of the present 1938 high school along with J.L. Spriggs, O.M. Whitley, and N.D. Chamberlain. For a total of 35 years, he helped with the preserving and caring for Yosemite National Park. (Author's collection.)

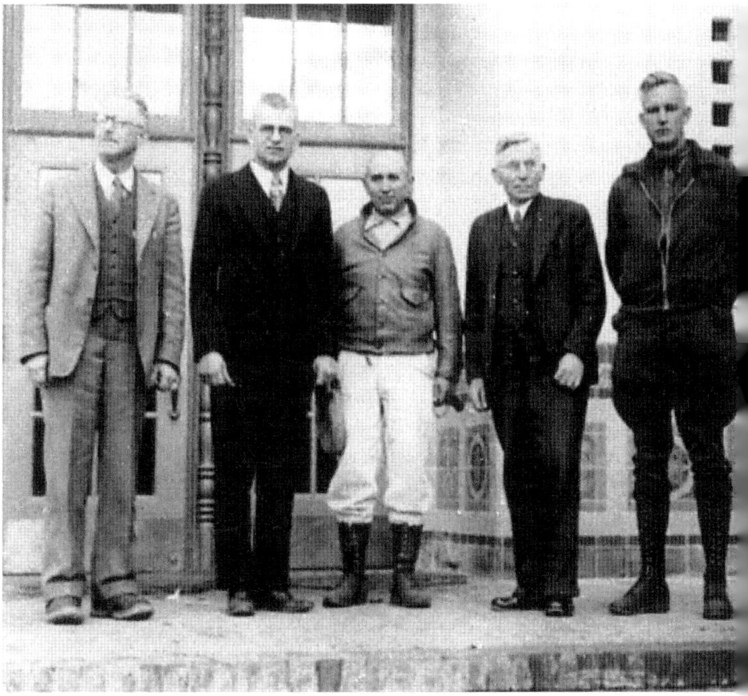

Gabriel Sovlewski, School Board Members, and Contractor

Shown from left to right are N.D. Chamberlain, board member; J.L. Spriggs, principal; contractor (who did not finish the job); Gabriel Sovlewski, board chairman; and O.M. Whitley, board member and later sheriff of Mariposa County. (Author's collection.)

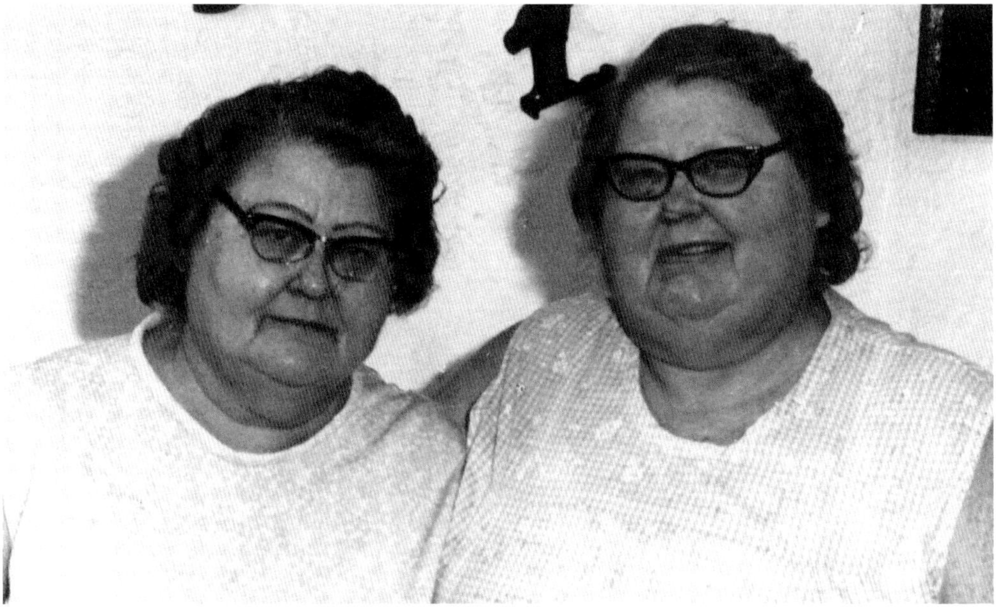

Arlene Ritter and Darlene Hibbs, Kontry Kitchen
Arlene Ritter (right) and twin sister Darlene Hibbs set up a breakfast restaurant in the old California Highway Patrol space downtown. Called the Kontry Kitchen, their biscuits and gravy, eggs, and ham attracted a lot of attention of early risers. Their big hearts saw to it that no one went away hungry. (Photograph by Andrew Cummings.)

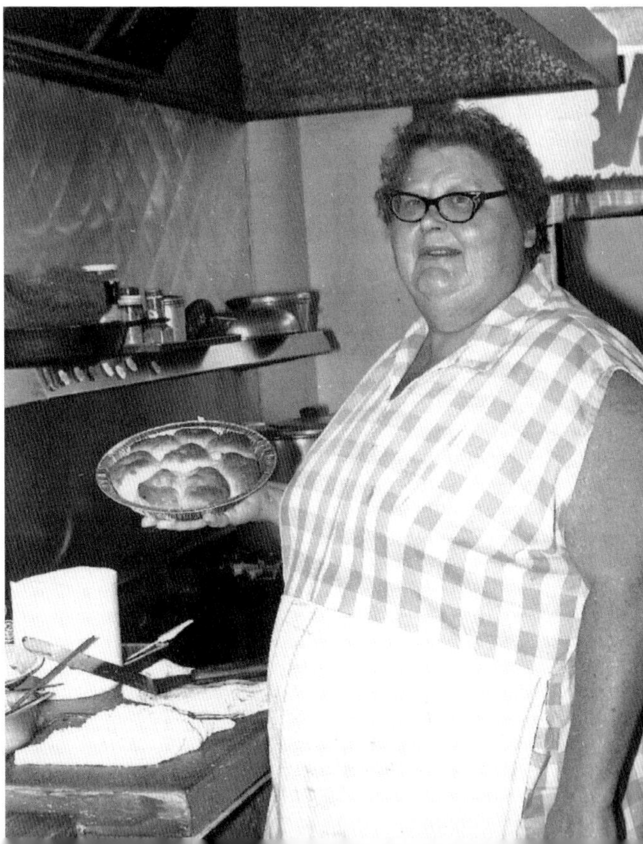

Arlene Ritter and Famous Biscuits
Born in Oklahoma City in the late 1920s, Arlene and Darlene spent their whole lives working at jobs that were not always lucrative but needed for the sustenance of life in the communities in which they lived. (Photograph by Andrew Cummings.)

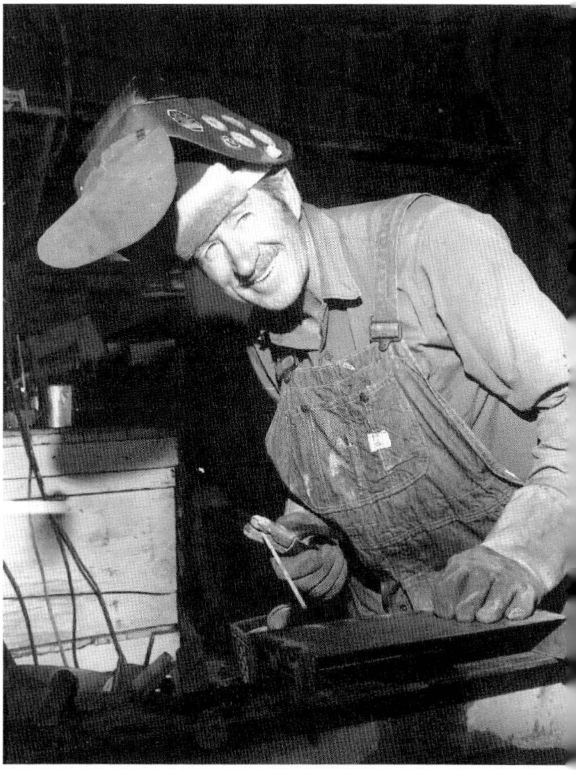

Bob Bissmeyer

The unofficial mayor of Bootjack, Bob Bissmeyer came to Mariposa to semi-retire, and with him came his wife and three sons. He opened a welding shop and set up the Missing Piston Auto Sales. He liked to fix up old cars and then offer them for sale cheap to anyone who needed transportation. The 1970s in Mariposa County was still a period of some growth with a number of new homes and mobile homes moving in. Major subdivisions had pretty much run their course leaving many lots to sell. The next phase of development included minor subdivisions or "four by fours." Bob set up such a development south of Bootjack Road but left the area to go fishing in Baja California. (Photograph by Andrew Cummings.)

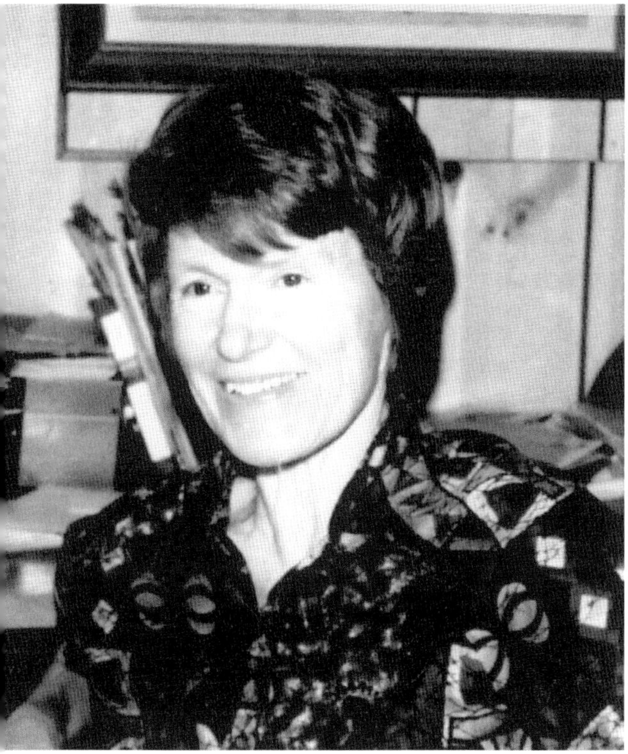

Shirley Sargent

Shirley's love of Yosemite traces back to the days when her father Robert was an engineer on the Tioga Road. As she became older, she was plagued with dystonia, a neuromuscular disease. Nothing stopped her from writing and publishing her memories of Yosemite and its pioneers. With Hank Johnson, they formed Flying Spur Press, named after the hill west of the Old Coulterville Road, just outside the Park where Shirley built her home.

It is as a prolific writer that Shirley must be remembered. Nine works of fiction, 20 major books of history, a great source for Yosemite, two Mariposa County guide books—plus she edited, wrote nonsyndicated stories and poetry, and had an uncountable number of published articles. Shirley is surely a legend in Yosemite and Mariposa County. (Author's collection.)

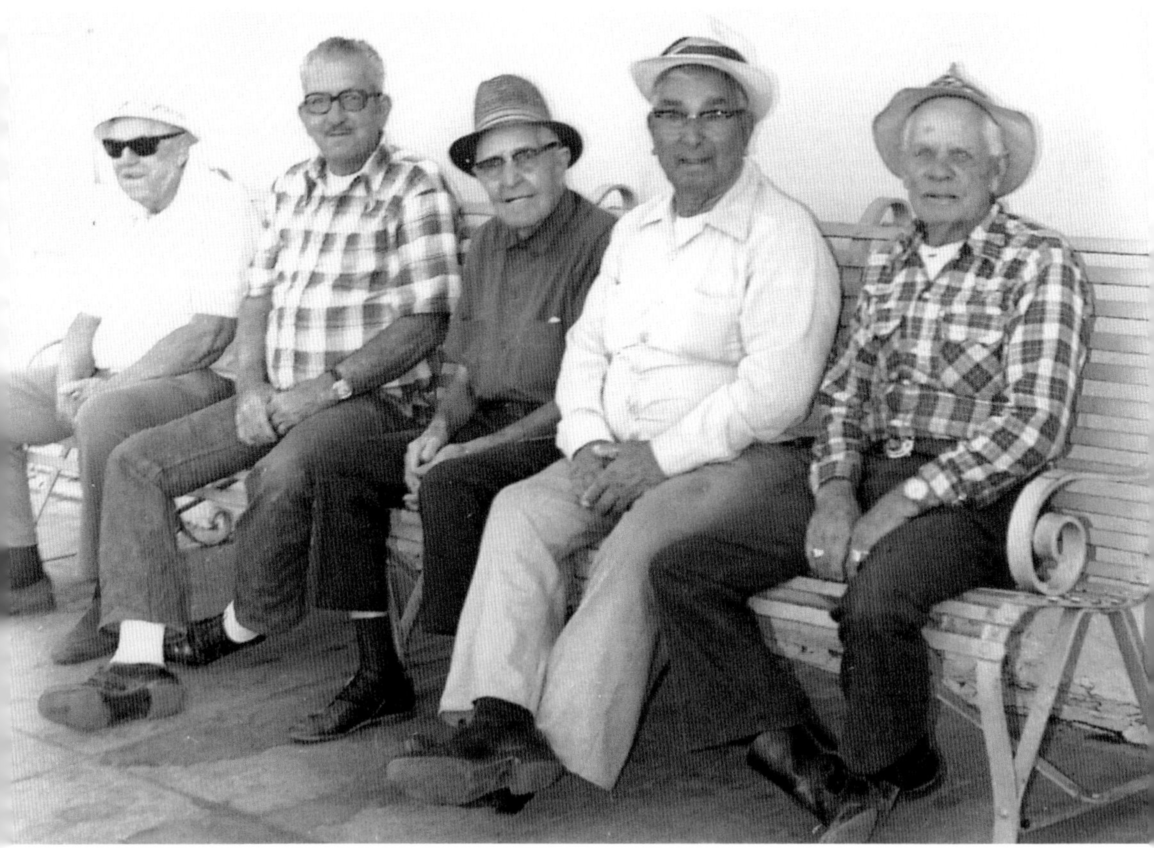

Sid Boyer and Friends
From left to right are Teofil "Ski" Kuzinski, Byrd "Pappy" Blunt, Pearlie Poor, Tony Soto, and Sid Boyer. These five old-timer retirees are representative of many generations who have spent part of each day in downtown Mariposa, perched on everything from benches to logs to Nehi cold drink boxes. Each had long work histories in Mariposa County, and earlier in their lives, they were gold miners, farmers, road builders, carpenters, and the like. Sid worked at the Madera Sugerpine Lumber Company and for Mariposa County Road Department, Tony did all kinds of labor and constriction, Pearlie finished his career with opening graves by hand at Mariposa's cemeteries, and Pappy and Ski worked many years at the California Youth Authority Camp on top of Mount Bullion. (Photograph by Andrew Cummings.)

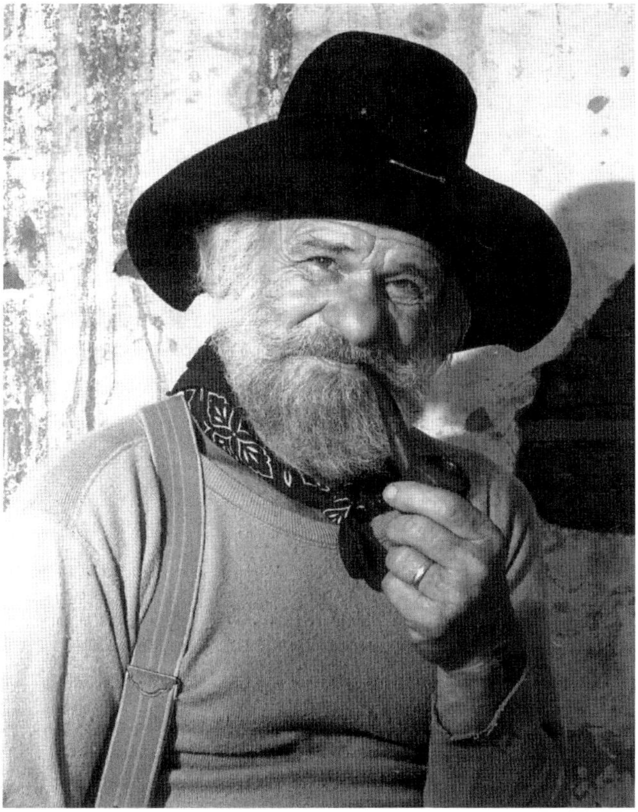

George Fournier
Born in Mount Bullion, George was related to the Fournier/Prairie families. He became a barber working with Bert Smith and Winnie Williams. When he retired, he spent many hours working at the Mariposa Museum and History Center guiding visitors and helping out on the grounds. He preferred to dress as a miner; his father worked at the Princeton Mine in Mount Bullion. (Photograph by Andrew Cummings.)

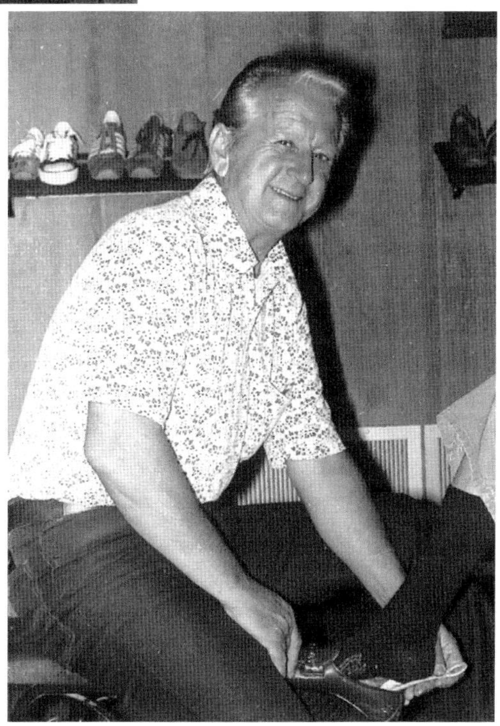

George Radanovich
Father of eight children, uncle of the author, and great story teller, George followed his older brother Roy to Mariposa after completing almost three years overseas in the South Pacific during World War II. (Photograph by Andrew Cummings.)

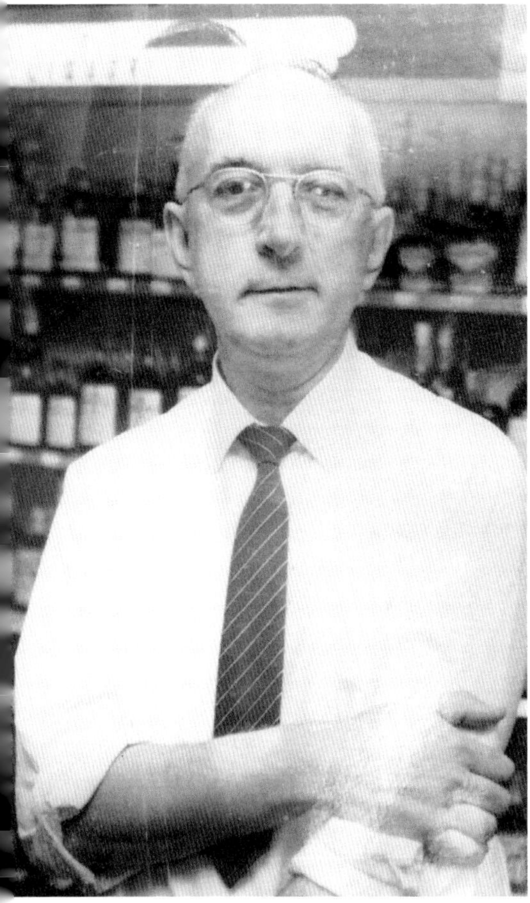

Roy Radanovich, Mariposa Drug Company
George joined his older brother Roy in the drugstore following World War II, met and married Joan Phillips, and proceeded to build a home and a family. But two brothers with growing families were more than one small drugstore could support. He opened the Fremont House, a men's clothing store. As a young man, George grew up in his father's and brother's shoe repair and sales stores, so he was not uneducated in the field of shoes and socks. In fact, he always told the story about on the day that he opened his new store that a logger came in telling him that he finally got a job but needed a pair of socks but had no money. While Joan was well on her way to delivering her fifth or sixth child, the cash box was a bit short. But George gave the logger the socks, and that was his only "sale" of that first day. In a couple of weeks, the logger got his first check and paid George. All of these young men at that time had been in World War II and knew how to depend on each other.

The brothers' generosity to the community, friends, and family continued their whole lives. When the drugstore moved into its new home across the street from the Independent Order of Odd Fellows Building, which was where it started in 1926, George moved his Fremont House into the space vacated by the drugstore, where it continues today. (Author's collection.)

Roy Radanovich and the great Red Bud Planting (OPPOSITE)
Pictured from left to right are Lydia Brady, Bill Brady, California governor Edmund G. "Pat" Brown, chamber of commerce president Bob Romine, and Roy Radanovich.

During the 1960s, the merchants along State Highway 140 formed the Highway 140 Association, which promoted the highway from the desert at Hawthorne, Nevada, to the sea at Monterey. Besides creating advertising brochures and then distributing them, the merchants and the chamber of commerce, assisted by Mariposa County government, took advantage of the skills possessed by Bill Brady for propagation of difficult species. One of the most difficult was a bush called red bud, so named by the deep-red composite flowers that introduced spring each year in the foothills. The process included gathering the seeds, refrigerating them to simulate winter temperatures, soaking them in acid to resemble the attempt to digest in the acid environment of a bird's stomach, and then planting the seed once sprouted in cans until they are established and ready for transfer. The whole community got behind the project by saving many coffee cans. When the number of cans was short, rancher Frank Long acquired many cans from canneries in Modesto and Stockton.

Bill Brady processed the seeds and turned the sprouting and planting over to the California Youth Authority inmates from Mount Bullion Camp. Ceremonial plantings attracted the governor, a congressman, and other dignitaries. Today, every spring, thousands of red bud bushes line the roads of middle Mariposa County and along Highway 140 to Yosemite. (Photograph by Harold Rowney.)

Planting

Harold "Biz" Johnson, center, is pictured planting one of first red buds. Roy Radanovich is on the left, and John Rotondo, Mariposa County recreation director, is on the right. (Author's collection.)

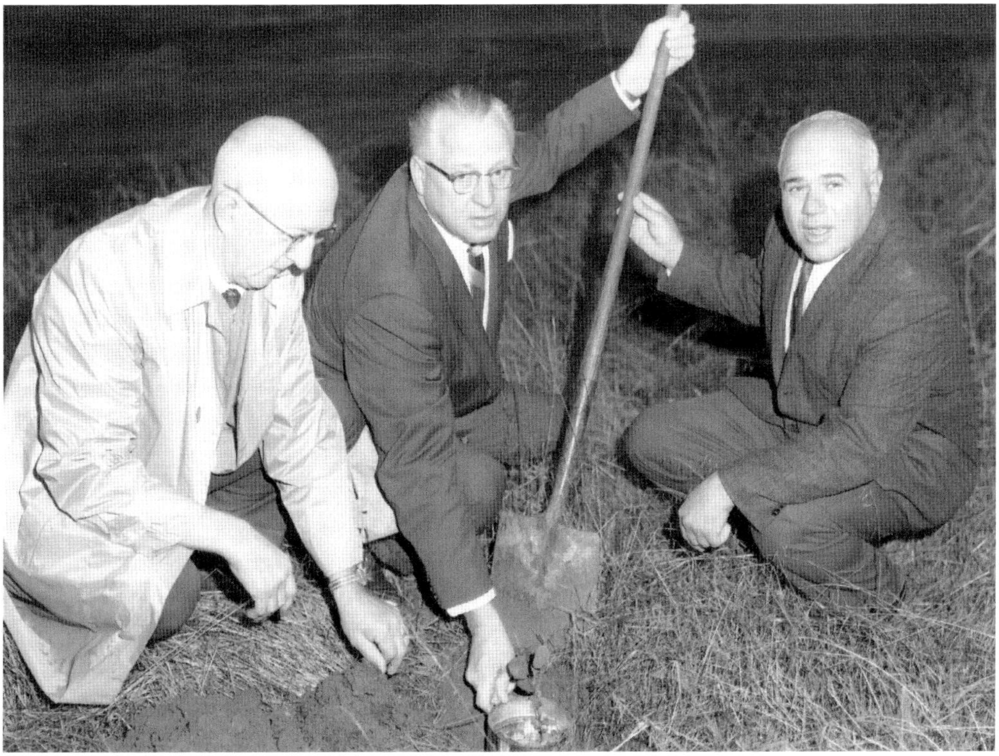

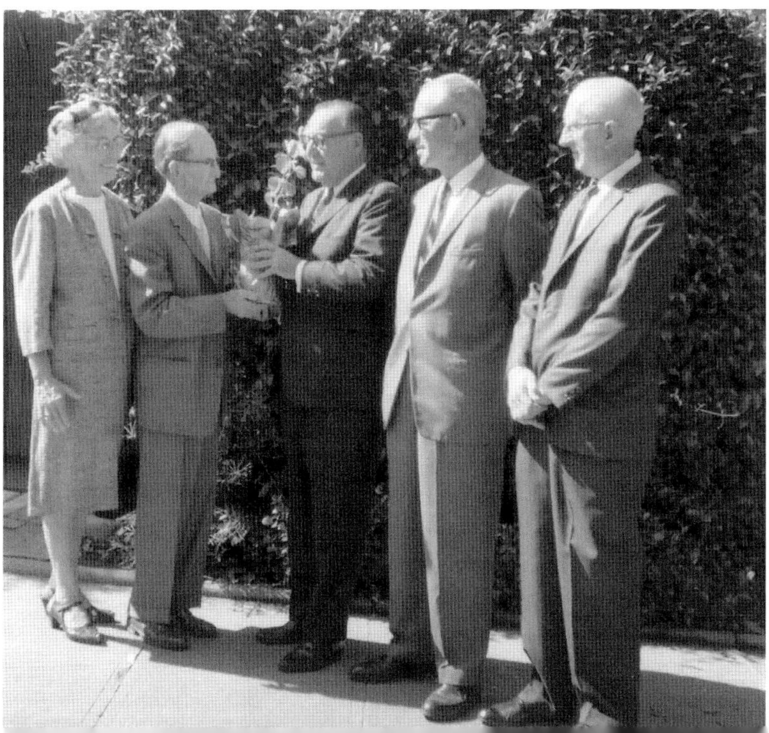

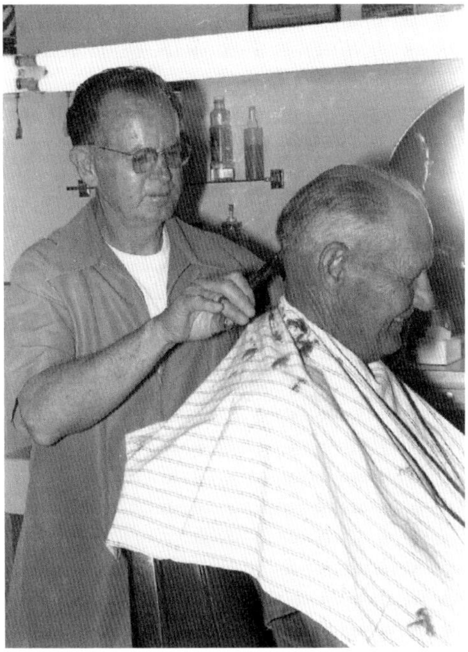

Winnie Williams

A native of Hornitos, Mariposa County, Winnie was the son of two pioneer families, the Williams and Catamartori. When it came time to go to high school, he rode a Model T Bus every day to Mariposa. Toward the end of his high school education, he rented a room in Mariposa so he could work after school. His most responsible job was at Schlageter's IGA Market and Fountain. When the owner had to take an emergency trip, Winnie, 18 years old, was placed in charge. Devoted to his family, church, and community his entire life, Winnie served in many ways. He became a barber and worked at first for Bert Smith. When Bert retired, the space the shop had occupied was needed for the new Western Auto Store, so Winnie moved a couple doors up the street. He continued to work into his nineties, having a shop in a side room of his son Trent's Styling for His & Hers. (Photograph by Andrew Cummings.)

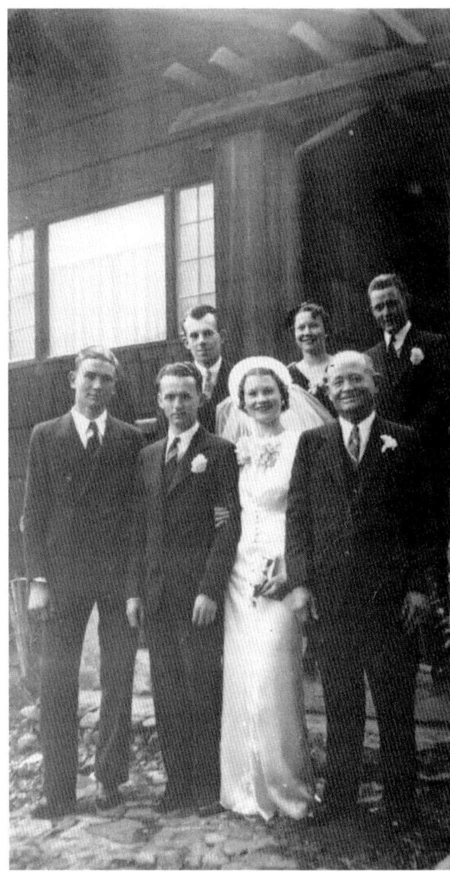

Winnie and Pearl, St. Joseph Church, 1938

Winnie married Pearl Carter, also a hairdresser who continued working well into her later years with son Trent. Winnie and Pearl had three sons: Gary, Trent, and Bill. They were raised having the same sense of commitment to their community, which was exhibited by their parents. Over the years, Winnie could be found cooking at Veterans of Foreign Wars dinners (though he was not a veteran); cutting hair free for old-timers at the hospital; working, often with Pearl, on projects around St. Joseph Church; participating in many community activities; and quietly helping many people, especially those with problems related to alcohol and hunger. The Mariposa Masonic Lodge made him an honorary member. (Courtesy of Pearl Carter Williams collection.)

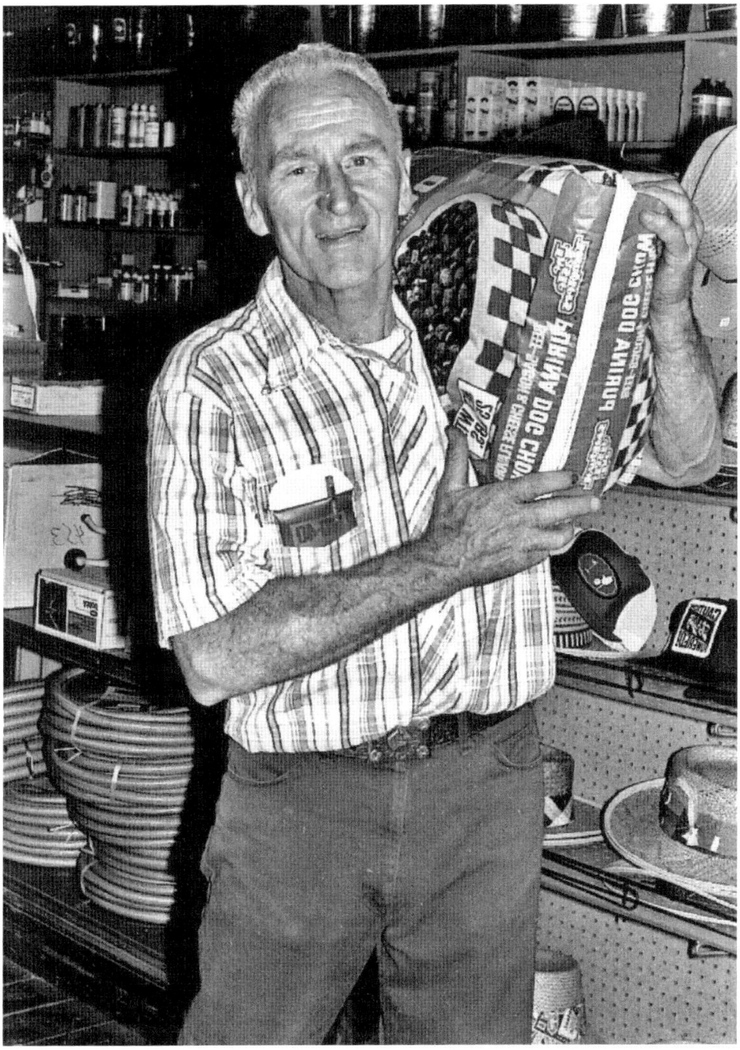

Jack Ritter

Jack and Pat Ritter came to Mariposa in the early 1950s to join the Webb family in forming Mariposa Enterprises. The company grew rapidly, providing diverse products and services to Mariposa. John and Reba Webb joined son Jack Webb, who came to Mariposa to become the agricultural teacher at Mariposa County High School. Jack Ritter was the point man of the company, helping to organize a number of chicken ranches and running the feed mill and feed store in Mariposa. Other collateral activities became associated with Mariposa Enterprises, such as Charlie Morse's Nursery and John Webb's auto repair shop. The repair shop brought two mechanics to Mariposa who went on to become contributing citizens. John Rotondo became the recreation director for Mariposa County, responsible for organizing and developing many community recreation sites throughout the county.

Mariposa Enterprises had difficulty in competition with larger egg producers and feed companies and, eventually, had to close. Jack and Pat Ritter salvaged the Mariposa Feed and Supply part of the company, and it is still operated by their son Tom Ritter who has added a fine nursery business. Pat went on to become county clerk of Mariposa County. They had five children, Joe, Greg, Steve, Monica, and Tom. Jack loved baseball and played shortstop for various teams. His support of school agricultural programs, 4-H, and Future Farmers was legendary. (Photograph by Andrew Cummings.)

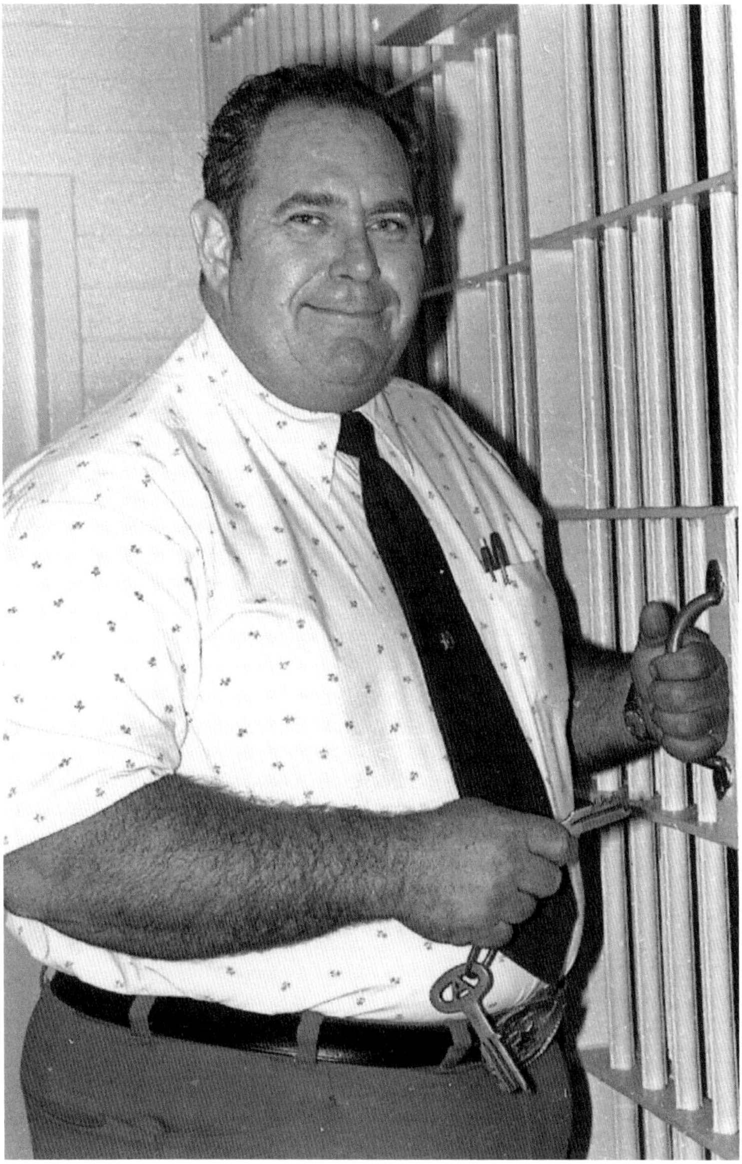

Sheriff Paul Paige
Paul and Mary Paige came to Mariposa to run the Perry Joel Ranch, a turkey operation. When the overall business ceased, Paul took on various ranching jobs and, finally, became a plumber for Posy Plumbing. As time went on, Sheriff O.M. Whitley hired him as deputy. In the mid-1970s, Paul was elected sheriff and served two terms.

During his eventful eight years, Mariposa and Yosemite changed a great deal. There was growth in the county as well as a significant increase in visitation to Yosemite. At this time, the use of illegal drugs posed as a challenge to law enforcement and county budgets. Many social and cultural changes were taking place, and a sheriff's department having to face many challenges tasked the leadership. Mariposa was no longer a quiet, old mining town. Paul responded. Those who knew Paul well appreciated his service during a very difficult time. Paul and Mary had four children, all born in Mariposa. (Photograph by Andrew Cummings.)

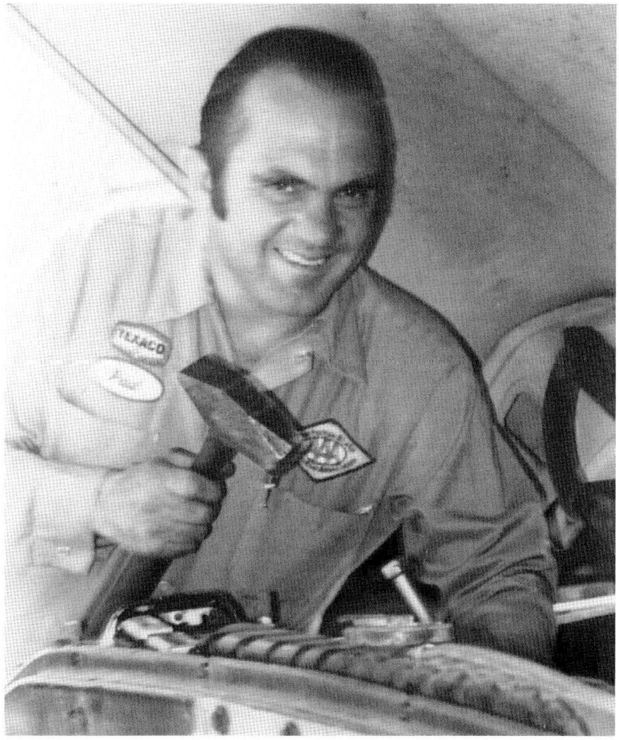

Paul Halencak

Paul Halencak, who came with Mariposa Enterprises, went on to purchase Sierra Motors and operated the towing and repair facilities serving Mariposa for decades. He and wife Shirley raised a fine group of sons who each learned trades in mechanical services and law enforcement. (Photograph by Andrew Cummings.)

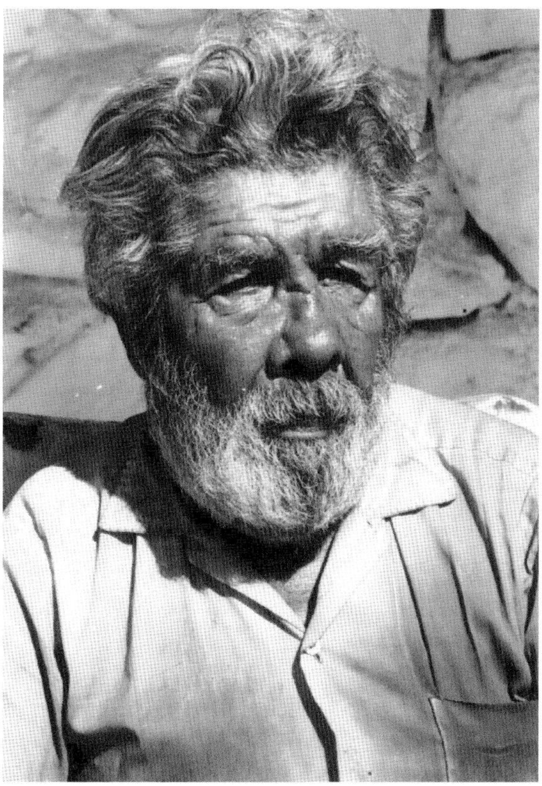

Henry Hogan

Henry was a Native American of Mariposa County, although his grandfather was an Anglo who came to Mariposa and Yosemite and married a Native American woman. He homesteaded on Yaqui Gulch Road, living and ranching there; that area was his family's home base for generations. Henry served his country during World War I and had been a prizefighter. This photograph is included to first honor Henry and second to show the fine work of Andrew Cummings. (Photograph by Andrew Cummings.)

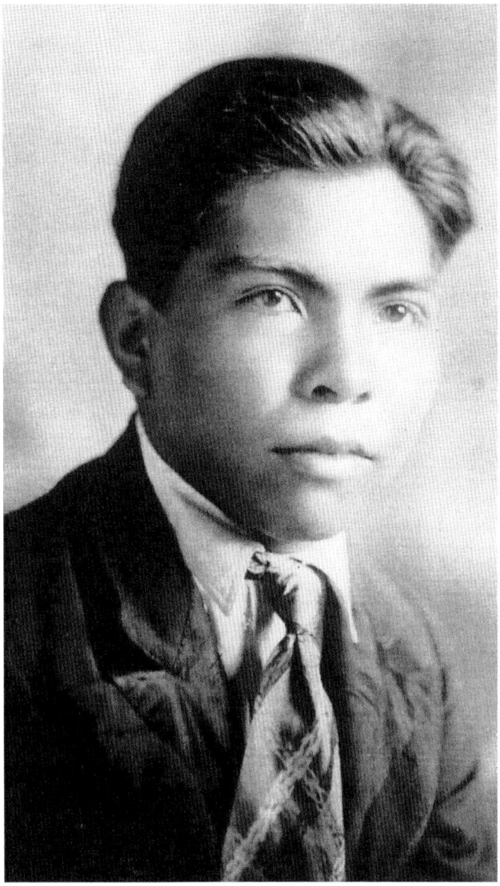

Andy Johnson

Andy was a Native American who was one of three first graduates of the 1918 Mariposa High School. A very bright student and athlete, he lived and worked around Mariposa for most of his life. He had a home at the Indian village north of town where he lived with his mother until she passed. Andy never married but had a sister and brother nearby who did have children with whom Andy enjoyed interacting with. Uncle Andy could usually be found passing out candy to his nieces and nephews. (Author's collection.)

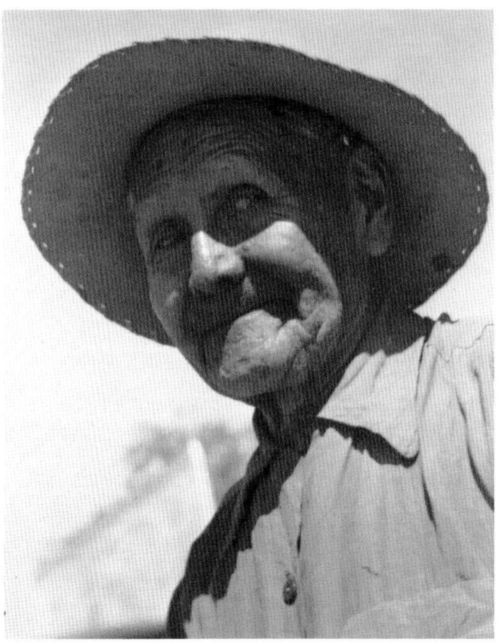

Antone Jose

Antone claimed that he was the last of the Awaneechees or Yosemite Indians, and no one quite knew what he meant by the claim. He lived along Mariposa Creek north of Mariposa and raised donkeys. In his donkey-pulled wagon, he would travel to town to buy supplies at Trabucco Shopping Center. This photograph, taken by the author's father, Roy, was obtained with a sitting fee of one silver dollar paid by Roy. Each subsequent Christmas, Antone would drop by the Drug Store in search of another silver dollar, which Roy gladly paid. Antone explained that the $1 paid only one year's use of his image and must be paid each year. Roy captured the dignity of this gentleman and gladly paid the fee. (Photograph by Roy Radanovich.)

David Radanovich

The brother of the author, David operated the Mariposa Drug Company from 1962 until 2007. His interests range from heavy equipment to restoring an old truck. He served Mariposa County on the Planning Commission and, for many years, has been a board member for the Mariposa Public Utility District. Two of his three children are pharmacists, and his wife, Heidi, is a pharmacy technician. His many contributions to the community include the quiet, private service and help that he gave to many unidentified citizens as the community druggist. (Photograph by Andrew Cummings.)

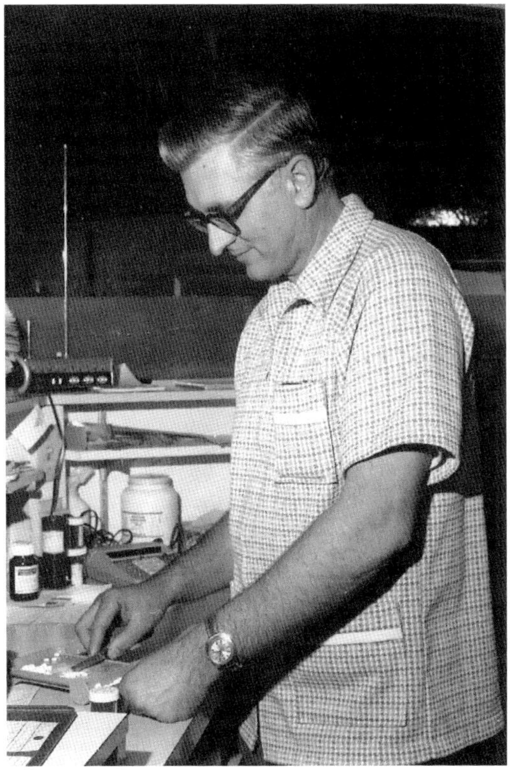

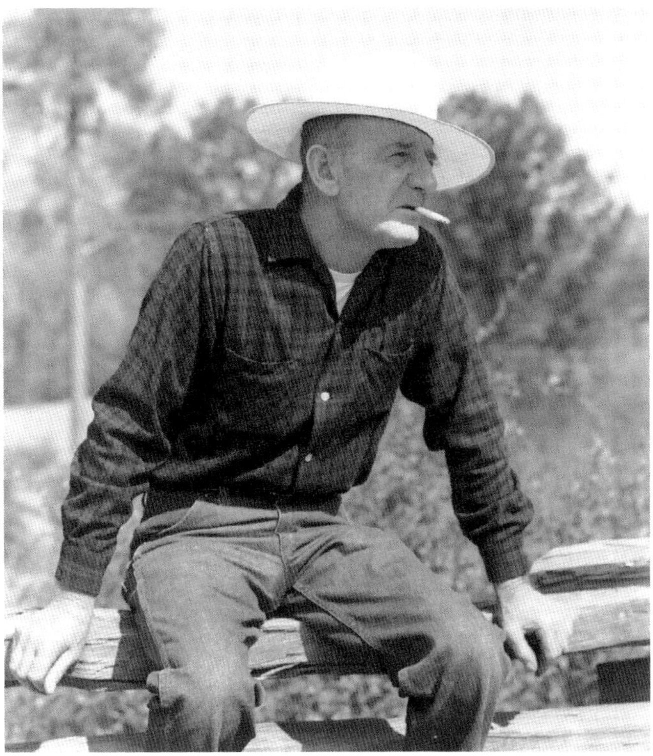

Scotty Taylor

As someone once said, Scotty was such a gardener that he could grow grass on red hardpan in the shade. Married to Bernice Abbott, a member of a historic pioneer family, he lived in one of the historic Abbott cottages along Mariposa Creek and was a good friend to everyone. (Photograph by author.)

Elmer Stroming

This portrait of Elmer Stroming was taken during World War II while Elmer was in the Merchant Marines. As a young man, Elmer worked at the mines in Mariposa County, and after the war, he and brother Walter started Stroming Machinery in Mariposa, which offered machine work, welding, and well drilling. Elmer and his brother had a great knowledge of Mariposa's underground formations and structures learned from mining. This knowledge was used in their understanding of water development when growth began in the late 1960s. They introduced the first hard-rock well drilling rig in Mariposa with Walter doing the drilling and Elmer running the shop, welding, and selling pumps. Elmer's greatest value to the author as a friend was helping the development of the Saxon Creek Project, which provides adequate water to the town of Mariposa. He shall always be remembered for his wisdom and service, responding to trouble any time day or night. (Author's collection.)

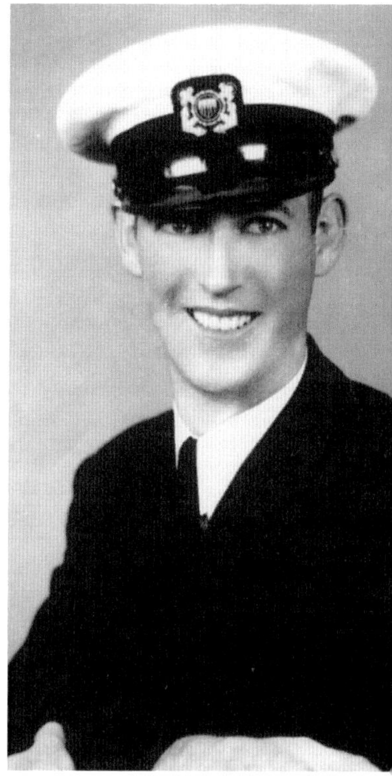

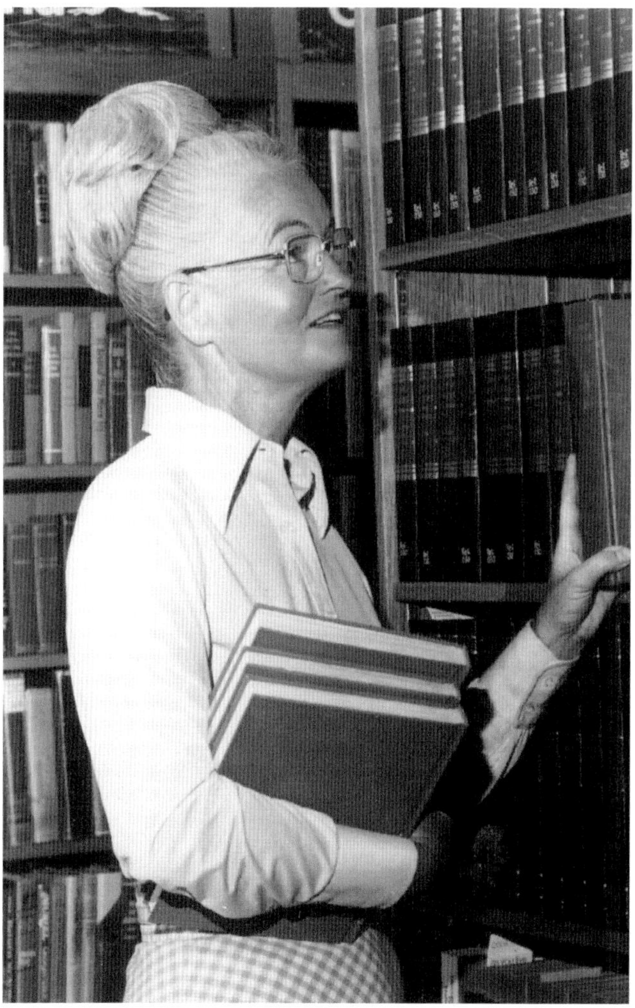

Dorothy Gibson

In 1968, a museum and library (today's Mariposa Museum and History Center) were established. The library was later moved and expanded to the government center. Dorothy Gibson was the well-received and respected librarian; she assisted in the library's growth and development. (Photograph by Andrew Cummings.)

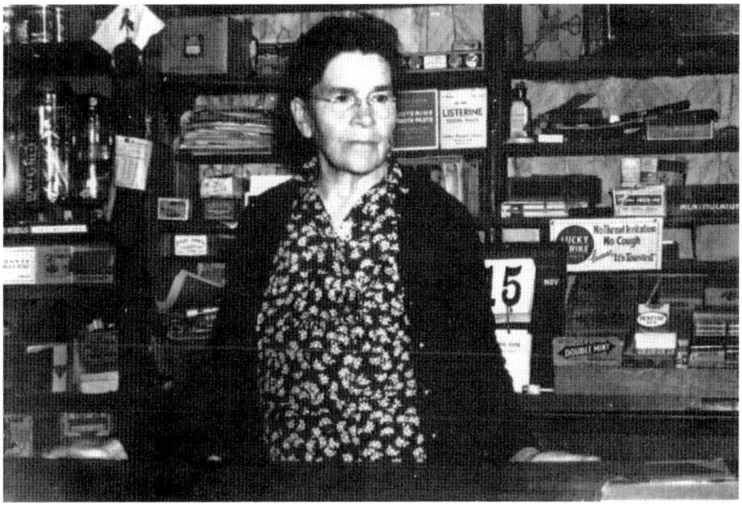

Eugenia "Jennie" Gagliardo
Hornitos merchants and ranchers, the Gagliardo family members operated a major merchandise store in Hornitos, which was started by Frank and Andrew Gagliardo in early 1852. In 1869, Jennie's father, Giuseppe, acquired the business with a partner Stefano Cademartori from his brother Frank and cousin Andrew. Jennie was the last of the family to operate the store, which closed with her death at 90 years of age in 1960. The contents of the store remained untouched until the new history center was built. Then, the family donated many of the store fixtures and merchandise to the Mariposa Museum and History Center, where it is prominently on display. Because Jennie preferred to keep much of the store intact, singular items of merchandise from the Gold Rush era are preserved and proudly on display. (Author's collection.)

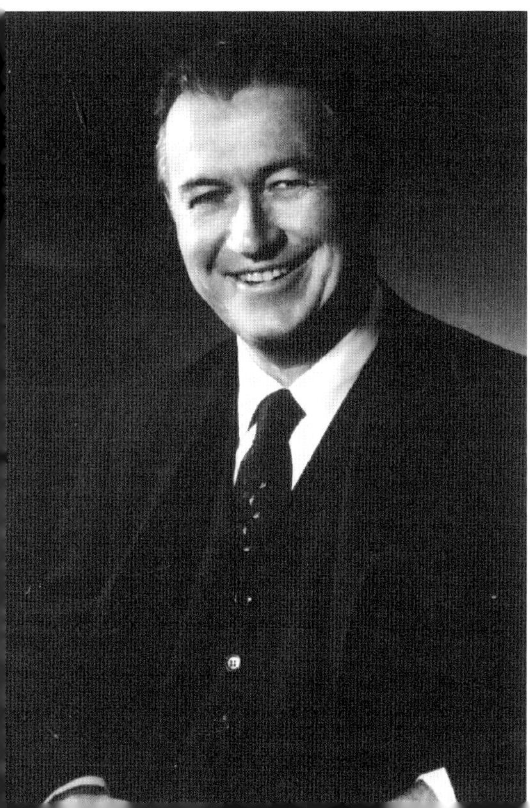

Judge Tom Coakley
Tom Coakley came to Mariposa County to be the fourth superior court judge in the county's history. As a young man, in order to pay for his education, Tom led a small dance band that played in the hotels of San Francisco. From 1953 to 1969, he sat on the bench of the Mariposa County Courthouse and was very active in the political and social life of Mariposa County. In 1954, Mariposa County celebrated the centennial of the building of the Mariposa County Courthouse and the inception of the *Mariposa Gazette* newspaper. Tom was overall chairman in crafting the celebration; he also helped start the Mariposa County Historical Society. Additionally, the Coakley family donated the land to Mariposa County as the site for the new Mariposa Museum and History Center and Library. Eventually, as both functions grew, the library moved to a new site near the courthouse. (Photograph by author.)

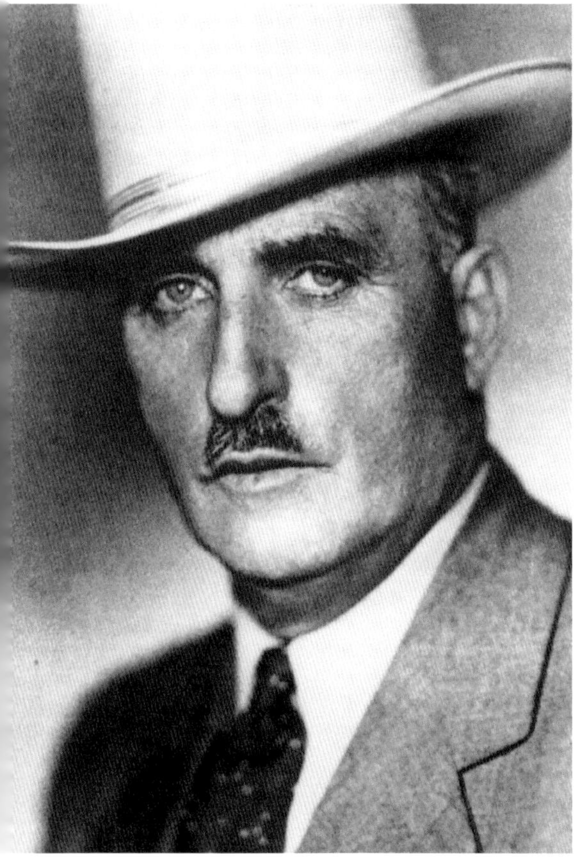

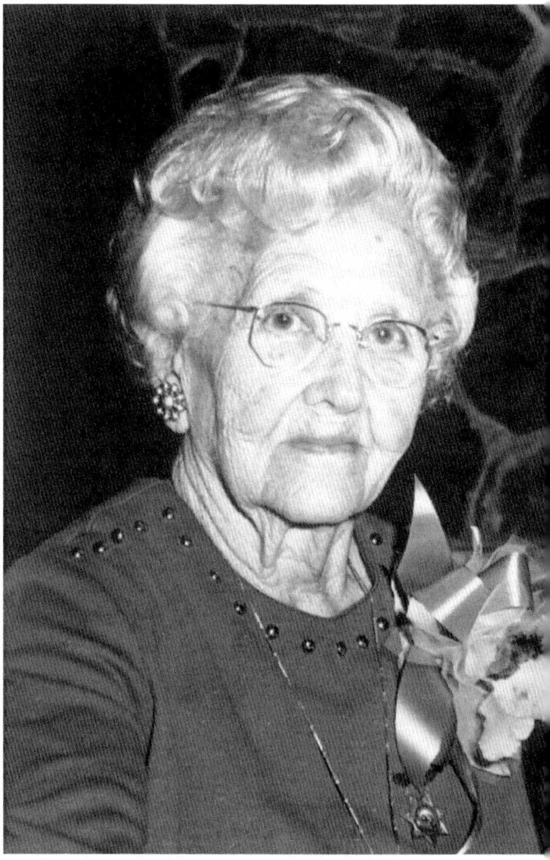

Sheriff John and Alta Castagnetto

John Castagnetto was born in Hunter's Valley near Hornitos. Both of his parents died when he was four years old. By the time he was 12, he was working in the mines of Hornitos. He married Alta Prouty, daughter of the sheriff of Mariposa County, Bob Prouty, who had served for 23 years. She served as matron for female prisoners from her father's time through the 17 years of her husband's tenure and beyond into the 1980s. She had a room in her home on Jones Street for the female prisoners. Few females were ever kept in the 1858 jail on Bullion Street. Alta and John had two children, Bob and Bernice.

John was well respected as sheriff being reelected without opposition for all of his 17 years in office until his death in 1946. John would frequently attend the flag raising on Friday morning at Mariposa Elementary, astride his Palomino horse, offering a salute as the Boy Scouts in uniform performed the ceremony. (Author's collection.)

Sheriff Orville M. Whitley

Probably the most beloved and respected public figure in Mariposa history was O.M. Whitley. Upon the death of Sheriff John Castagnetto in 1945, the board of supervisors appointed "Whit" as sheriff. At the time, he was the owner-operator of the Tide Water Associated Station at the corner of Seventh and Charles Streets in Downtown Mariposa. He served on the school board during the building of the new high school and was involved in the construction of Highway 140 in 1924–1925. A tall, very handsome man who had premature gray hair, he and under sheriff Mart Tresidder were the county law enforcement. They provided their own cars and weapons. He did have help from the California Highway Patrol and constables. But his approach to law enforcement was first let people work out their differences, and if that did not work, he would step in and use his wisdom and common sense.

During Whit's tenure, World War II ended, meaning the return of many feisty young men; many state laws relating to gambling and use of alcohol had to be enforced. He took a measured approach to restore a bit of calm to the community in the face of a fair amount of resistance. Nonetheless, he was respected, and most everyone complied. The county even began providing the sheriff and deputy with a car; it was sometime before his office had more than one telephone. (Photograph by Harold Rowney.)

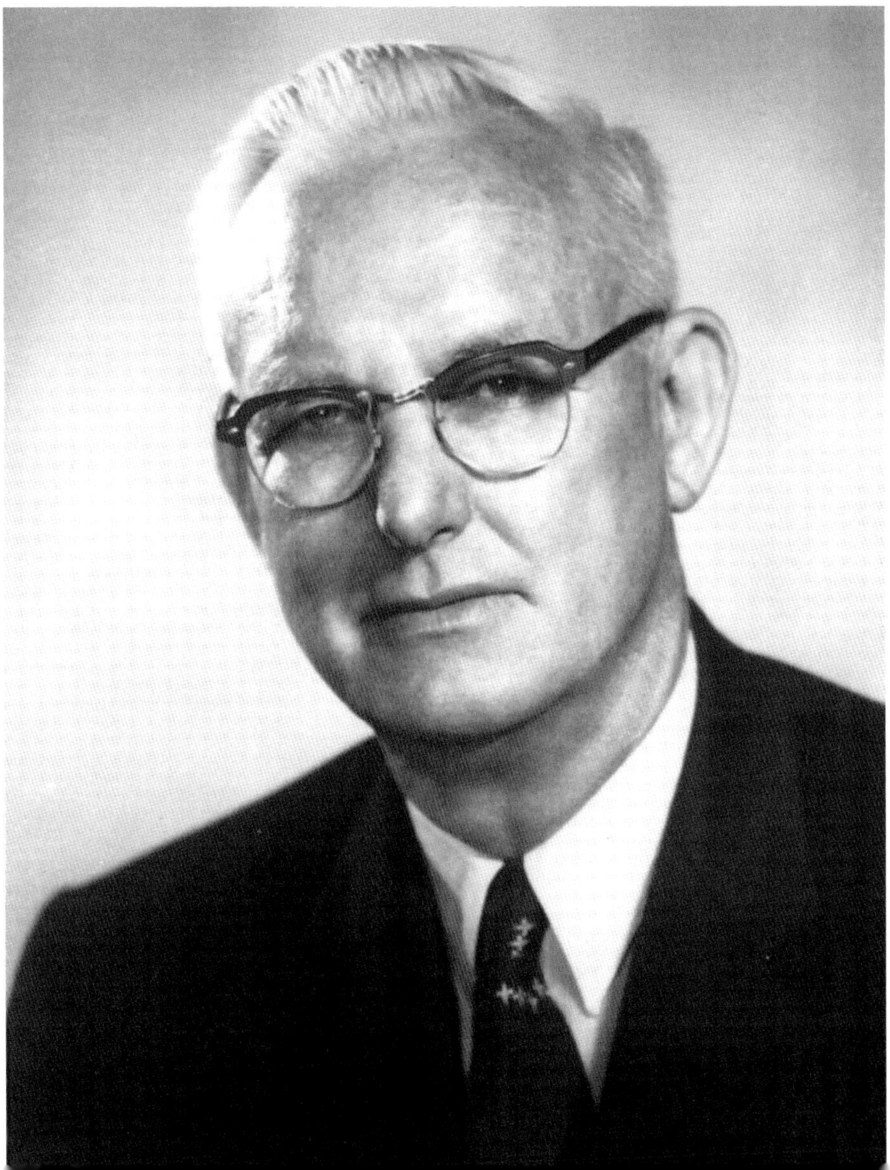

Rebecca Ching

In the late 1930s, a group of Seventh-Day Adventists came to Mariposa County with the goal of establishing a home for their families to flourish. Rebecca Ching's family purchased a large parcel of land near Big Spring Hill, and the Ching Ranch was established. The beautiful gardens and orchards of the Ching Ranch were well known and respected in Mariposa. (Photograph by Andrew Cummings.)

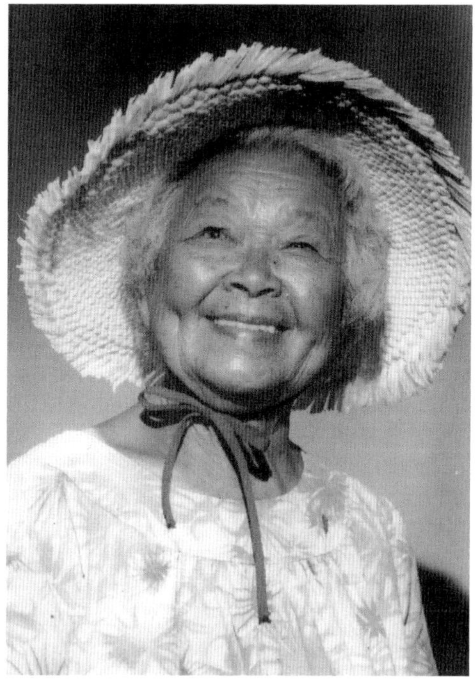

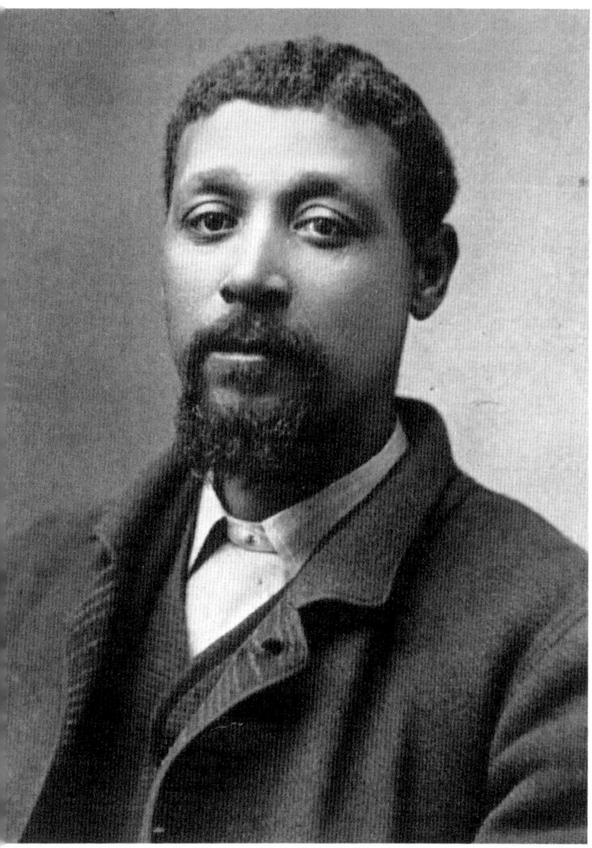

George Monroe

Stage driver George Monroe worked for Albert Henry Washburn driving from Wawona to Yosemite Valley on the Mariposa Road. Opened in late 1876, this was the main wagon route from Mariposa at first; it brought passengers who rode the Central Pacific Railroad to Raymond. From Raymond, the stage went first to Wawona and then to Yosemite Valley.

Monroe was known for the care he took of both his passengers and horses. A rockslide below Inspiration Point caught his coach throwing Monroe to the ground. More worried about his passengers; he saw to it that they were safely in Yosemite Valley before heading home near Mariposa. His parents had a homestead on Pea Ridge southwest of Mariposa, and it was there his apparent internal injuries claimed his life.

His funeral was held indoors at the Methodist church in Mariposa, which was not a common occurrence for a black man in those days. (Author's collection.)

CHAPTER FIVE

The Legendary Educators

Schools were mentioned in early sources about Mariposa. Each school hosted multiple grades, and in most cases, the schools had only one room, which would accommodate the first through twelfth grades. There was no separate high school until the turn of the 19th century, when one was established in Mariposa. Mariposa County had a school superintendent who basically assisted the elementary schools. But each of the schools was independent from each other, often in establishments built and owned by the community on private land.

Students wishing a higher level of education and coming from established families often were sent to the San Francisco Bay area. In 1852, a school tax of 3¢ per $100 in assessed valuation was established. This was raised to 25¢ by 1854. There are two school districts, one central and one west, with the county assessor serving as superintendent.

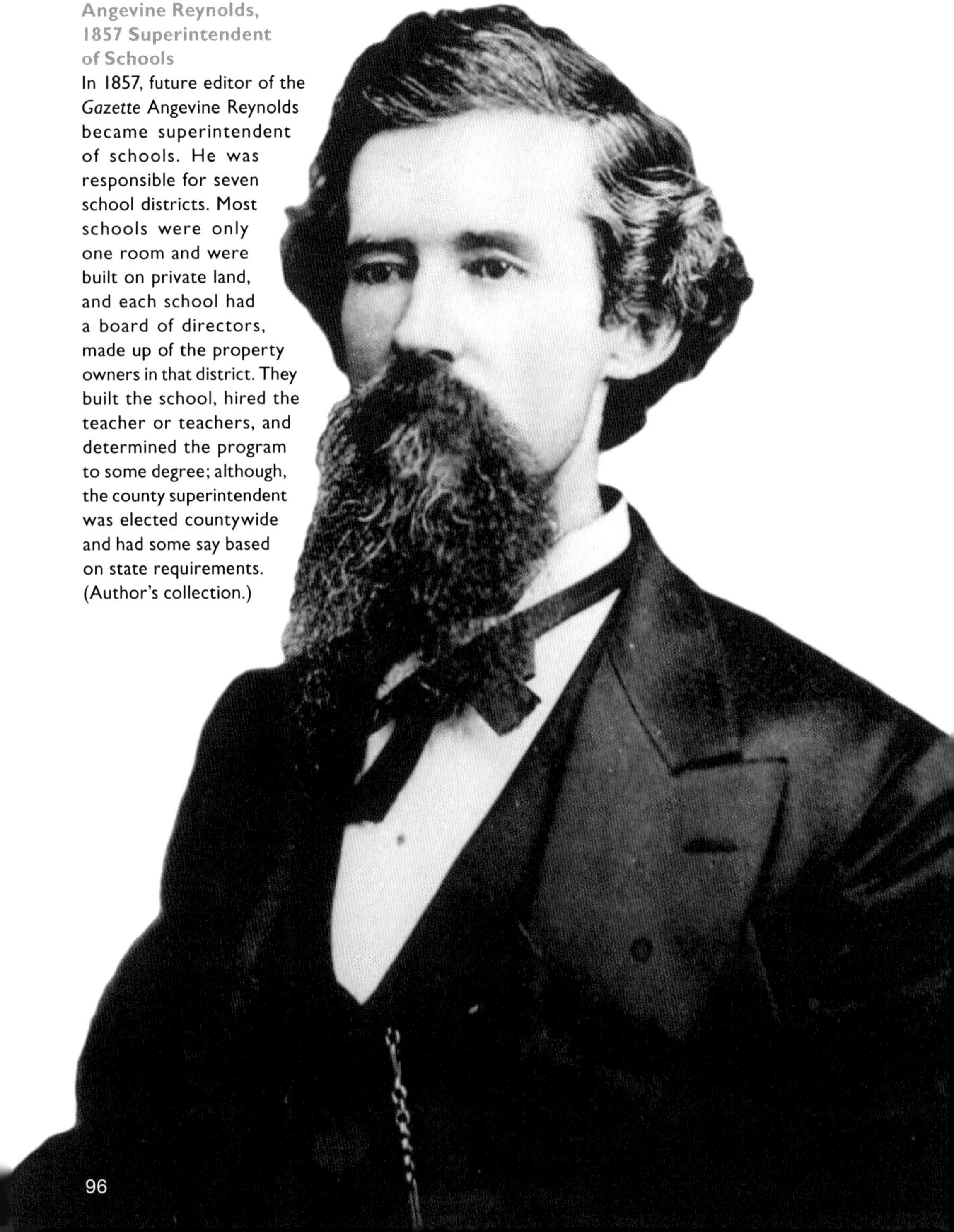

Angevine Reynolds, 1857 Superintendent of Schools

In 1857, future editor of the *Gazette* Angevine Reynolds became superintendent of schools. He was responsible for seven school districts. Most schools were only one room and were built on private land, and each school had a board of directors, made up of the property owners in that district. They built the school, hired the teacher or teachers, and determined the program to some degree; although, the county superintendent was elected countywide and had some say based on state requirements. (Author's collection.)

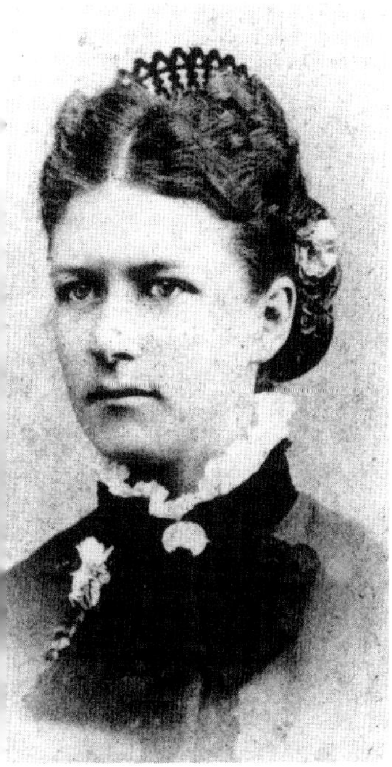

Julia Jones, Mariposa County Superintendent of Schools

In 1897, Julia Jones, who was the daughter of justice court judge Lewis F. Jones, became superintendent of schools. Revenue for the school district was unstable since the mining companies had a difficult time paying their taxes. Small mining claims were short-lived, and the miners moved on failing to register to vote or file claims and thus were often unknown to county government. Perhaps to offset the shortfall, the mining company donated land in Mariposa for the first elementary school. Later, more land was donated for the 1918 high school. The Mariposa Commercial and Mining Company, started by the owner of the Fremont Grant in 1880, was an English-based company that did not always do well. The mines run by the company were the primary employer. Price of gold, lack of water, and in general, the economy of the country interfered with the ability for the company to meet its obligations. As time went on, some revenue was gained by leasing mining and grazing properties or the sale of parcels. The problem was that all of this activity took capital, of which there was little locally. Outside of mining, subsistence farming was the main occupation to support one's family. This left little cash for more than basic necessities. Julia is pictured below on the left in the carriage, holding the reins on a trip to the Yosemite Valley school. (Both, Author's collection.)

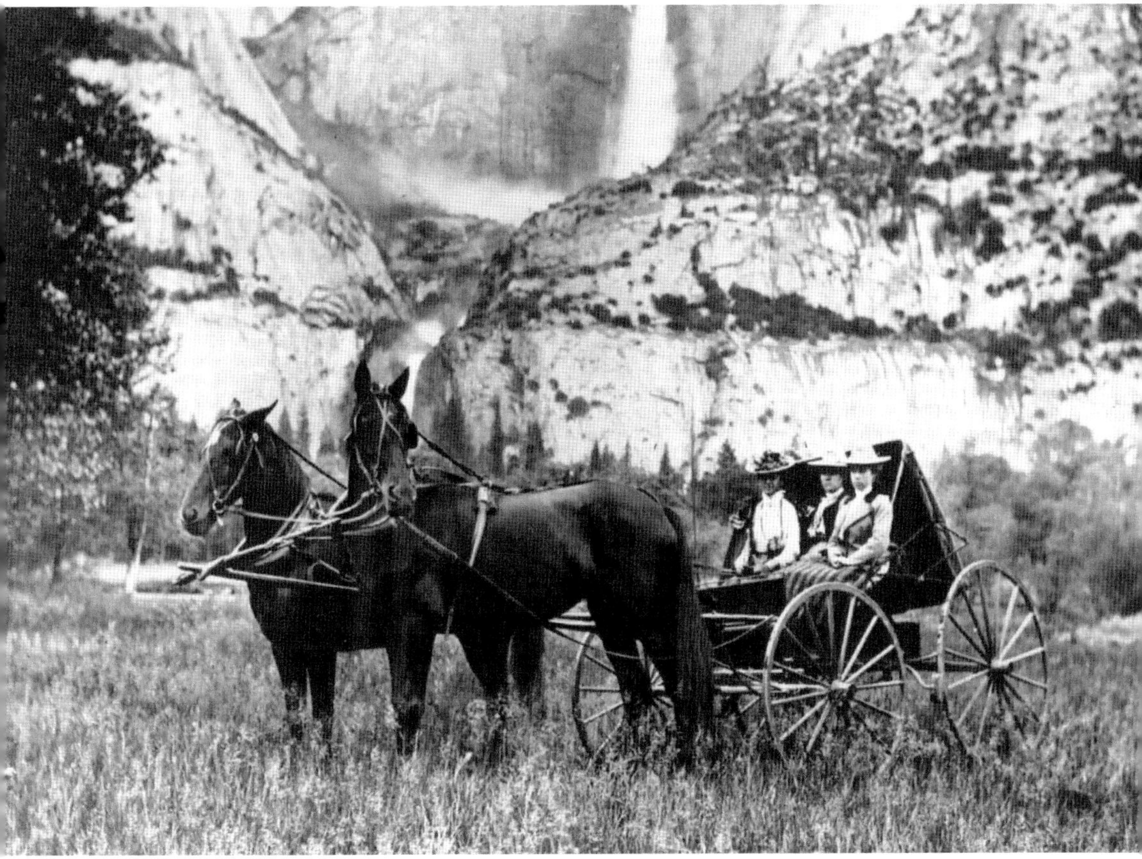

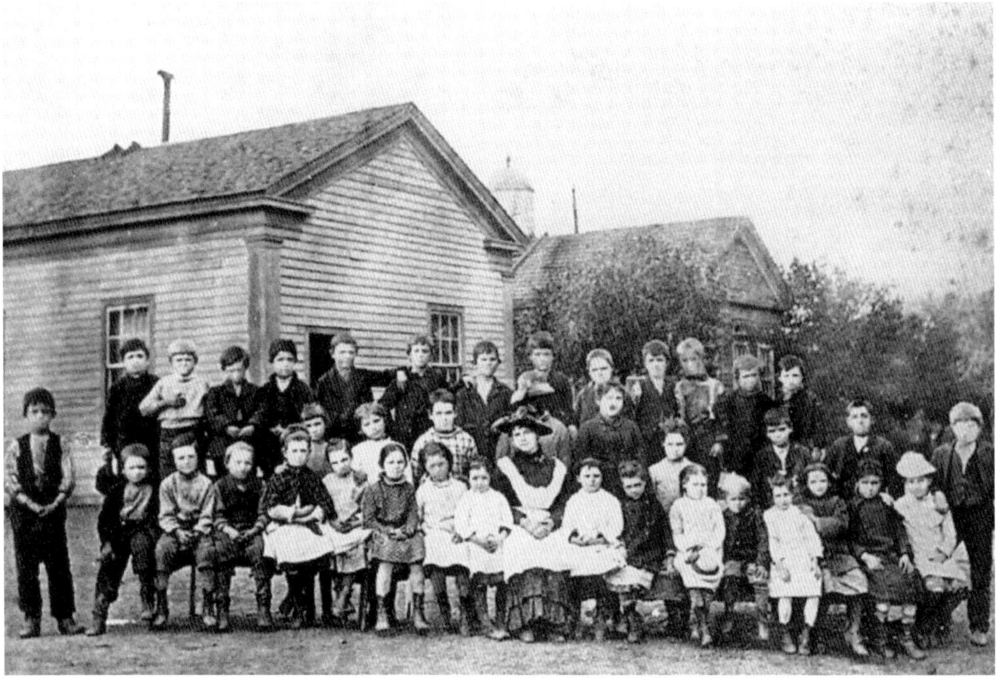

The First School in Mariposa Town
Located on mining company property at the end of Seventh Street in the unincorporated town of Mariposa, it was some time before transference of title went to the county. For example, streets in the town of Mariposa were still owned by the company until 1956. But it was better for the mining company to donate the land than pay taxes on what was considered useless land or at least had already been worked out. Teachers were poorly paid and usually were young women or wives of miners or ranchers. The number of children in a class varied almost from day to day. The stable population came from the few merchants and mine managers. Teachers often taught for a few years before moving to other schools or to other professions or sometimes to raise a family. Marrying a young teacher was quite a prize. (Author's collection.)

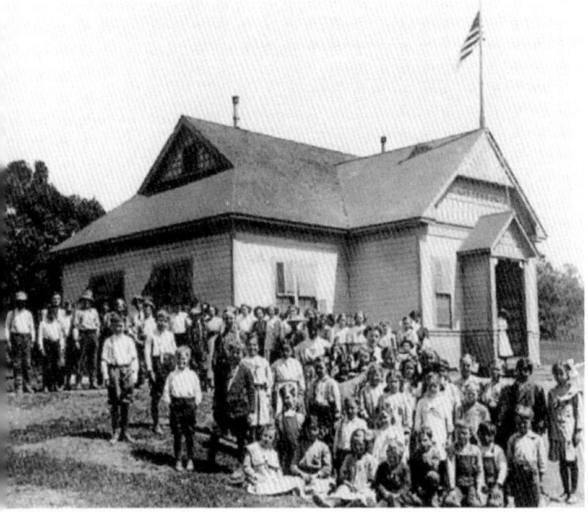

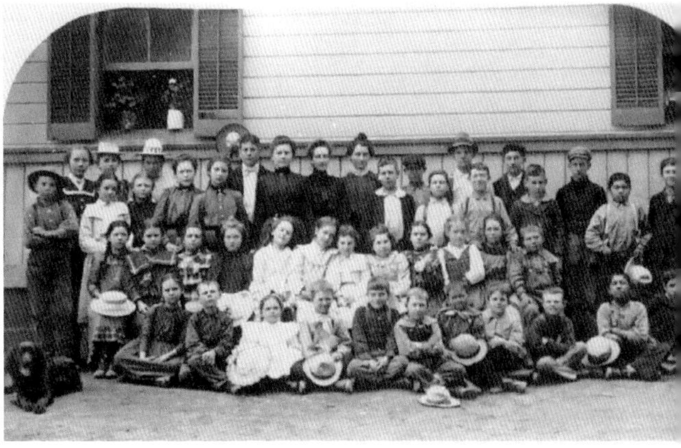

New Grammar Schools 1890s
Pictured at left is a class at one of the new grammar schools created in the 1890s. Mrs. Converse was principal. At right is the 1896 class at Mariposa Grammar School. (Both, author's collection.)

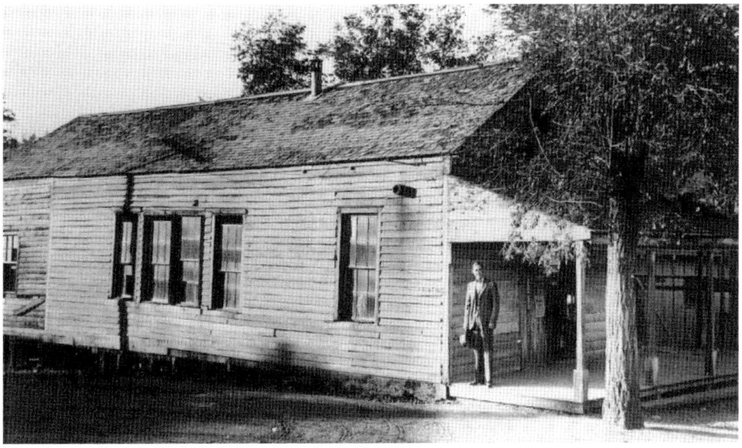

John L. Dexter

Even the position of superintendent changes frequently. By 1914, John L. Dexter became superintendent, and after the county voted to have higher education come to Mariposa County, his task was to start a high school. The new high school opened in 1914 in Mariposa in the Larew Building and the basement of the Presbyterian Church on Bullion Street between Sixth and Seventh Streets. Dexter, the editor/publisher of the *Mariposa Gazette*, is pictured on the porch of the newspaper building, which had been moved in from the Whitlock Mine. (Author's collection.)

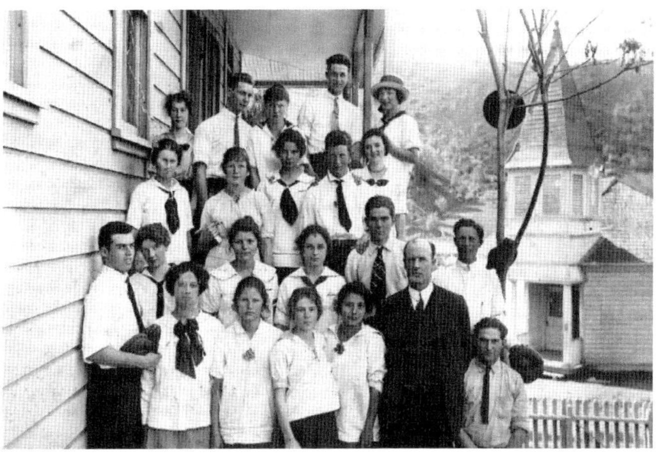

Professor Offield

Professor Offield came to Mariposa to teach and direct the new high school. With him came his daughter who went on to be the first graduate of the new school. A fire in 1916, started in the opera house next door, destroyed the Larew Building and most of the school. Classes continued in other structures and private homes until a new high school was constructed on property provided by the Mariposa Commercial and Mining Company. Its first class graduated in 1918, at last a proper high school program comes to Mariposa County. Problems during the construction of the main building involved the community in finishing this lath-and-plaster building. Problems, like the lack of proper drainage in the boys' shower room in the basement and leaking elsewhere, caused the high school board to begin thinking about a proper educational plant. This building was used in some capacity until 1949.

Professor Offield, in suit, and the student body of Mariposa High School are pictured about 1914 next to Larew Building with Presbyterian church in background. The boys in back row are Henry Garber (left) and Martin Tresidder (right). (Author's collection.)

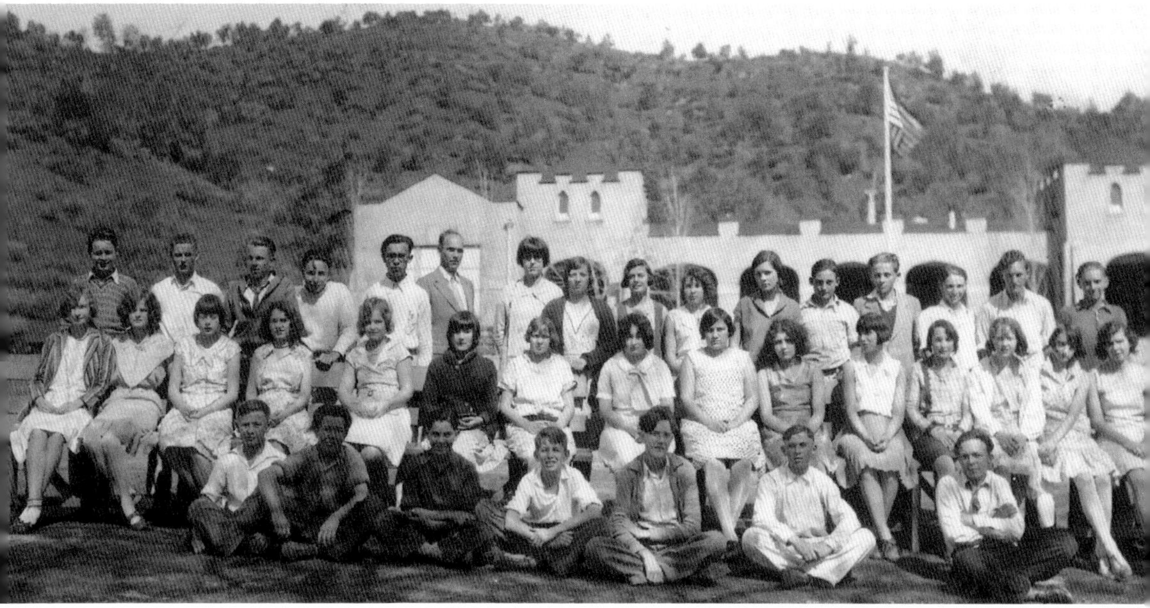

A New School

Shown here is the student body at the new 1918 high school, which can be seen in the background. Around 1920, the school had not grown with additional buildings. From 1918 until the opening of the Yosemite All-Year Highway from Merced to Yosemite Valley in 1926, school's populations were small and the economy of Mariposa County was weak. The mines were closed and little timber was being harvested. The strongest element of the economy was stimulated by the Yosemite Valley Railroad and shipping logs to the mill at Merced Falls. Many local men worked in Yosemite National Park in the woods and on the railroad. (Author's collection.)

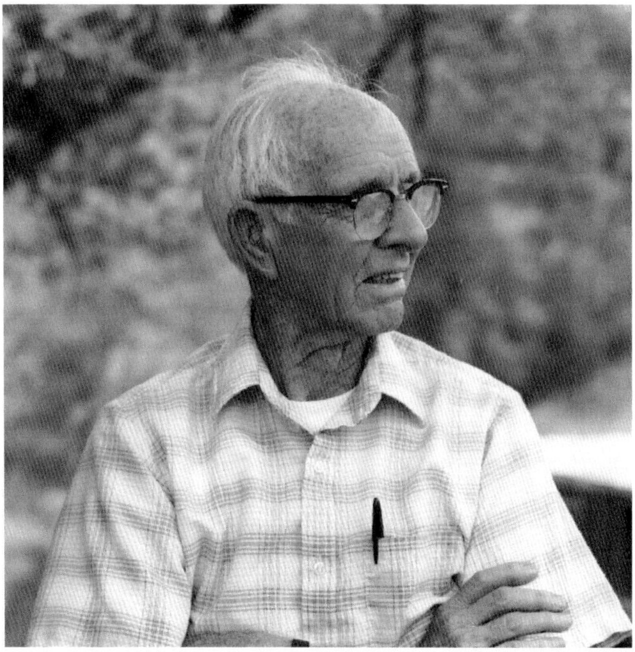

Cleo G. Adelsbach, Longtime Educator and Community Benefactor

Cleo G. Adelsbach came to Mariposa in 1931 as a mathematics teacher. Trained at Stanford, he rapidly demonstrated his skill and intelligence. He had an interest in being principal but was considered too young. By 1935, he formed a working and personal relationship with J.L. Spriggs. (Photograph by author.)

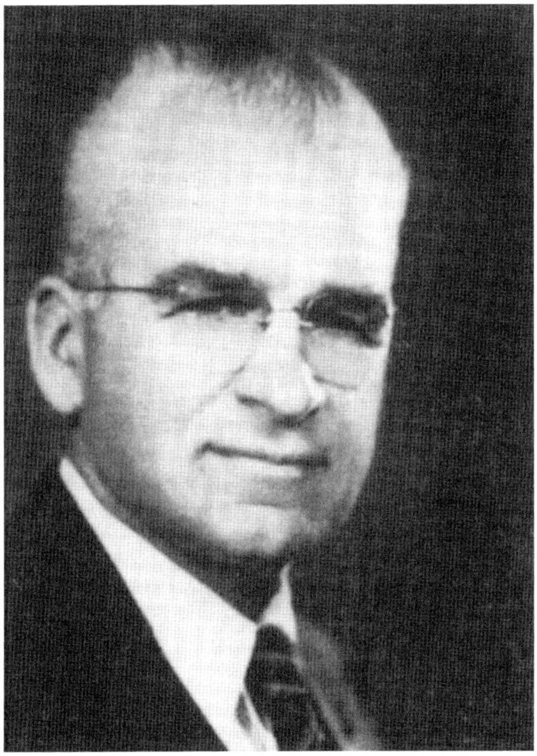

James L Spriggs

In 1935, James Lewellyn Spriggs came to Mariposa and became principal. His task was to begin building a new high school, which was not going to be easy because the previous year a bond election failed and the principal discharged. Cleo was appointed vice principal. The Depression was under way and the federal government began building schools as Works Progress Administration efforts. A number of projects occurred in Mariposa, including Mariposa Elementary, Sebastopol (Bootjack) School, Mariposa High, the renovation and addition of the second-floor and indoor bathrooms on both floors of the addition to the Mariposa County Courthouse, and cement rain gutters along Sixth Street and along Bullion Street south. Rock walls were built at Mariposa Elementary and at the new high school. The high school project appears to be the largest and most important. Many local men worked on the projects especially doing cement and rock work around athletic fields.

J.L. Spriggs was a very conservative leader, who was followed by Cleo Adelsbach as principal in 1947. Both of these gentlemen took educating young men and women very seriously. They served the county of Mariposa for all their adult lives. J.L. was involved in building the Methodist church while Cleo was very involved in the Salvation Army and the John C. Fremont Hospital Foundation. Both administrators were frugal and saved enough money to pay cash for Mariposa High's first and only gymnasium built in 1950. While there have been complaints about its size, facts are that the economy of Mariposa County prevents a replacement being built.

Cleo and J.L. understood how to educate young men who were a little rough around the edges. Most of the male students came from the sawmills, mines, and farms. Many did not have running water, electricity, or modest housing. They treated them like men, and when necessary, they could impose very impressionable discipline. Such things as painting backstops, hoeing weeds, digging ditches, and pouring concrete were employed to get the gentlemen's attention. Nonetheless, all the students respected both teachers because they basically spoke the same language. Many of these young men became World War II and Korean War participants and often remarked later how the skills and discipline learned from J.L. and Cleo, helped them survive. (Author's collection.)

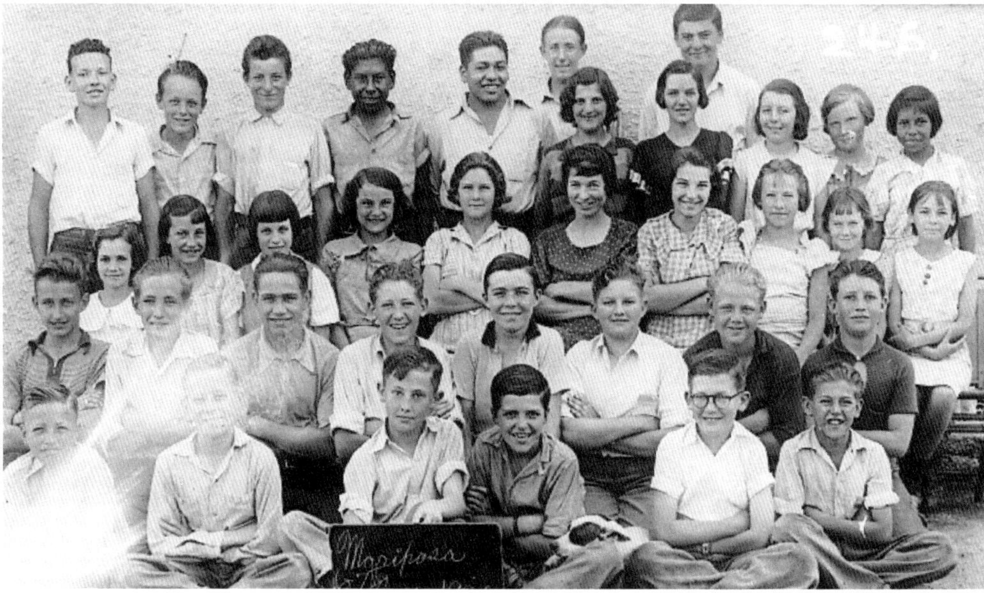

A Strong Influence

Alice Ellingham started an after school program of teas and various social events attended by all children within the community. For these events, children dressed in their best. The yearly Halloween parade was anticipated each year by a school full of hobgoblins; they would invade downtown Mariposa for the two-block-long parade, which stopped traffic and brought everyone to town.

Here, young Alice Ellingham is pictured with her sixth-, seventh-, and eighth-grade students from 1936 at Mariposa Elementary. The girl second to her right is June Tresidder. (Author's collection from Alice Ellingham.)

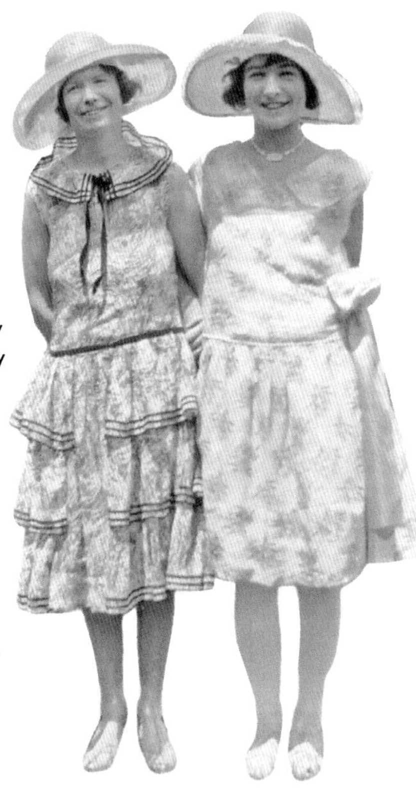

Alice Hampton Ellingham

Another key teacher and principal came to Mariposa County about 1930. Alice Hampton Ellingham, a graduate of University of California, came to Mariposa County to teach first at the Bagby School and then at Mariposa Elementary. Lovingly referred to as Mrs. "E," she served the children of Mariposa for over 40 years. She was married to highway patrolman and Mariposa native John "Chic" Ellingham, and although they never had any children of their own, all of the children who went through Mariposa Elementary were hers to nurture. Generations of Mariposa children benefited from her kind but firm hand and her ability to influence young minds. She is pictured here (left) with her sister. (Author's collection from Alice Ellingham.)

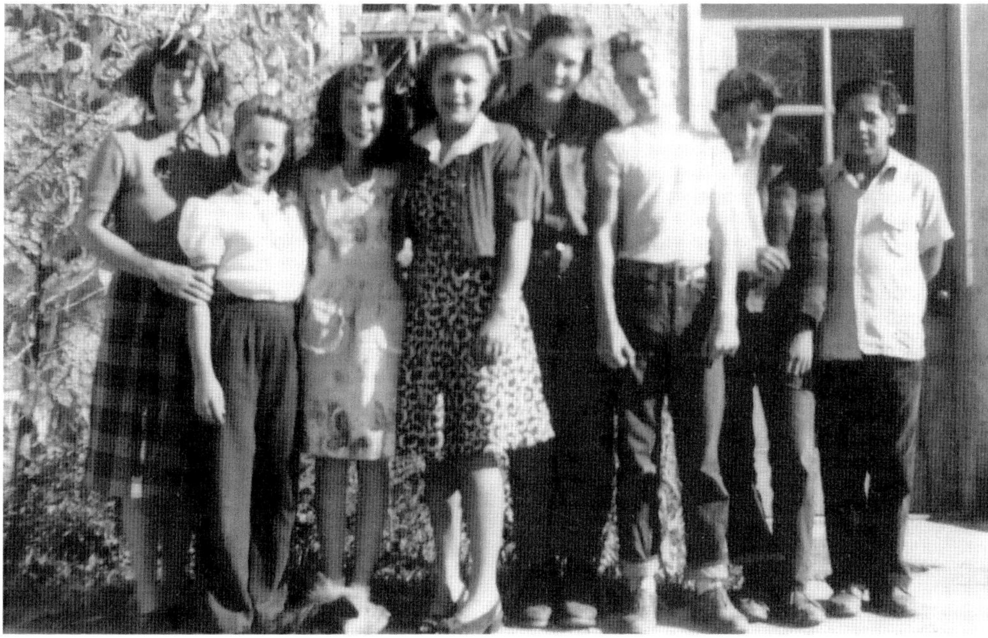

Loved by All

Alice Ellingham not only had the love and respect of all of her students but also of all of her teachers. Many of the teachers were young and just out of school and needed seasoning, which she was quite able and willing to do. Pictured below are, from left to right, Mariposa Elementary teachers Gladys Bolton, Eleanor Hastings (Richards), and Alice Ellingham. (Both, author's collection from Alice Ellingham.)

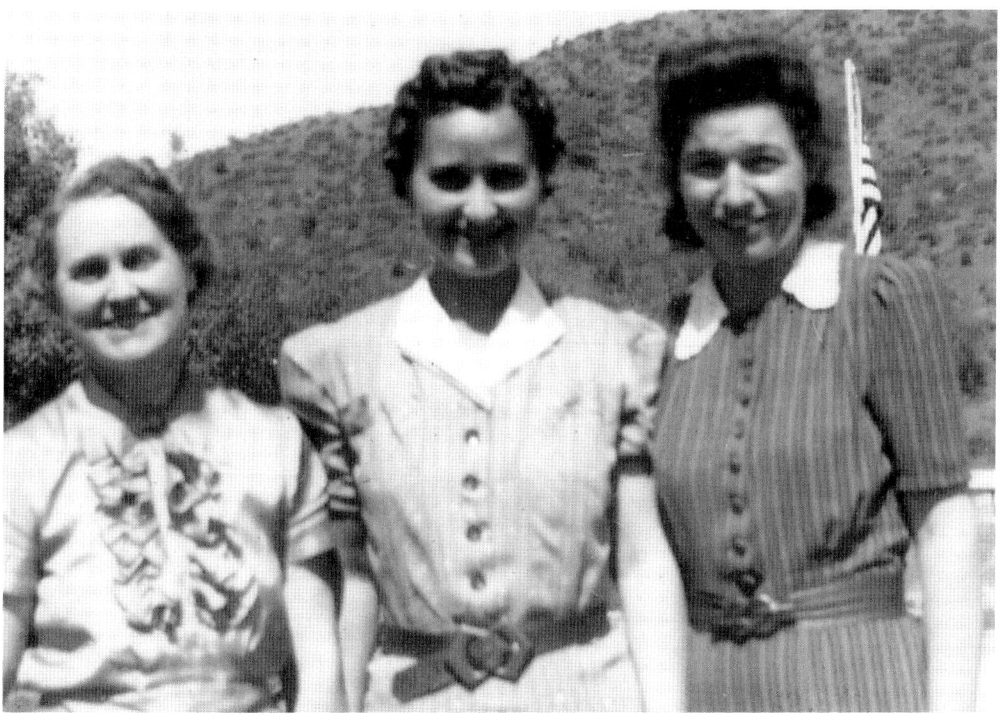

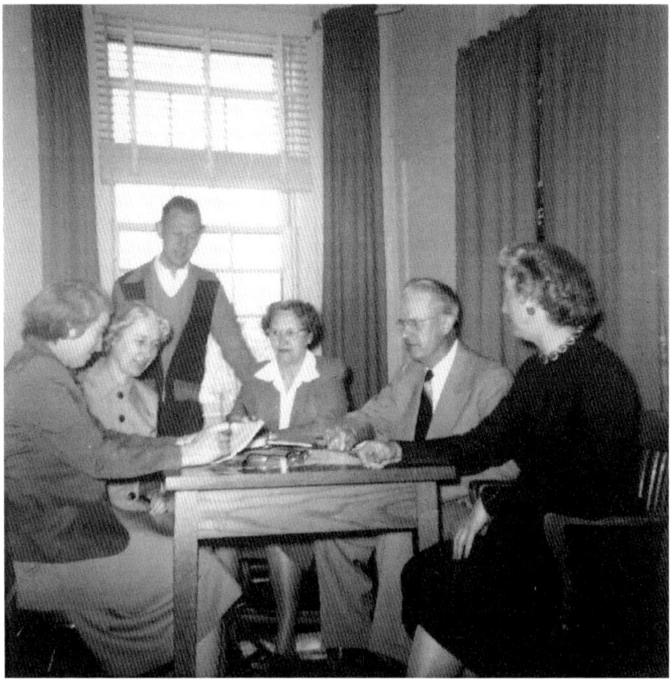

Continued Service

Alice Ellingham also served for a period as assistant superintendent of schools. Here, she is in a meeting with other principals and Supt. Thomas Price, sitting directly across the table from her. (Author's collection from Alice Ellingham.)

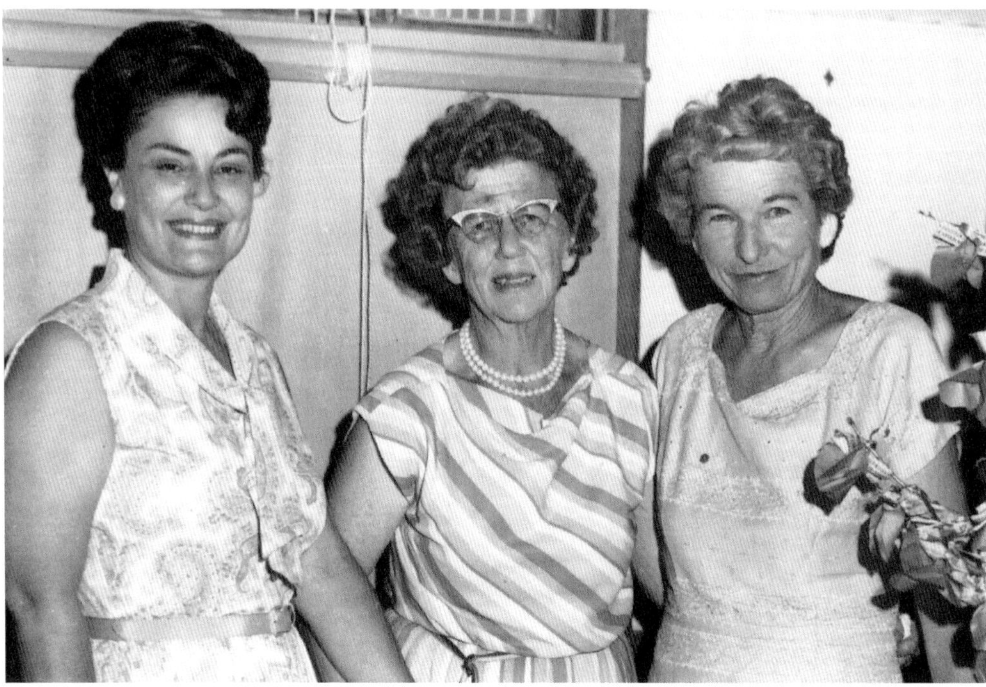

Stepping Down

Alice finally retired to join her husband, Chic, at their cabin in Wawona. With her was her great friend and colleague Rhesa Bagby. Participating was her friend and former student June Tresidder Meagher from the 1936 class. June Tresidder Meagher, Rhesa Bagby, and Alice Ellingham are pictured after many years of service to the community. (Author's collection from Alice Ellingham.)

CHAPTER SIX

Further Legends of Mariposa County

The first constitution of the State of California was adopted in 1849 before California became a state. That first legislature divided California into 27 counties, with Mariposa being the largest. The best-known area within the county was a Mexican land grant known as Las Mariposas, owned, or at least claimed, by Col. John C. Fremont. When California was accepted into the Union in September 1850, Fremont had no interest in the local politics of the county; he only wanted to gain clear title to his 44,386-acre Mexican land grant located at the end of the Mother Lode gold region.

Even though Fremont did not have clear title to Las Mariposas Mexican land grant under American let alone Mexican law, he nonetheless established his claim and began leasing out land for establishing towns, ranches, and mining properties. The promise was that those who leased from Fremont would receive clear title once his claim had been established. Thus, the towns of Mariposa, Princeton (Mount Bullion), and Bear Valley were established without clear title. Those creating the towns laid them out on a proper grid, unlike most Mother Lode Mining camps. Mariposa, for example, has streets running north and south that are straight and 60 feet wide and those east and west 50 feet wide.

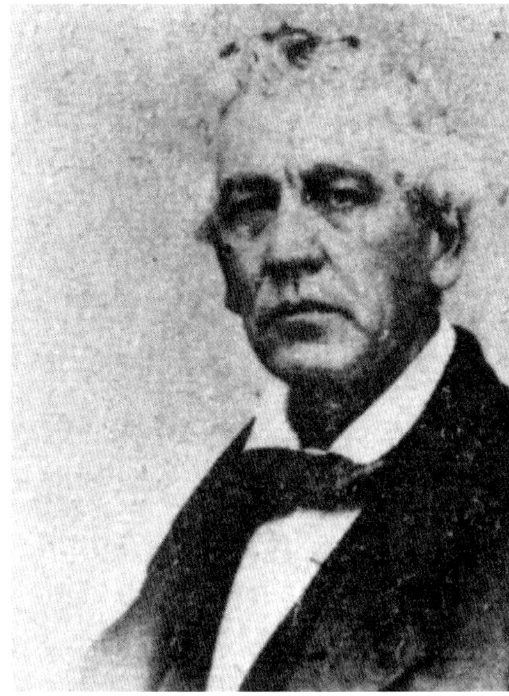

James A. Bondurant, County Judge

The first constitution of the state created a three-judge panel, termed the court of sessions, which was to govern both the judicial and legislative affairs of the county. James A. Bondurant was the first county judge. The court of sessions was made up of the county judge and two justices of the peace. For the first few years, many changes took place in who held the county offices. The promise of gold was stronger than public service. (Author's collection.)

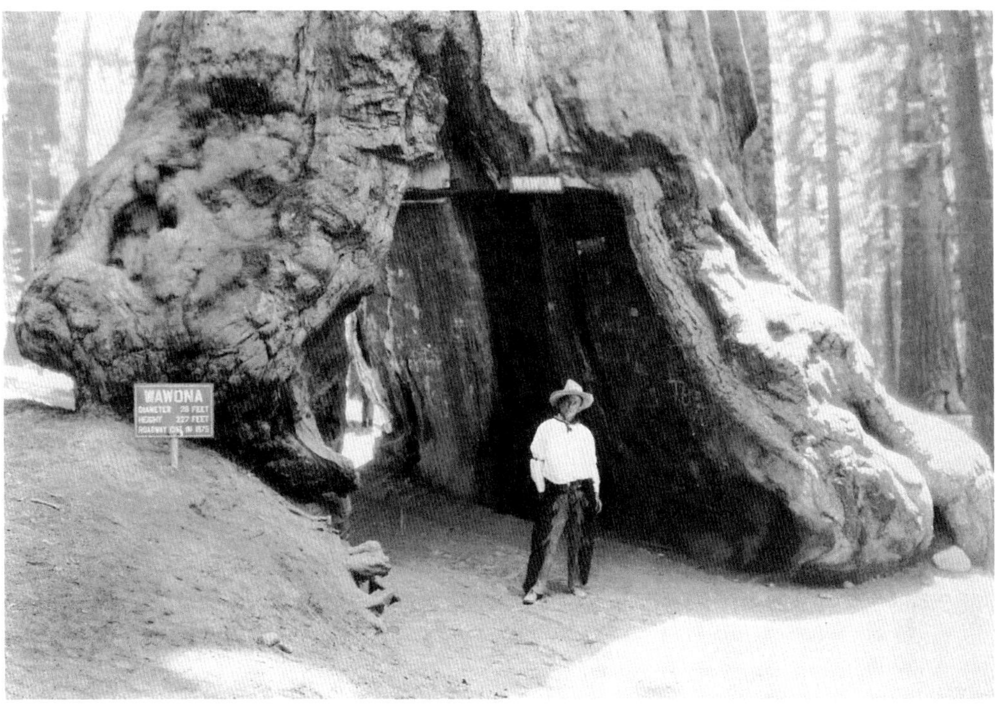

Eddie Gordon, Stage Driver

For at least two generations, members of the Gordon family were stage drivers to Mariposa Grove of Big Trees and to Wawona. Here, driver Eddie Gordon is shown in the tunnel through the Wawona Tree in the Mariposa Grove. (Author's collection.)

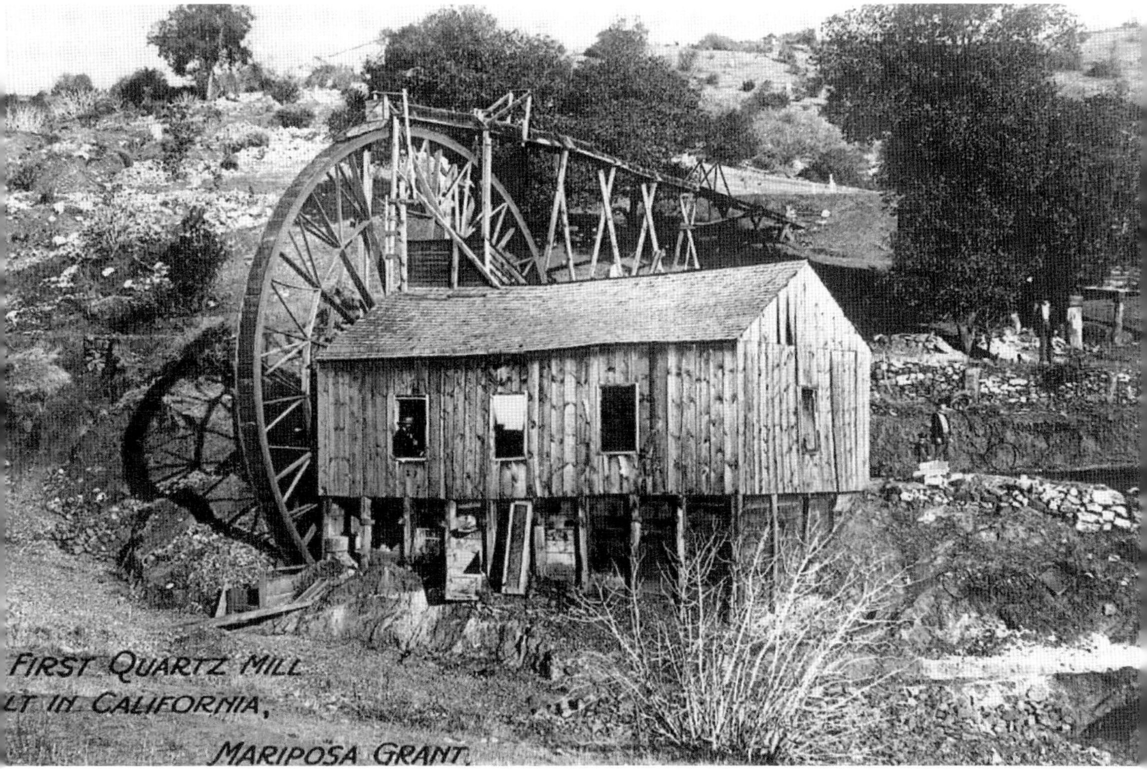

James Duff and the Mariposa Mill, 1861

Almost immediately upon locating the boundaries of his grant, Fremont formed a relationship with Palmer Cooke and Company of San Francisco. This investment firm came to Mariposa with managers, miners, engineers, surveyors, cooks and boardinghouse keepers, Ferro dealers, and others needed to begin a town and an industry strong enough to support its existence.

It became apparent that the crude mining machinery that was first brought from the East was not going to be able to handle the hard quartz ore that came from the mines. Soon, much stronger mills were invented and installed at the Mariposa Mine and hard-rock underground mining got its start in California. Water was still an issue. James Duff introduced the hard-rock mill at the Mariposa Mine and dug a ditch around the east side of the hill east of town, stretching up Stockton Creek, to bring water to the mill. This ditch received the name Duff Ditch, and the water that it carried drove the mill as well as washed the crushed ore. (Photograph by Carleton E. Watkins, author's collection.)

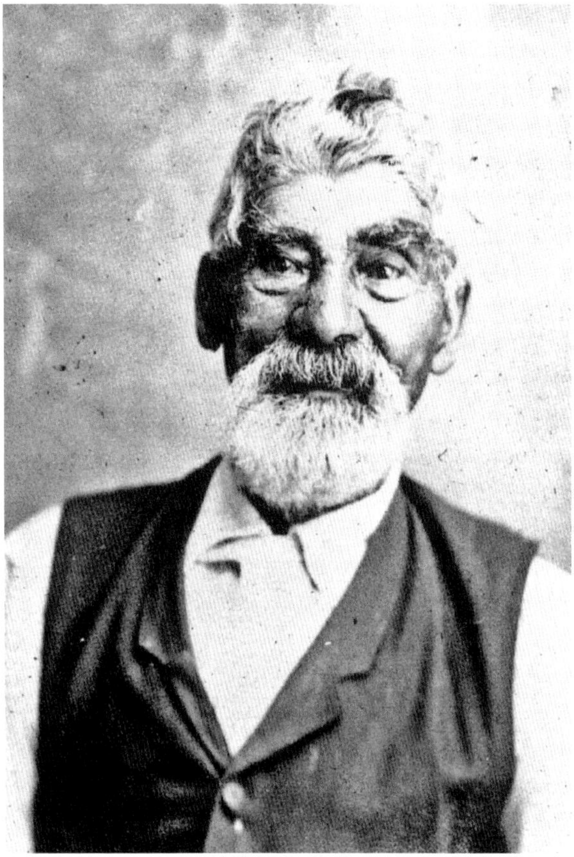

The Miner Who Brought the First Successful Stamp Mill to Mariposa and California: James Duff

The short supply of water plagued gold mining in California. The presence of springs at the headwaters of Stockton Creek helped extend the gold mining season, but to run all year was still a challenge.

Steam engines soon provided power to the mills in California. The engines came from the steam-powered sailing ships that arrived in San Francisco only to be abandoned by their gold-seeking crewmen. The bay of San Francisco was choked with abandoned ships, and soon they were stripped of their engines and hardware. (Preston collection.)

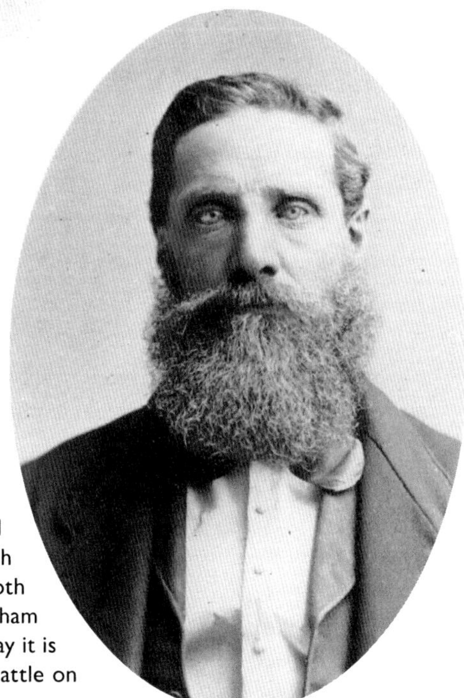

Capt. James Cunningham

One of the ship captains who had to watch his crew disappear was James Cunningham. But instead of hanging around San Francisco looking for a new crew, Cunningham spent his time exploring the country on the western edge of Mariposa County, in what was to become Merced County. He acquired large tracts of land for future ranching purposes. The method of acquisition was preemption by which boundaries were set and the land filed on. This was the method used prior to the Homestead Act of 1962. Cunningham's ranch became an important livestock and farming area in both Merced and Mariposa Counties. At its peak, the Cunningham Ranch covered 16,000 acres. No longer that size, today it is still the fourth generation of Cunningham's pasture cattle on what remains. (Courtesy of Jim Cunningham.)

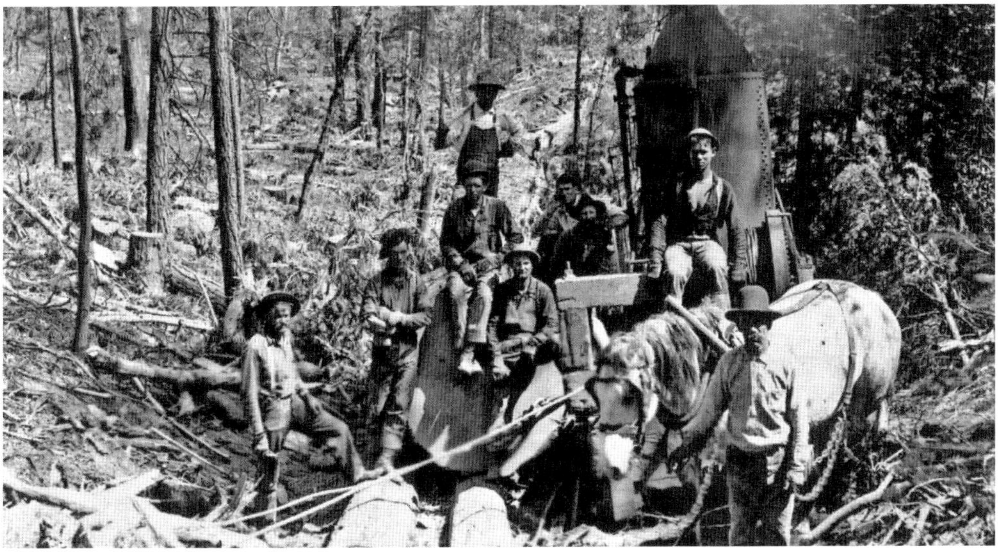

Logging in the Sierra

Preemption was the federal and state method of putting the large acreages to use during the development of the West. The claimant had to put the land to good use. Timberlands were also acquired by the similar method; although, some of these properties were called timber allotments. Once established, these stands of timber could be harvested or sold to others for harvest. Large tracts were filed on and held well past the time of the establishment of National Parks and Reserves. Thus, logging went on within Yosemite National Park as a result of these early claims. This steam donkey engine moves the logs to the mill. (Author's collection.)

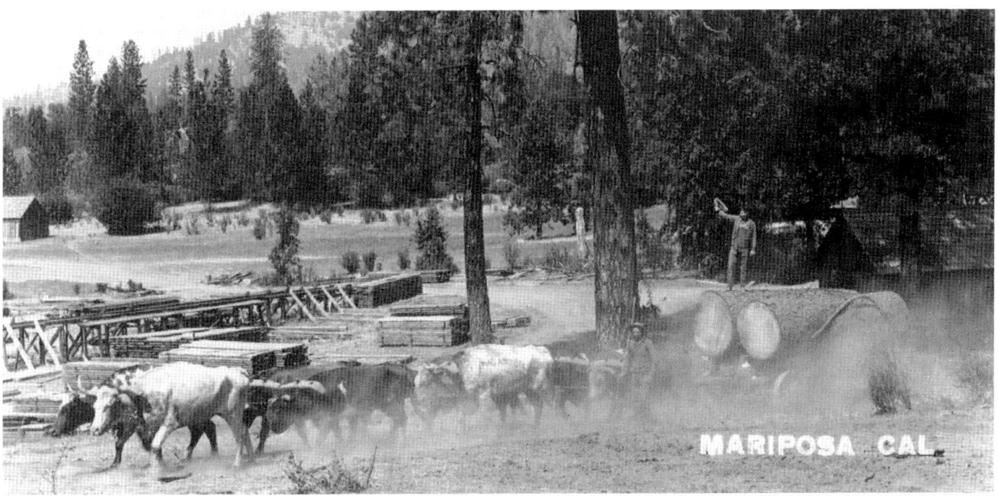

Dick Wass and Logging in Clarks Valley

At times, land went with the timber but not always. The village of Fish Camp in eastern Mariposa County started as an allotment. Thousands of acres of timberlands were acquired in that fashion. Once harvested, the sawmills closed, and the land returned to the federal government or sold. Only those parcels that had other uses remained in private hands. Grazing and residential use both for recreation and as primary residences were common uses of smaller plots. Dick Wass is pictured logging on a logging dolly. (Photograph by Robinson, author's collection.)

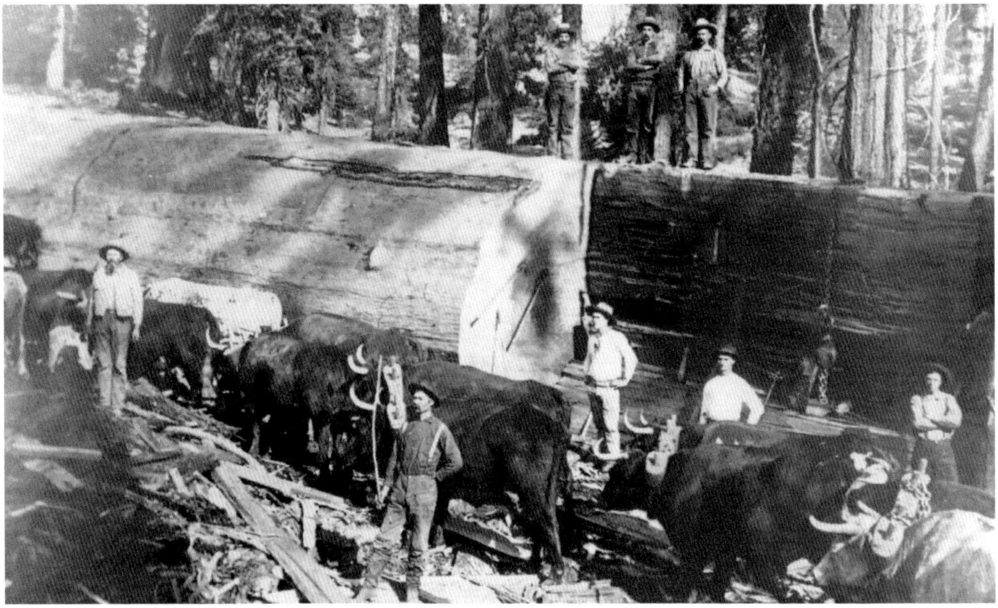

James C. Lamon

James C. Lamon was one of the earliest pioneers in Yosemite Valley. Noted for his ability to run a sawmill, he was the first white man to spend a full season living in Yosemite Valley. He worked with David Clark and others running sawmills near Mariposa and then went to Yosemite Valley. There, he constructed a log cabin in the east end within sight of Half Dome. There he planted, in various locations, apple and fruit orchards and gardened. Shown here are giant sequoia logs being reduced to a size that could be moved. It was found that the sequoia could not make good dimensional lumber, and thus, the trees were reduced to grape stakes. (Author's collection.)

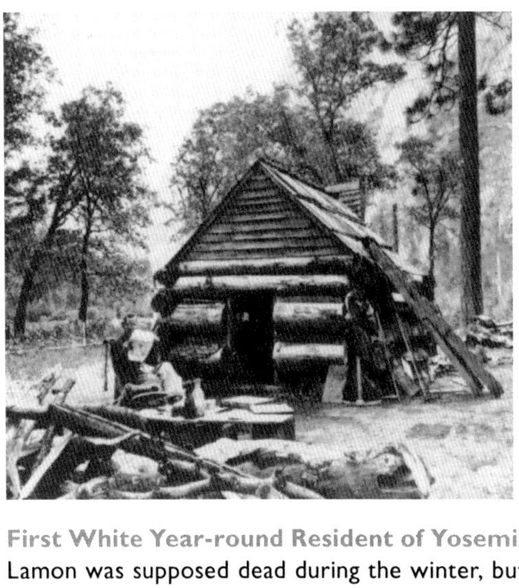

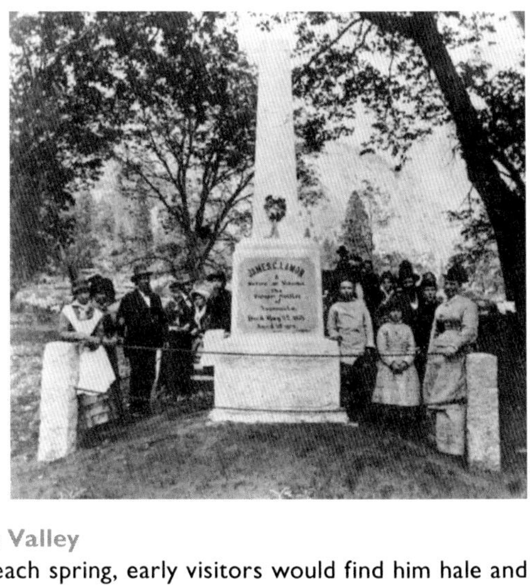

First White Year-round Resident of Yosemite Valley

Lamon was supposed dead during the winter, but each spring, early visitors would find him hale and hearty. During the winter, he would welcome the occasional Indian late in leaving the valley before the heavy snow. Both of his orchards still produce fruit; one is located behind the Yosemite Stables, and the other is at Camp Curry parking lot. Upon his death, Lamon was buried in the pioneer cemetery attended by a great stone obelisk. (Both, author's collection.)

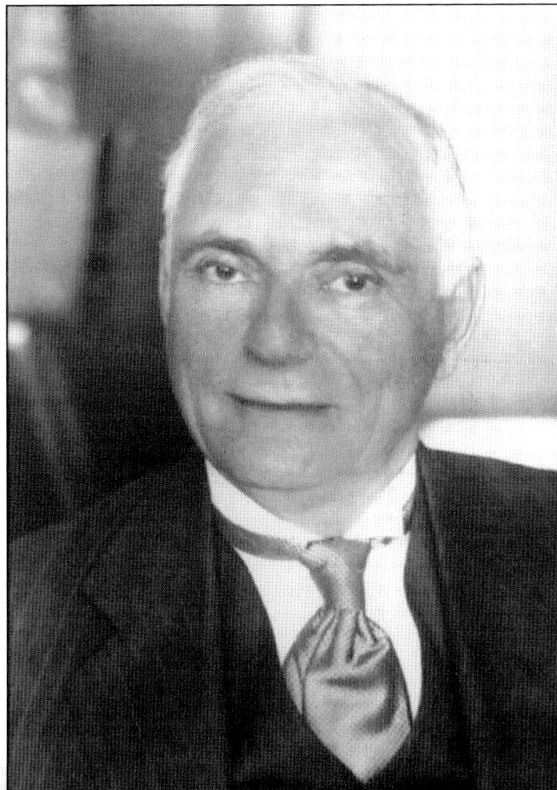

Judge Joseph J. Trabucco

Superior court judge Joseph J. Trabucco was the son of Eleanor and Louis Trabucco, pioneer merchants of Bear Valley. Having a fine reputation as a jurist, he served Mariposa County and the State of California for 35 years on the bench. As the record attests, he never had a decision overturned. For many years, judges sat in other counties when the caseload was light in Mariposa and heavy elsewhere. Criminals hated to learn that Trabucco was to be their judge because of his knowledge of the law was so intense that lawyers seldom questioned his decisions. He is pictured below at his desk in the 1854 Mariposa County Courthouse. (Both, author's collection.)

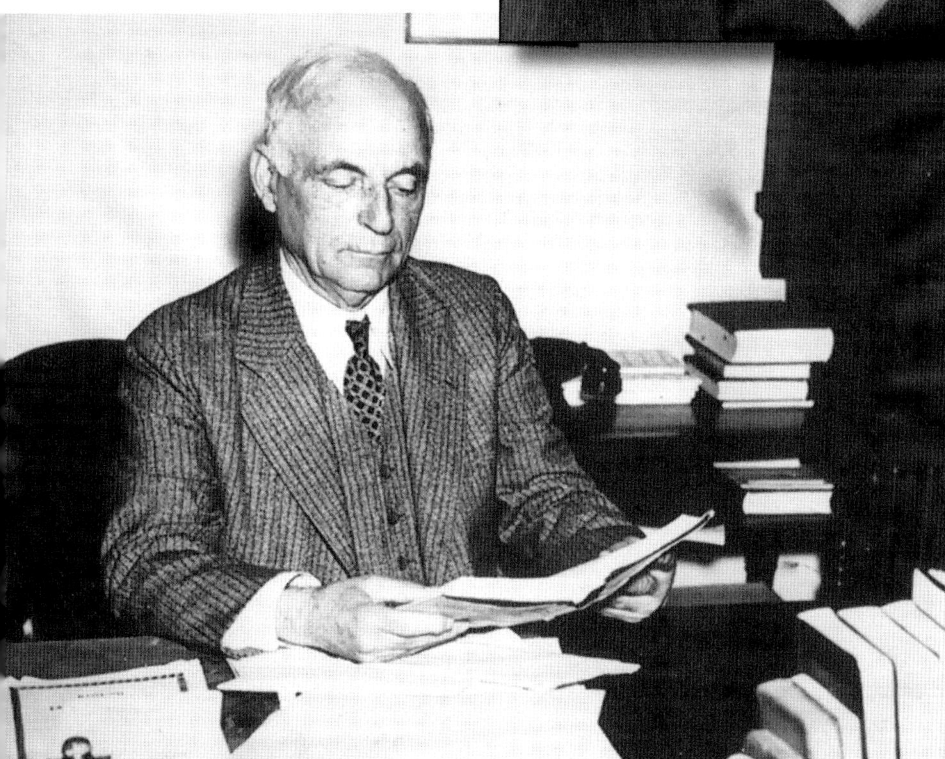

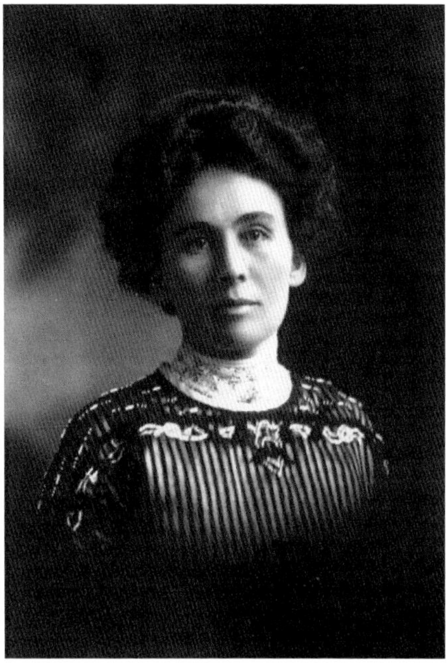

Edith Ridgeway Trabucco and Family Residence

Trabucco was married to the beautiful Edith Ridgeway, and his mother built them a fine Victorian home one block away from the courthouse. J.J. and Edith raised their family in the house near the courthouse. Edith lived there far beyond Joseph's death, tending to the garden and many trees. The house still stands, and little has changed over its 113 years. (Both, author's collection.)

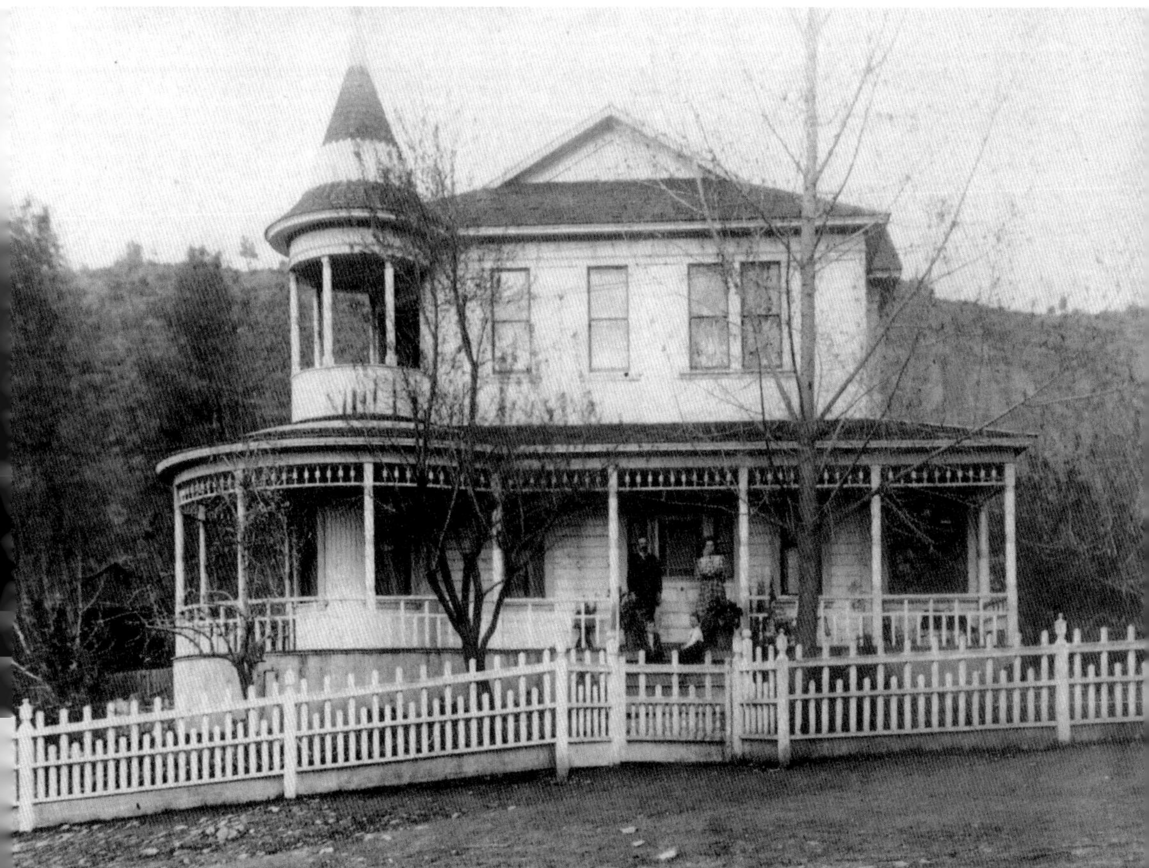

CHAPTER SEVEN

Legends of Character in Mariposa County

The population of Mariposa County has always been small, but the cast of characters and the diversity of their endeavors have been very significant.

Part of the reason for a great deal of turnover has been the nature of gold mining and the economy that accompanies the effort. Then, there is the constant turnover in personnel in Yosemite National Park and the political and social demands of federal management. The most stable institution in the park was the concessionaire Yosemite Park and Curry Company. Not all of the many legends associated with Mariposa and Yosemite can be included here.

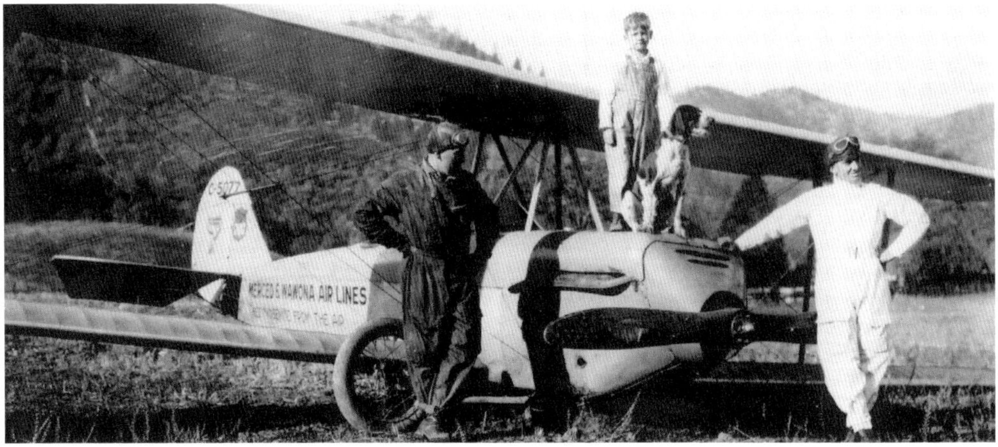

The Gallison Family

Gallison family members were true pioneers of Mariposa County. Coming in the 1850s, they settled on land in the town of Mariposa. The Gallisons became carpenters, miners, county officials, rangers in Yosemite National Park, and most interesting, an aviator. Frank Gallison's love of flying came early, and by the 1920s he had his own biplane flying out of Merced. Mariposa did not have an airport until 1935.

Sometime after the formation of Yosemite Park and Curry Company and the ascendancy of Donald Tresidder as president, Gallison created Merced & Wawona Airlines. Almost immediately, the airline provided a variety of services to the park, both inside and outside. Don Tresidder had become president of Stanford University and needed a quick way to get to Yosemite on weekends. He would meet Frank in Merced, and they would fly to Wawona, landing in the meadow above the golf course.

On one such trip, not with Tresidder, a problem developed with the plane, and Frank and copilot Leland "Tiny" Tedrow had to land in the town of Mariposa in an open field north of the 1854 courthouse.

In 1927, Frank Gallison (right) and Tiny Tedrow are pictured after being the only pilots to ever land in the town of Mariposa. The young man on the engine cover is Lloyd Milburn with his dog. Lloyd was the son of Louis Milburn, district attorney of Mariposa County. All was well, but the plane had to be trucked out of town. (Author's collection.)

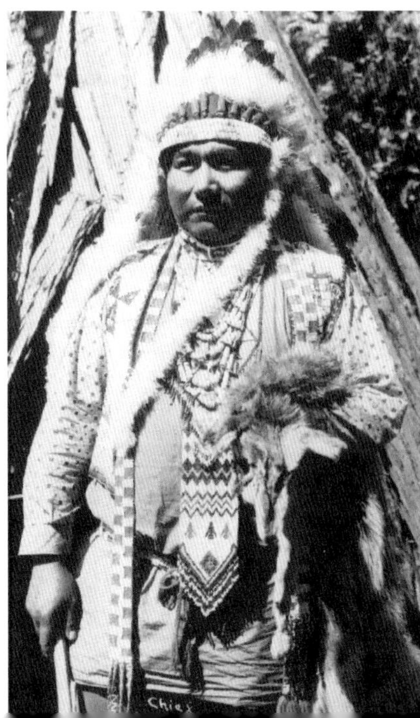

Chris "Chief LeMee" Brown

In less than 50 years after the discovery of gold in the foothills, John and Lena Brown, Indians living along the Merced River near today's El Portal, had four children: three boys and one girl. One of the boys was named Christian "Chris" Jorgensen Brown. This name was chosen to honor an artist by the name of Christian Jorgensen living in Yosemite Valley. At some point, Chris Brown acquired knowledge of various traditions existing before the arrival of the gold miners and hotel builders. He was given or adopted the name "Chief LeMee."

Here, he is pictured in early costume. The headman would wear a headdress made of feathers much like the Sioux. He gave traditional dances at the museum in Yosemite Valley. (Author's collection.)

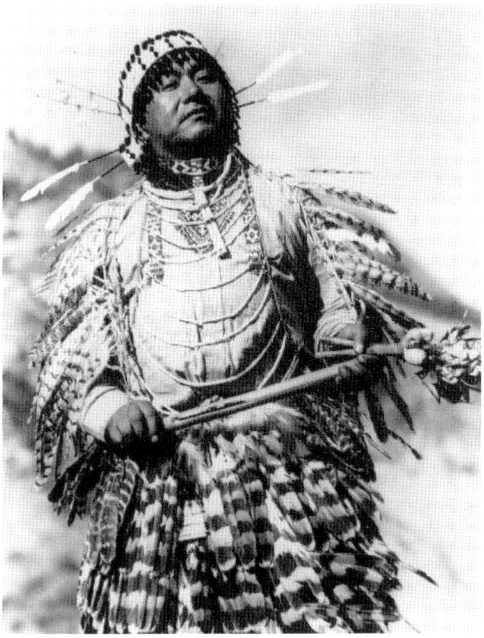

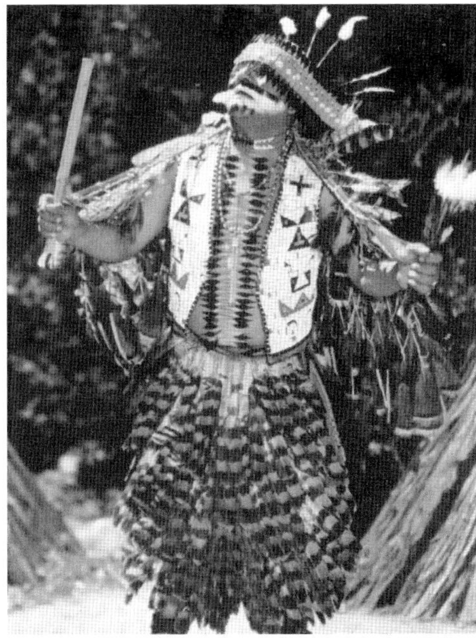

Chief LeMee Wears Evolving Costume
He also demonstrated various traditional activities, such as using soap root solution to capture fish. At some point, he began adopting more of the Miwok traditional costume. (Both, author's collection.)

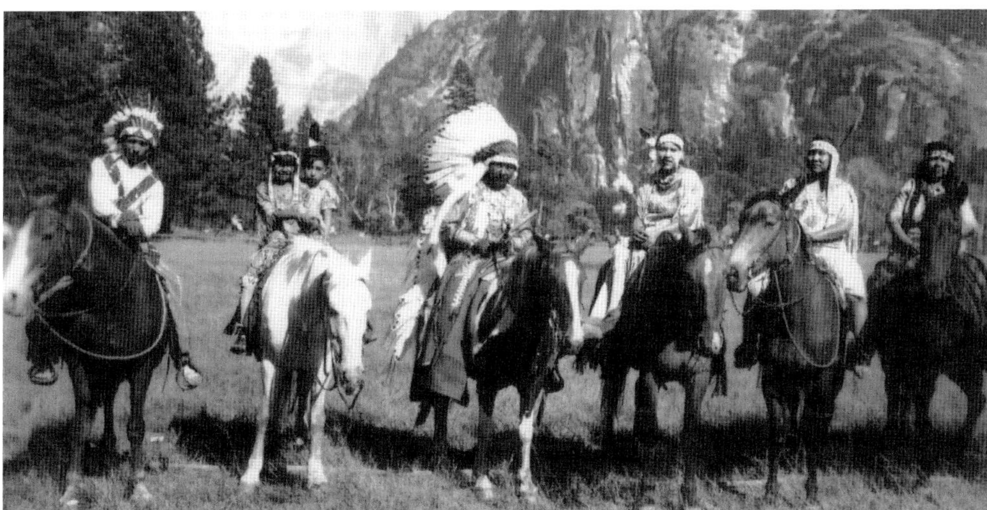

Yosemite Natives Dressed for Indian Field Days
The natives had always been exploited for their ability to gather food, such as fish or deer, and later as packers, maids, and servers. No particular interest was paid to the culture they possessed upon the white man's arrival. When the Indians' ability to entertain was discovered, a Merced transportation company helped sponsor events called "Indian Field Days." Native crafts, such as basket making, were on display for purchase. The natives were dressed at first to resemble Midwest tribes with which most Americans were familiar. Chris Jorgensen Brown ("Chief LeMee") had talent to entertain, and at first he and his brethren dressed like Plains Indians. (Author's collection.)

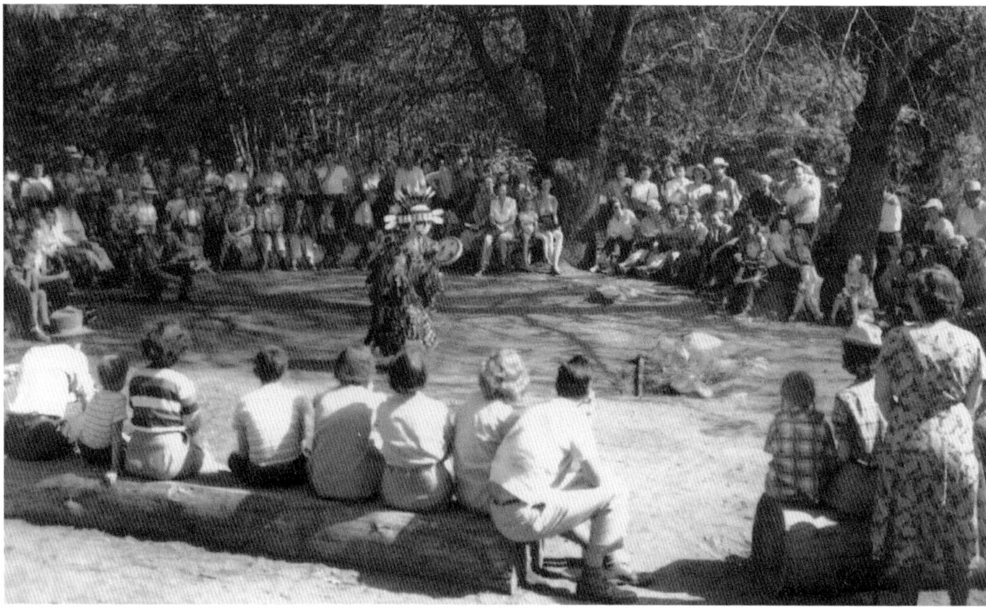

A True Showman

Brown was a showman. He taught dances and costuming to young Indian children and would appear in the Mariposa County Fair Parade each year and often at the fair. He is pictured dancing for tourists behind the Yosemite Museum in an area that is now the Indian Village. (Courtesy of Ralph Anderson, NPS.)

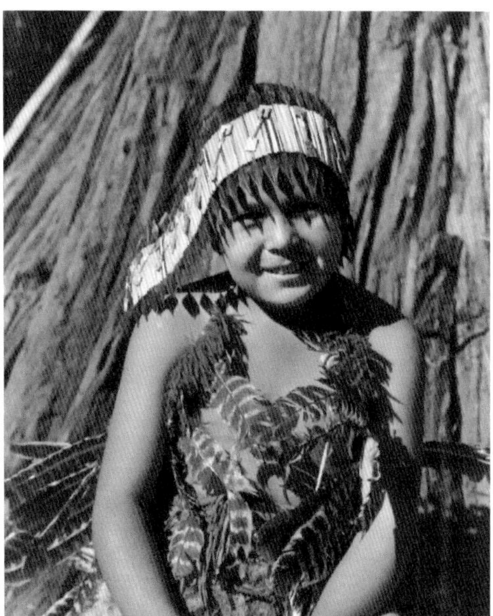

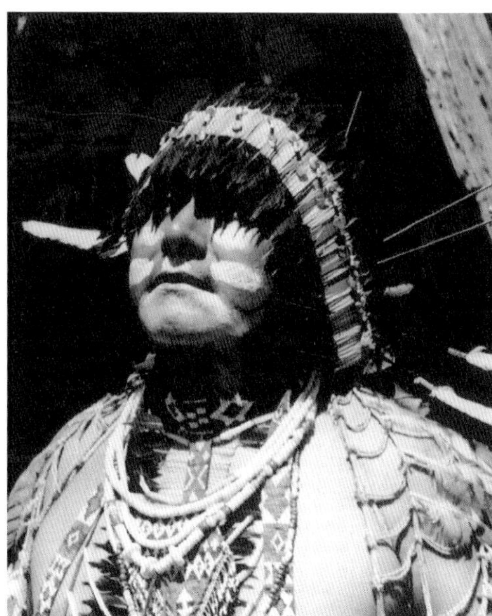

Jackie Oliver-Young with Chief LeMee

Jackie Oliver-Young was a Yosemite Indian. At left, she is pictured preparing to dance with Chief LeMee (right). Note the Indian Village in the photographs; it was located behind Yosemite Museum. (Both, courtesy of Ralph Anderson, NPS.)

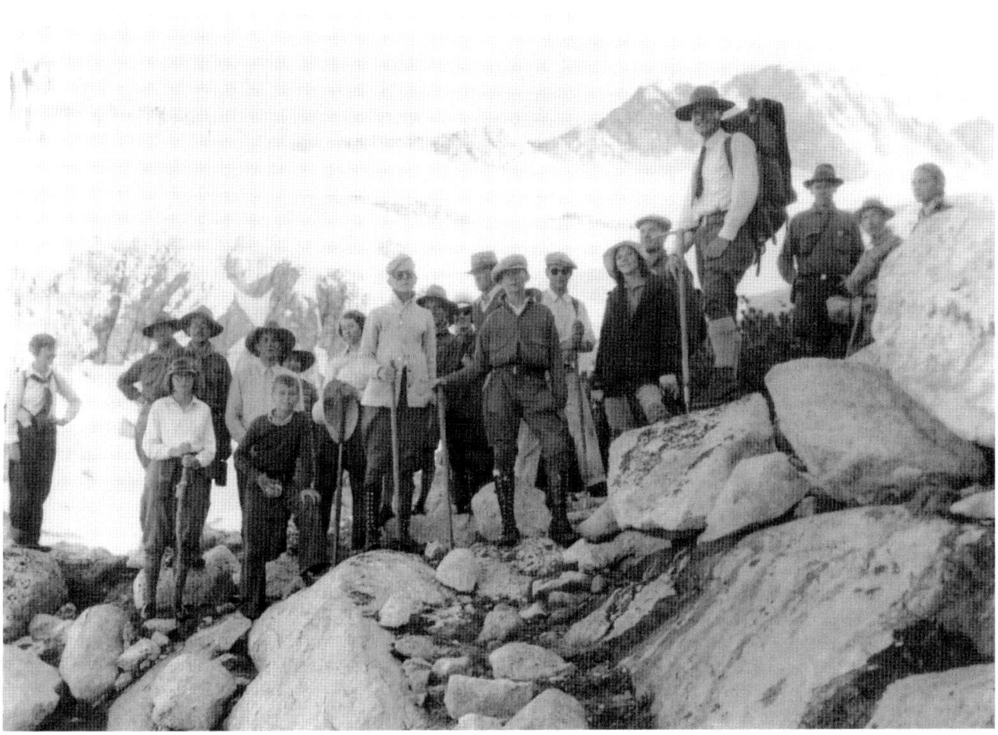

Carl Sharsmith

Yosemite has always been blessed with individuals who studied and interpreted the environment based on a passion for the mountains. Carl Sharsmith, even as a young man and student, saw glaciers and geology as his overwhelming interest. While studying and teaching were his main focus, he served as a summer naturalist in Yosemite. Tuolumne Meadows was Carl's base. In 1931, while assigned there, he and Helen Katherine Myers took a short trip to Reno to be married. They quickly returned to Tuolumne Meadows for their honeymoon and camped in a park service shack with only candlelight and a little water. Helen was a zoology major at University of California where Carl was enrolled, and their mutual love of the Sierra brought them together. Here, Carl is pictured with a group on Mount Conness in 1932. (Author's collection.)

Lifelong Ranger

Carl continued to offer the summer ranger naturalist programs for more than 50 years of his life. As time went on, he offered winter ecology programs in Yosemite Valley. Although he retired from being a ranger in 1973, he continued to give walks and talks for the balance of his life. He was featured in Robert Redford's film *Yosemite: The Fate of Heaven* searching the winter landscape for flora most often missed. He died at his home in San Jose, California, in 1995. Carl, toward the end of his life, is pictured enjoying a laugh with a group investigating his favorite home in Tuolumne Meadows—Yosemite National Park—on a walk 1989. (Courtesy of Yosemite Museum.)

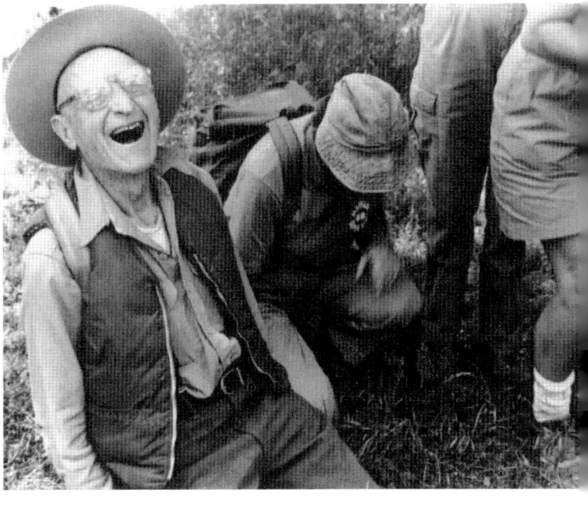

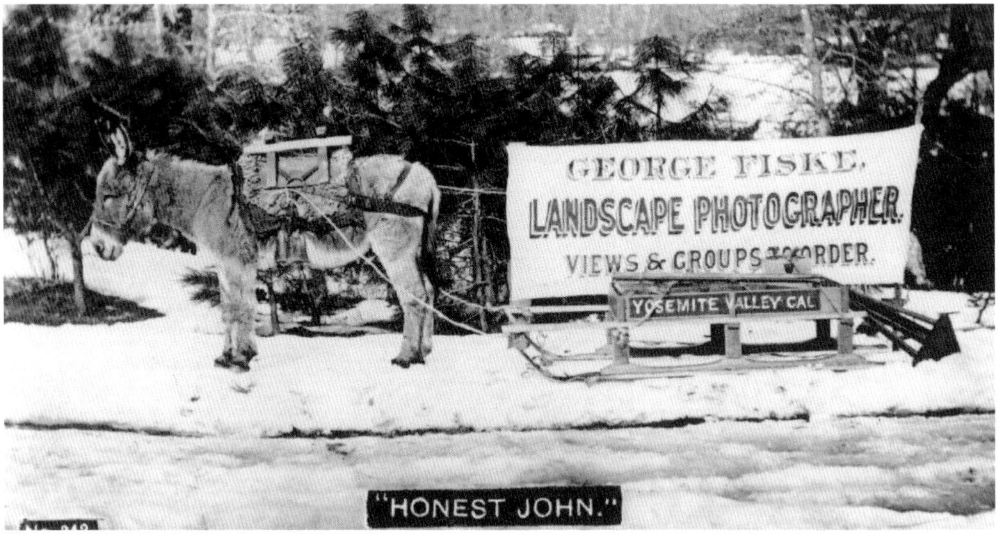

George Fiske, Landscape Photographer

Photographer George Fiske came to Yosemite in the early 1880s with his first wife, Elmira. He determined that he should live in Yosemite Valley year-round because no one was photographing Yosemite in the winter. Elmira died of cancer in 1896; her two sons who died of cholera preceded her. Fiske subsequently married Caroline Paull, and they had no children.

After fire destroyed his studio and most of his negatives, George opened his third studio in the Upper Village. There, he no longer developed customers' negatives and prints but determined to survive on the sales of only his own photography. Fiske sold individual prints, exposed, processed, and printed to the highest quality. He prepared albums of five-by-seven contact prints, and it is from one of these albums that the author started his collection. He formed a friendship with Galen Clark and James Mason Hutchings who published many of his photographs. Below, Fiske and his wife, Caroline, are pictured in the drawing room of Cedar Cottage. (Above, author's collection; below, courtesy of NPS Museum.)

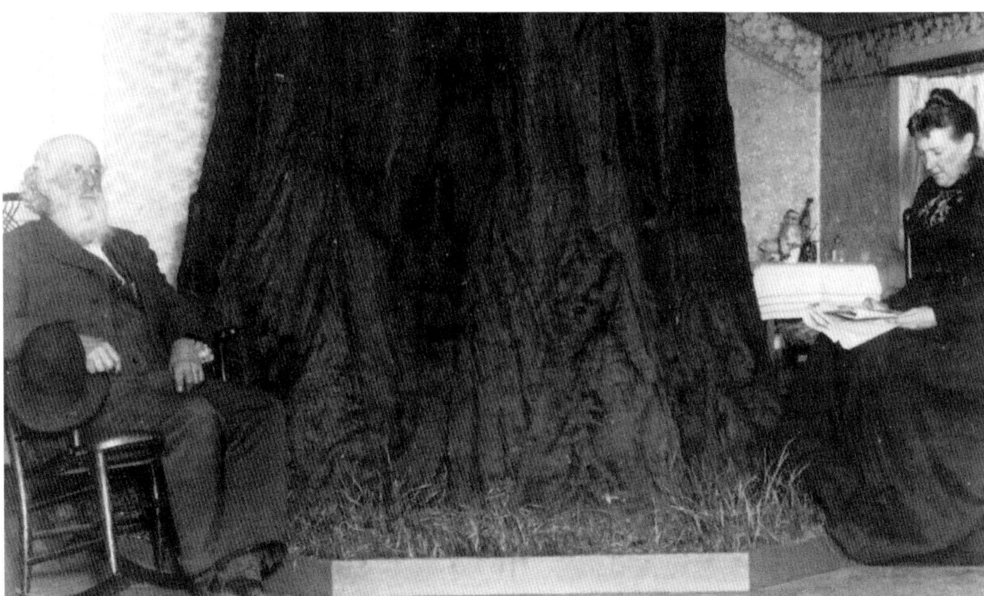

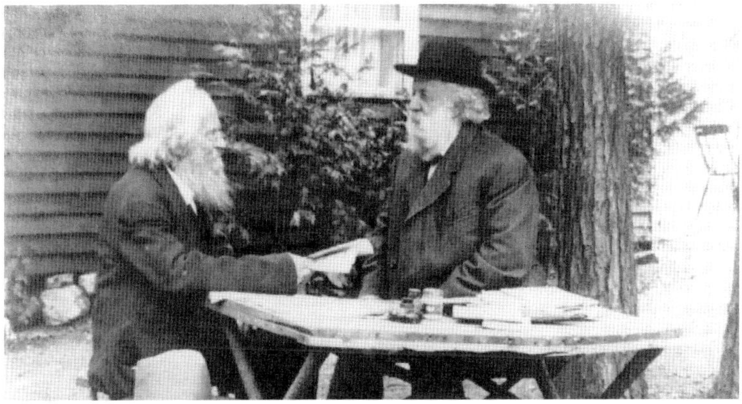

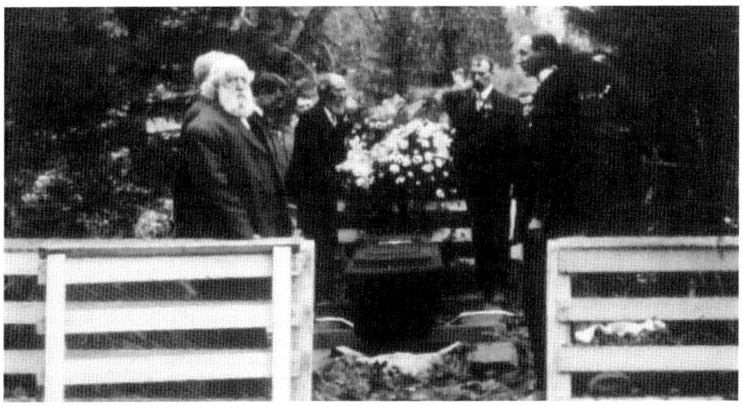

Fiske and Galen Clark's Funeral
Galen Clark (left) and George Fiske were longtime friends. When Fiske attended Clark's funeral, he had his assistant photograph the funeral and burial, which took place in the Pioneer Cemetery. (Both, author's collection.)

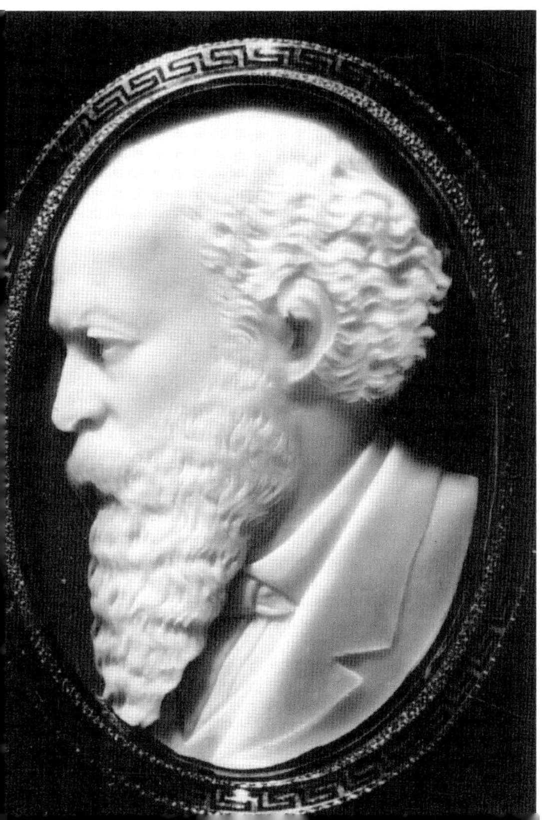

Carleton E. Watkins
Fiske and Watkins well established the artistic interpretation of the environment of Yosemite. Both were connected because they were both from San Francisco, both worked at Vance Studio, and it is believed that Fiske worked for Watkins.

Carleton E. Watkins was one of the early developers of the glass-plate negative process that made the multiple reproduction of single images the basis for rapid dissemination of photography both popular and in quantity. (Courtesy of Yosemite NPS Collection.)

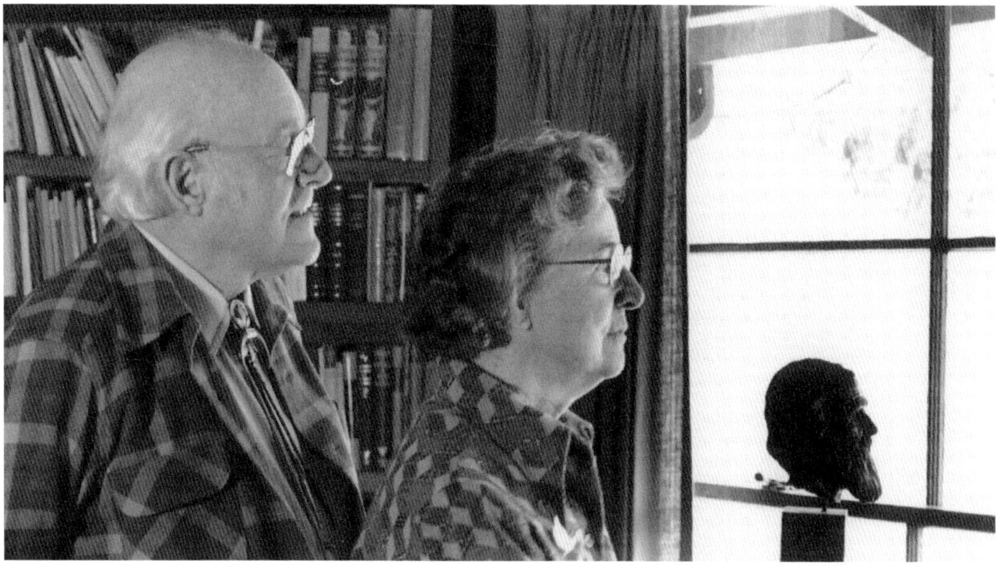

Bill and Mamie Kimes

Bill and Mamie Kimes came to Mariposa in the early 1980s to retire from teaching. It had always been Bill's goal to index for publication all of John Muir's written efforts. Bill had an extensive library of Muir's work; therefore, the task, though not simple, was a delightful retirement project. Writer and producer Tom Devries and the author interviewed and photographed Bill and Mamie for the *San Francisco Examiner.* Bill and Mamie Kimes are pictured at home with the bust of John Muir. (Photograph by author.)

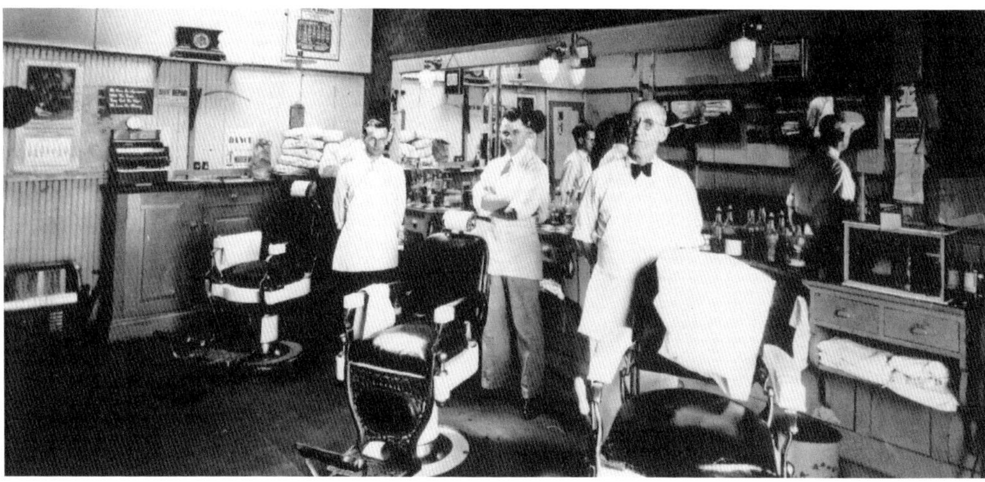

Bert Smith

Bert Smith was a longtime barber in Mariposa. He married Rose Hogan, and they had two girls: Penny and Mildred. Bert began the barbering careers of George Fournier and Winnie Williams. He and Rose were very involved in raising daughter Mildred and son-in-law Mickey McDonald's four boys. Bert was very interested in Mariposa history, and at an earlier time, he brought the first motion pictures to Mariposa. From right to left are Smith, George Fournier, and Winnie Williams; Winnie was just out of barber school. Eventually, Winnie bought the barbershop when Bert retired.

Rose Hogan's brother Sam was well known in Mariposa, too. Sam and his brothers lived on the family homestead on Yaqui Gulch Road. (Author's collection.)

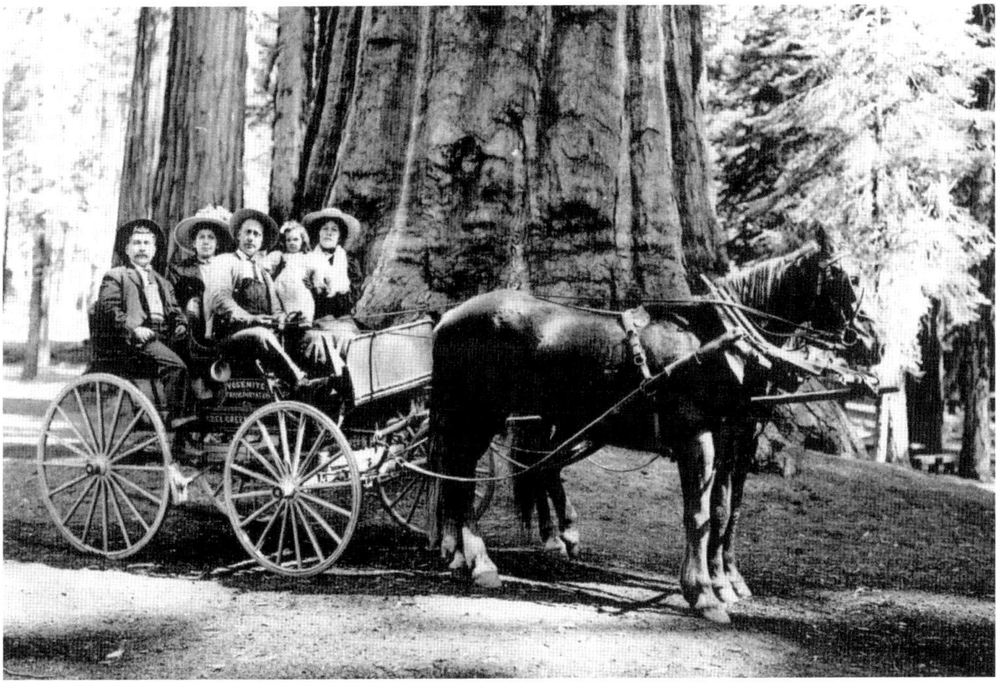

The Smith Family

Bert Smith; wife, Rose; and daughter Mildred visit Mariposa Grove of Big Trees in a rented Yosemite Transportation System coach. In the back seat are Rose's brother Sam and his wife. (Author's collection.)

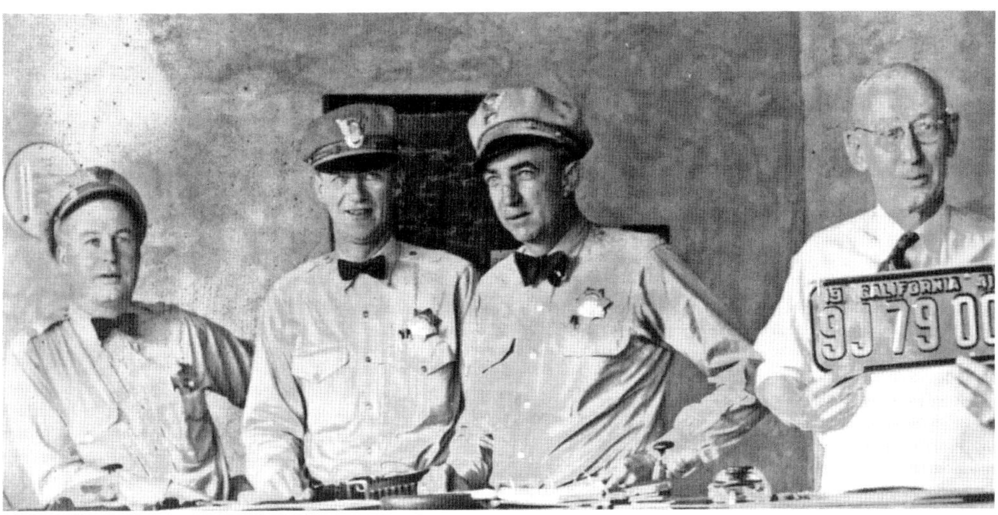

Bert Celebrates the California Highway Patrol

Bert was a well-respected businessman with a sense of humor. When the county patrol was folded into the new California Highway Patrol, Bert joined in celebrating the opening of their office in downtown Mariposa. Bert, holding the license plate, is pictured with, from left to right, Earl "Bub" Johnstone, Harry Eckert, and John "Chic" Ellingham. Soon World War II began and traffic to Yosemite virtually stopped, Harry was transferred, and Bub and Chic carried on during the war. (Author's collection.)

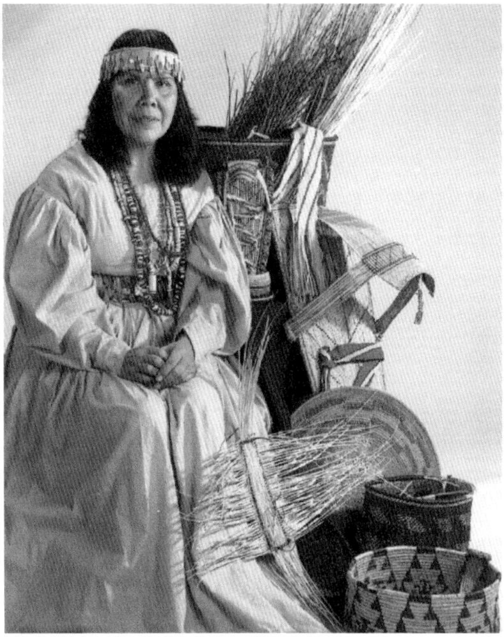

Julia Parker, Yosemite Basket Maker

Julia Parker came to Yosemite as a young member of the Pomos group of northern coastal California. She married Ralph Parker, and they raised a family in Yosemite. In the process, she became acquainted with the traditional basket makers of Yosemite. Her skill shows the necessary love and intelligence for the craft. For many years, she has demonstrated her skill in the India Room at the Yosemite Museum. The author was very honored to photograph her with examples of her craft. (Photograph by author.)

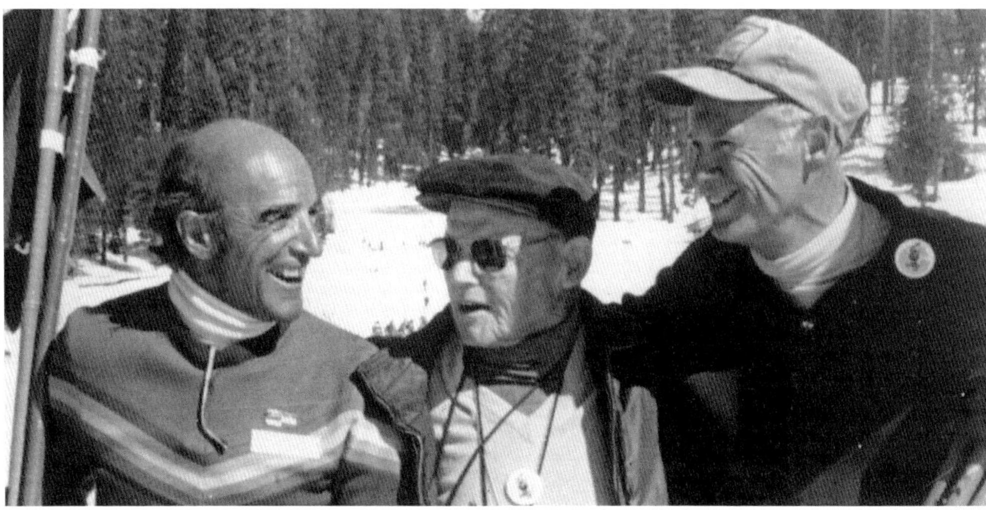

Nick Fiori and Leroy "Rusty" Rust

Leroy "Rusty" Rust (right) is pictured with Nick Fiori (left). The two were great longtime friends and taught skiing together as soon as the first snowflake fell.

Nick Fiori, a French Canadian, came to Yosemite about 1948 to join the staff at Badger Pass Ski Resort. His skill as a skier and as an instructor and his friendly personality made him a legend in Yosemite. During the summer months, he was in charge of the High Sierra Camps. He made his way around Yosemite Valley on a bicycle, and in the high country, he would travel from camp to camp on foot with only a water bottle. The High Sierra Camps were less than a day apart, and Nick could be seen running along the trail dreaming, no doubt, about the fine dinner that awaited him.

"Rusty" Rust was the son of a stage driver in Yosemite, Jess Rust; Rusty spent most of his life working in Yosemite. He eventually became the postmaster in Yosemite, but most people remember him for his involvement in the ongoing winter sports program, including skiing and skating, among other activities. (Photograph by author.)

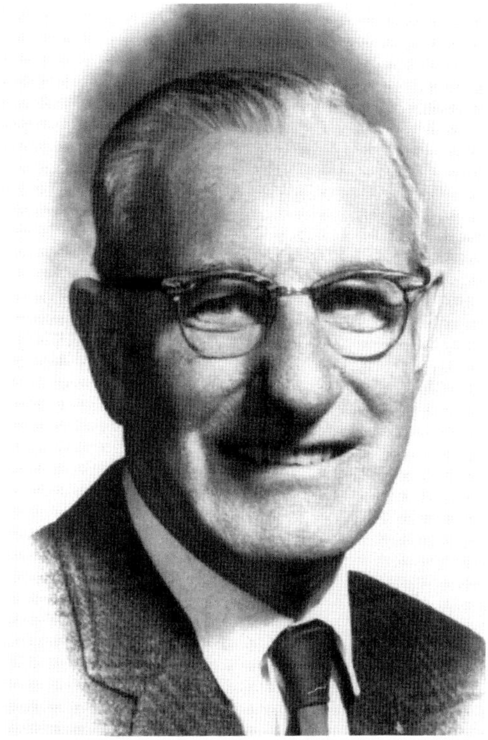

John Menzies

John Menzies, a native of Scotland, came to Mariposa County to operate a Shell service station along the Merced River in El Portal. There, he and his wife, Gertrude, started a family by giving birth to twin boys Robert and Ronald. In 1936, the family moved to Mariposa to operate a new Shell station and dealership at the Tenaya Motel. Right from the beginning, John became involved in the community. He and Gertrude had a third son, Harold, in 1938. As the boys grew, they joined their father serving the community as youth leaders and firemen. (Author's collection.)

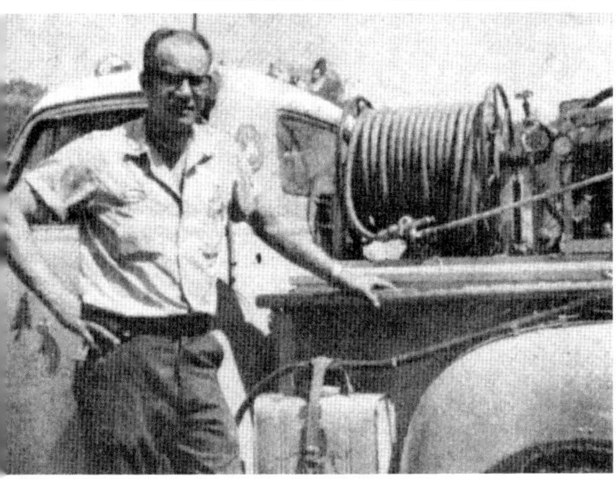

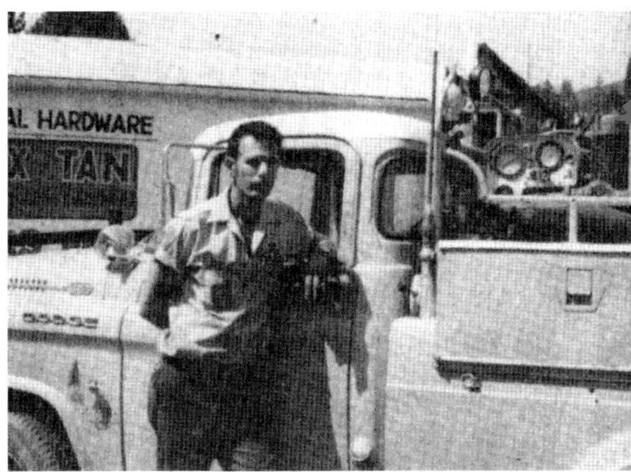

Ron and Harold Menzies

Ron and Harold Menzies are pictured with their fire trucks. The trucks were built on each fireman's personal pickup. Ron's truck was a Chevy with a 70-gallon water tank, and Harold's was a Dodge with a 150-gallon tank. At the time that the Menzies brothers provided the fire service, the California State Division of Forestry manned their stations only during fire season, usually May through October. The Menzies brothers, who would leave the gas station often unattended to respond, augmented limited emergency services. If a patron were in the station getting gas and the Menzies took off, the patron would stay and guard the station and its cash register until one or both returned.

Anytime there was a need at the schools, the Menzies family was there. Often, there were difficult meetings deciding school issues. The Menzieses were always there supporting the schools. In later years, John would be the caretaker at the Mariposa Museum and History Center; each morning, he opened it and swept the floor. (Both, courtesy of Ron Menzies.)

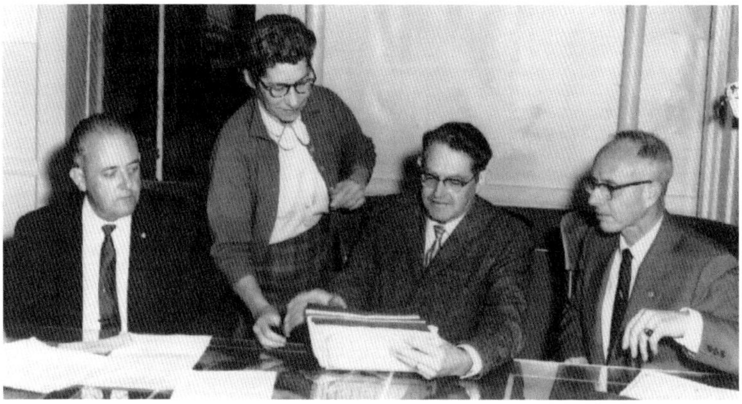

School Bond Committee

Only once in Mariposa County history did the voters pass a school bond. This occurred in 1957. That year, postwar growth plus the burning of Sebastopol School caused the school district to expand. Supt. Cleo Adelsbach and the school board proposed a school bond that would provide funds for the building of a new shop building and an agriculture building at the high school, Woodland Elementary School in Bootjack, plus a few other needed items. Cleo traveled throughout the county convincing the voters that all of these improvements were needed. When the election was held, the bond measure passed. Other bond elections before and since have never won the approval of the voting public, with the exception of a small election that created Mariposa County High School in 1914. Pictured are the citizens responsible for selling and issuing the bonds. From left to right are John Mentzer, Mariposa County treasurer; Gabe Wilson, county clerk; Perlie Barnes, manager of the Bank of America; and Cleo Adelsbach, superintendent of schools. (Photograph by Harold Rowney.)

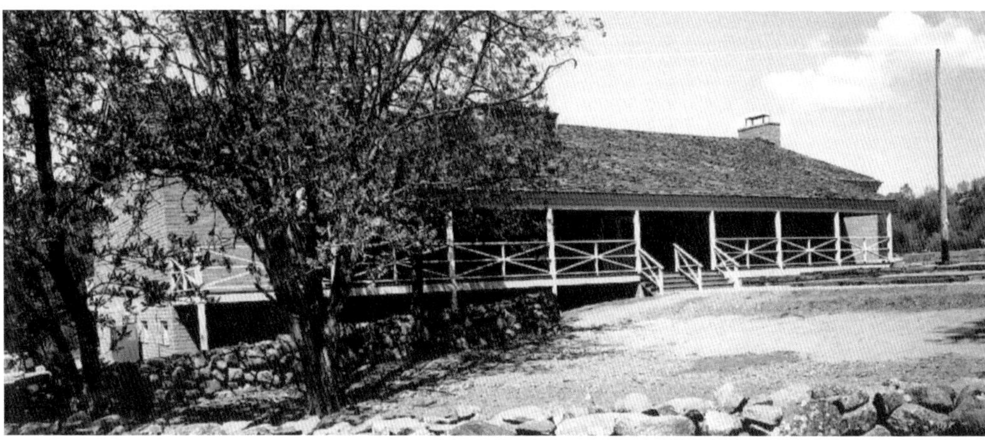

Judge Thomas Coakley and the Mariposa Museum and History Center and Library

The Mariposa Museum and History Center and Library was a community effort. Started in 1968, Judge Thomas Coakley took charge, just as he had during the centennial. A balloon launching at the courthouse lead to a parade of the county's schoolchildren downtown supporting the need for a library. The Coakley family donated the land for the building, and families from throughout the area, including from other counties that had been part of Mariposa County in 1850, all contributed to the project.

Today, the history center no longer holds the library; the library was given its own building in the civic center. The museum has been developed to include a wide-ranging collection of historical artifacts, a large archival vault, a stamp mill, and many other buildings all from Mariposa County's past. The Smithsonian has judged this museum as one of the finest small museums in the United States. (Photograph by author.)

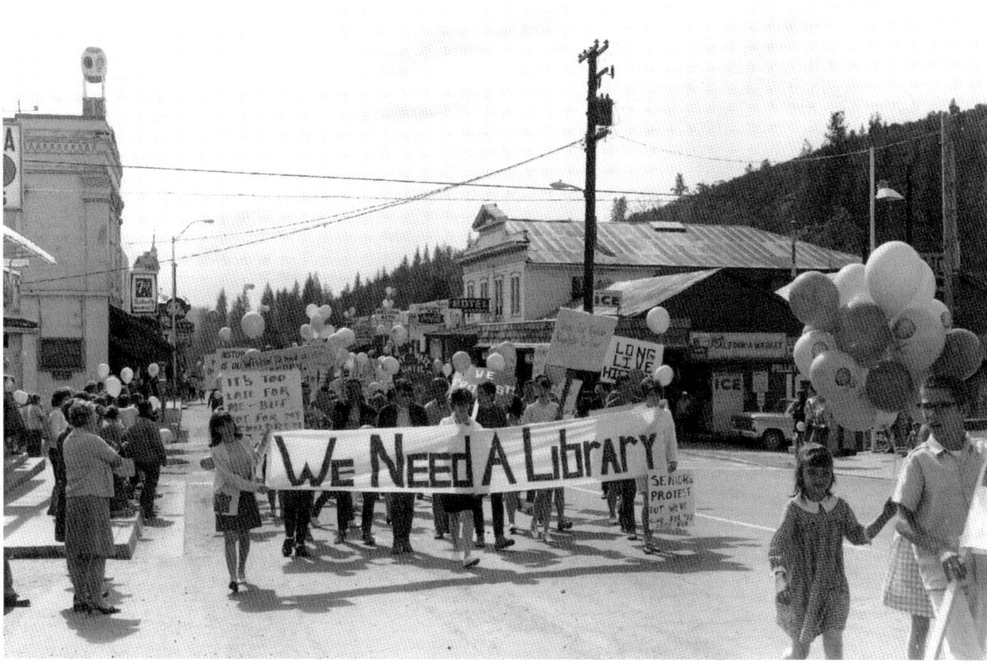

Honoring the Local History
Shown here is a parade through downtown Mariposa supporting the construction of the new history center and library. (Photograph by author.)

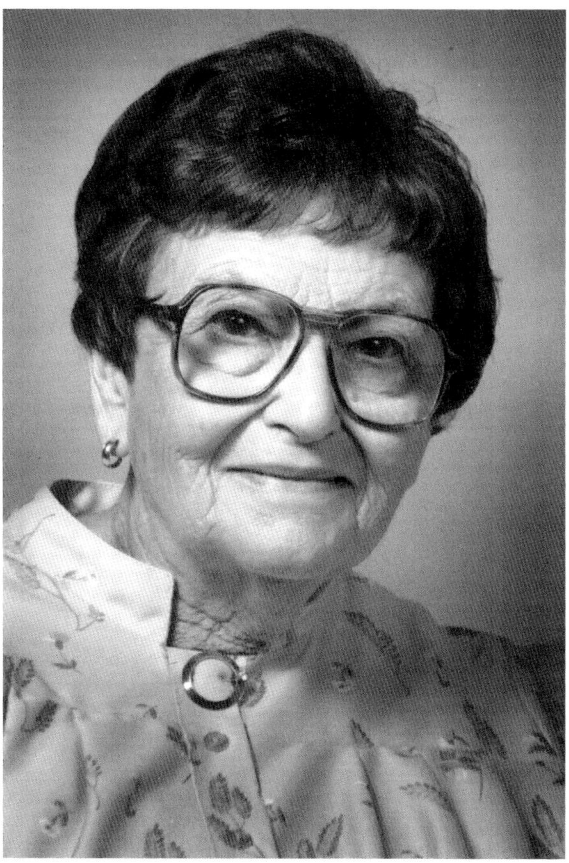

Edith Turner
Edith Turner was the wife of a Hornitos rancher and mother to four outstanding children. Edith was not only a mother, wife, and grandmother, but she was also a prime mover in the Hornitos School Patron's Club, which also took the preservation of Hornitos and St. Catherine Church. Her involvement in school activities extended from lessons to sports; she was known for never having missed a football game or any other school-related activity. (Photograph by author.)

Flossie Thomas

Flossie Thomas and her husband, Merritt, lived on a hillside of Mount Bullion halfway between Bear Valley and Mount Bullion town. She participated in many community activities, raised a huge garden, had a large family, and took great care to know and understand the history of the northern half of the Fremont Grant. She served on the Board of Directors of the California State Mining and Mineral Collection and was considered a very valuable colleague and friend by many, including the author. (Photograph by author.)

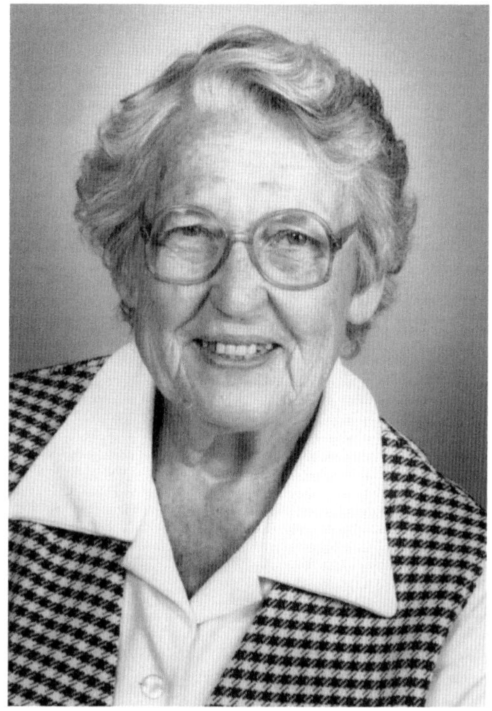

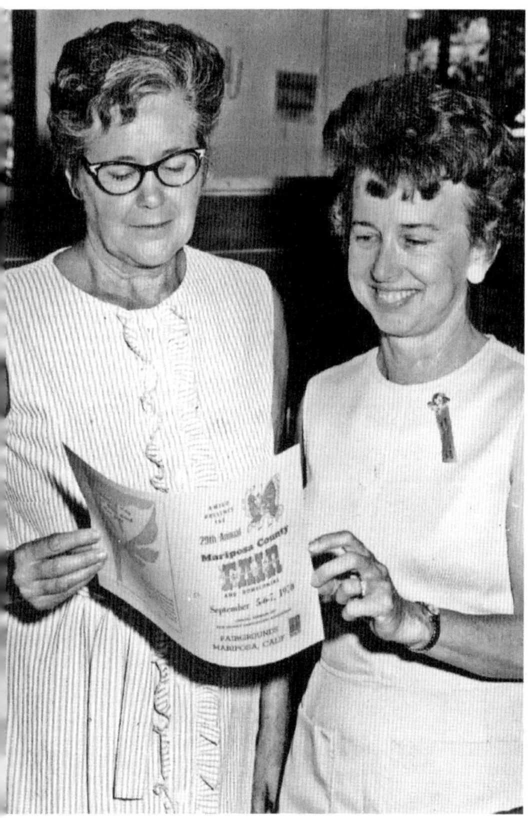

Marguerite Campbell and Tillie Stroming

Marguerite Campbell was editor and publisher of the *Mariposa Gazette* for decades after the death of her father, John Dexter. She kept the newspaper alive and informed the county on everything happening. The *Mariposa Gazette* is the oldest newspaper of continuous publication in California. She had three children and many others that she took in, raised, and helped educate. Her special editions of the *Mariposa Gazette* for the town's centennial, the 125th anniversary of the publishing of the *Gazette*, and for the building of the Mariposa County Courthouse will serve as valuable records of Mariposa County history into perpetuity.

Tillie Stroming, married to Walt Stroming, managed the Mariposa County Fair for many years and was a staple in the community. With Elmer Stroming, she was an owner-operator of Stroming Machinery. She fully demonstrated her love of Mariposa by leaving sizable gifts to St. Joseph Church, the California State Mining and Mineral Museum, the Mariposa County Library, and others in her estate. (Photograph by Harold Rowney.)

INDEX

Adelsbach, Cleo G., 39, 124
Agua Fria, 39
Ahwahnee Hotel, 100
Army Troop Wawona, 35
Barnes, Perlie, 124
Bissmeyer, Bob, 79
Boling, John, 11
Bolton, Gladys, 103
Bondurant, James A., 106
Boyer, Sid, 80
Brown, Chris "LeMee," 114–116
Campbell, Marguerite, 126
Castagnetto, Alta and John, 92
Chamberlain, N.D., 77
Ching, Rebecca, 94
Clark, David, 40
Clark, Galen, 1, 20, 21, 119
Clark's Ranch, 20
Coakley, Thomas, 91, 124
Whistling Billy, 52, 53
Cummings, Andrew and Betty, 70
Cunningham, James, 108
Curry, David, 64–68
Dexter, John, 99
Diltz, John, 46, 47
Duff, James, 107
Dulcich, Jim and Marjorie, 72, 73
Eckert, Harry, 121
Ellingham, Alice, 102
Ellingham, John, 121
Fellows, George and Lucille, 76
Fiori, Nick, 122
first rangers of Yosemite, 38
Fiske, George, 118, 119
Fournier, George, 81, 120
Fremont Adobe, 61
Fremont Grant Map, 14, 15
Fremont, Jessie, 12
Fremont, John C., 12, 61
Freschlag, Winifred Bagby, 76
Gagliardo, Eugenia "Jennie," 91
Gallison family, 114
Gibson, Dorothy, 90
Glacier Point Hotel, 67
Goday, Alexander, 14
Gordon, Eddie, 106
Hatcher, Beth, 76
Halencak, Paul, 87
Helm, Jim, 66
Hibbs, Darlene, 78
Hite, John, 44, 45
Hite, Lucy, 46
Hogan, Henry, 87
Hogan, Sam, 121
Howard, William J., 30
Hutchings, James Mason, 16
Hutchings Sawmill, 17
Hutchings Upper House, 17
Johnson, Andy, 88
Johnstone, Earl, 121
Jones, Julia, 97
Jose, Antone, 88
Kimes, Bill and Mamie, 120
Lamon, James C., 110
Lauritzen, Dean C., 71
Lind, Joseph, 33
Mariposa Gazette, 42, 71, 91, 96, 99, 126
Mariposa Mine, 24, 32, 34
Mather, Stephen T., 8, 63, 68
Mary Harrison Mine, 52
McElligott, Bessie, 75, 76
McElligott, Charles, 74, 76
McElligott, Ellen, 76
McElligott, James P., 74–76
McElligott, Maynard, 74, 76
McElligott, Mervin, 74, 76
McSwain, Myrtle Schlageter, 76
Mentzer, John, 124
Menzies, Harold, 123
Menzies, John and Gertrude, 123
Menzies, Ronald, 123
Michaels, Ansel and Virginia, 76
Monroe, George, 94
Murietta, Joaquin, 28, 29
Muir, John, 17, 18, 34–37, 62, 63
Roosevelt, Theodore 36, 62, 63
Mount Bullion, 51
Nilson, Gabe, 124
Northrup, Gladys, 76
Offield, Professor, 99
Oliver-Young, Jackie, 116
Olmsted, Frederick Law, 18, 19, 48, 62
Parker, Julia, 122
Paige, Paul, 86
Pinkerton, Beverly, 76
Radanovich, David, 89
Radanovich, George, 81
Radanovich, Roy, 82, 83
Red Bud Planting, 83
Reynolds, Angevine, 43, 97
Richards, Eleanor Hastings, 103
Ritter, Arlene, 78
Ritter, Jack, 85
Rogers, Lorella, 56
Rogers, Mose, 56, 57
Rust, Leroy "Rusty," 122
Sargent, Shirley, 10, 79
Savage, James, 10
Sharp, Jane, 76
Sharsmith, Carl and Helen, 117
Smith, Bert and Rose, 120, 121
Smith, Mildred and Penny, 121
Sovlewski, Gabriel, 10, 11
Spriggs, James L., 77, 101
Spriggs, Vesta, 76
Stroming, Elmer, 90, 126
Stroming, Tillie and Walt, 126
Swartz Painting, 41
Taylor, Scotty, 89
Thomas, Flossie and Merritt, 126
Thorn, Thomas, 57
Trabucco, Edith Ridgeway, 112
Trabucco, Emile, 59, 60
Trabucco, John and Katie, 59
Trabucco, Joseph, 2, 58
Trabucco, Leslie, 60
Trabucco, Louis and Eleanor, 58,
Trabucco, Victor, 59
Trabucco Warehouse, 61
Tresidder, Donald, 65
Turner, Edith, 125
Washburn, Albert Henry, 21
Wass, Dick, 109
Watkins, Carleton E., 20, 23–26, 119
Wawona Hotel, 22
Whitley, Orville M., 77, 93
Williams, Pearl, 84
Williams, Winnie, 84, 120
Womack, Ruth, 76
Yosemite National Park Army, 37